Richard Poston
THE GANG AND THE ESTABLISHMENT

THE GANG AND THE ESTABLISHMENT

Other Books by Richard W. Poston

Democracy Is You
Democracy Speaks Many Tongues
Small Town Renaissance

THE GANG
AND
THE ESTABLISHMENT

Richard W. Poston

HARPER & ROW, PUBLISHERS

New York • Evanston • San Francisco • London

FIRST EDITION

STANDARD BOOK NUMBER: 06-013401-1

LIBRARY OF CONGRESS CATALOG CARD NUMBER: 72-144186

TO THOSE WHO LABOR WITHOUT ILLUSION IN
THE TASK OF HELPING AMERICA'S GHETTO
YOUTH FIND ALTERNATIVES TO THE STREETS

Contents

Introduction

1967 was the year forty-three people died in the Detroit riot, the fourth year of ghetto violence then sweeping the country. The police and the military were bracing for more to come, and the nation was jittery with threats of anarchy. Predictions of guerrilla warfare were being reported in the press. Crime in the streets was a national issue. Racial desperation seemed to have passed the breaking point. Not even excluding the 1965 holocaust in Watts, the year 1967 was the most violent the cities had managed to live through up to that point in the decade of the sixties. It was in November of that violent year that I was informed by friends in Washington and New York of a new development that offered not only to calm the violence, but also to provide dramatic solutions to many of the ills of which the violence was symptomatic. It was a kind of modern reform twist to *West Side Story*.

The gist of it was this: On the initiative of their own leaders, two powerful street gangs that had been at war with each other, that had been involved in murder and other violent crimes, and that had long terrorized the Lower East Side of New York City, had formed a truce, turned away from illicit activities, and were applying themselves to constructive neighborhood development. Because of their unusual talents acquired from years of predatory operations in the streets, these self-determined gang leaders were said to be so effective in dealing with ghetto youth they had been able to successfully establish a half dozen youth-managed business enterprises, provide legitimate youth employment, and with the help of outside contributions, were then generating enough income to support several youth-directed social services: an effective riot-prevention force, a housing program, a day-care and baby-sitting service, and their own independently operated school, in which they were reported to have enrolled two thousand high school dropouts and other neighborhood residents.

These once-violent gangs were said to have been so successful in this bootstrap effort, they had won the respect of their own community, gained the backing of the police and other arms of the city government, and attracted financial support from private foundations and several leading business firms totaling nearly a hundred thousand dollars. Their leaders had been featured guests on a dozen university campuses, and they were then being accorded recognition in Washington that in all likelihood would bring them a large grant from the federal government. Already the story had received considerable newspaper coverage and had appeared as a major article in one of the nation's largest circulating magazines. Now the gang leaders were said to be pushing programs similar to theirs in other parts of the country, and had decided to establish an organization that would promote such action among street gangs nationwide.

This story of spontaneous action by traditionally delinquent youth gangs, supported by substantial financing from wealthy private organizations and by the federal government, was in itself extraordinary enough. But beyond that I began to realize that what I had encountered was a growing mood among individuals and institutions in the field of grant-making to look upon urban street gangs as proper recipients of large sums of public and private money aimed at the social and physical rehabilitation of the ghetto and the prevention of delinquency.

Underlying this growing mood among grant-makers was this simple theme: Positive change within the ghetto must be self-motivated and internally directed, and as was being illustrated on the Lower East Side, youth gangs were a prime source for this motivation and direction. This New York model, it was being said, was a live demonstration of what could be accomplished by street gangs in cities everywhere; that despite their history of crime and violence—or, more appropriately, as a result of that history—these gangs represented a previously untapped reservoir of leadership that enabled them to instill new dignity in ghetto youth and assume a leading role in the general improvement of ghetto life. These gangs, according to this theme, were not just another route to ghetto youth, they were ghetto youth. They therefore presented an unparalleled opportunity for the development of needed social action, if the federal government and other grant-making institutions would simply accept them, not as gangs, but as bona fide community organizations, or indigenous youth groups, and respond to their initiative with supporting financial resources. With this kind of recognition, street gangs across the nation, usually regarded by the police as bands of hoodlums, could become bridges of understanding and cooperation between alien worlds—the ghetto and the larger society. That was the essence of the rationale. It was a theme that carried enormous appeal, and it was gaining widespread acceptance both in and out of government.

I had never heard anything quite like it. And after more than twenty years of professional work in the field of community development, I was impressed. The action on the Lower East Side was represented not as an unrealized dream, but as an operation that was actually taking place. Near the end of November 1967, I went to New York and Washington, talked to several of the gang leaders themselves and to other interested persons; the more I heard, the more impressed I became. This, it seemed to me, was one of the most significant social phenomena yet to emerge out of the urban despair of the sixties, which if sufficiently cultivated could become a major preventive for such despair in the seventies, and beyond.

At that time I was not able to begin any serious research of the story, but over the next several months I kept in touch. In February

1968, I attended a weekend meeting in Milwaukee with the gang leaders from New York and several of their friends from other cities. A short time later I was instrumental in getting Southern Illinois University—where I am a research professor—to provide the gang leaders with facilities for a conference in East St. Louis. That meeting was held in May and lasted almost a week. Then, beginning in July 1968, I spent the better part of a year and a half making a detailed study of the operation on the Lower East Side and its related activities, and taking a long second look at the amazing story to which I had been introduced eight months earlier.

Gradually, as I dug deeper and observed the action, I began to discover that I was dealing with a story that in reality was very different from that which had been described to me and reported in the press. I never lost my concern for the desperate needs of America's ghetto youth, but reluctantly, indeed painfully, I had to recognize that in accepting the widely publicized New York model as a basis for federal and private grant-making, I, along with a good many people who effect the annual distribution of millions of dollars of grant funds, had been taken in by an incredible job of myth-making.

This book is an account of what I discovered. It begins, not with the point at which I was initially exposed in November 1967, but with the beginning of the story itself a few years earlier.

Richard W. Poston

THE GANG AND THE ESTABLISHMENT

1

Angelo

Mr. Heisler was a kindly old gentleman who had settled into his retired years on a modest pension with his wife Eva in a fifth-floor apartment of the Baruch Houses, a sprawling eighteen-building public housing complex on Manhattan's Lower East Side. In keeping with his daily habit, he had gone to the synagogue, and was on his way home. It was about eight o'clock on a Monday evening in May 1961.

He stepped into the elevator in his apartment building and exchanged greetings with a fellow tenant. Four teenagers stepped in behind him. At the second floor the other tenant said good night and got off. The elevator door closed, and Mr. Heisler was the victim of a New York street gang.

Between the second and fifth floors he was attacked, shot, and robbed. The assailants fled down the stairways and disappeared into the streets.

Their loot, $2.60.

Bleeding and faint, Mr. Heisler staggered to his apartment and told his wife what had happened. About three hours later, in Bellevue Hospital, he died.

The police at Clinton Street Station moved into the streets asking questions and picked up the trail. Two days after the murder the assailants were apprehended. The oldest, who confessed to firing the fatal shot, was sixteen. Two of them were fifteen, the youngest fourteen.

In a story headlined, "Cops Say Youth Admits Killing Man, 76, in Lift," the *Daily News* reported the reaction of the sixteen-year-old killer: "Flippant and insolent, . . . [he] seemed unaware of the seriousness of his situation, except once, when he asked if he would get the electric chair.

"At that point he broke down and cried."

The news story concluded:

> Services for Heisler will be held at 2:30 P.M. today in the Windsor Park funeral home, 202 Broome St. After the funeral, Robert Provda, president of the Baruch Tenants Association, said a delegation will march on the City Housing Authority, 299 Broadway, to demand more protection from hoodlums.
>
> "In the last month more than 20 persons have been assaulted and robbed here," Provda said. "These bums prey on the elderly. More than 20% of our people are retired and living on pension checks. The halls, the stairways, the elevators are traps."
>
> Provda said his group complained to the Housing Authority last March and was promised protection—when the budget permits.

The sixteen-year-old was convicted of murder and sentenced to life in prison. The others were convicted of lesser charges and drew shorter terms.

Some years later one of the fifteen-year-olds who was the leader of the gang, and who beat the old man with the butt of a sawed-off shotgun, gave me his version of the crime and told me some of his own life story.

Angelo Gonzales was born in New York City of Puerto Rican parents on October 16, 1945. He grew into a handsome kid—bright personality, quick mind, a husky five feet ten, and exceedingly popular with the girls. He had two younger brothers, a younger sister, and one older sister. His father, a disabled veteran of World War II, and his mother, a very devoted woman, did what they could to support the family.

"But it was tough," Angelo told me. "I'm proud of my parents because they stuck together and stuck with us even though they had real bad times to go through. They always had trouble paying the rent. Let me put it this way, man, my sister and myself had to go robbing to bring home food."

At an early age Angelo was indoctrinated into the life of the street gangs and never finished high school. Within a few years his prowess as a street fighter, his ability to brag and cheat and con, made him a warlord in the Dragons. Nobody ever knew how many members this gang actually had, but like most of the street gangs, it boasted numbers ranging from several hundred to several thousand.

"As a warlord," said Angelo, "I was the guy who said when we would fight another gang. I had to be the first cat on the scene. I had a suicide squad we called the Magnificent Seven that took the most dangerous risks. Man, we did about everything, fight, mug, steal."

Had Angelo not been caught, the Heisler affair would have been just another experience in his world of the streets on the Lower East Side—a world in which the police and all other symbols of established society were seen as enemies, and in which a police record, like the ability to talk tough and act violently, was a badge of prestige.

"What happened that night," Angelo told me, "a friend of mine was in trouble with his parents. They gave him some money to buy a pair of shoes, but he went to a carnival on Delancey Street, spent part of it on a girl, and was scared to go home. So I called some of my boys in the Magnificent Seven to make a holdup to get money for the shoes. We spotted this old guy, a Jewish guy, and followed him into the Baruch project, and we made the robbery in the elevator.

"We didn't mean to kill him, but he grabbed my boy Joe by the neck and wouldn't let go. I started beating him with my shotgun, but I didn't pull the trigger. Joe got so uptight he shot him point blank. Then we cut out."

Angelo said it wasn't a very good scene because the "take" was pretty small. They rendezvoused later that evening, spent part of the money for a joy ride in a taxi, and gave what was left to their friend.

"That's about it," he said. "Joe is doing life. I already had a record for armed robbery, assault, anything else you could think of, but I was only fifteen at the time. They could of held me until I was considered an adult, but they could take me as a juvenile delinquent. So that's how I got out of it. They gave me three and a half to five years."

Angelo entered prison with contempt for the authorities who had separated him from his life in the streets—the only life to which he had ever really adjusted—and with deep inner feelings of persecution, assumed that for him and all like him the last door of hope had been forever closed.

"The whole thing was I had this big nasty attitude," he told me. "The way I saw it there didn't seem too likely a chance for guys like me to make it. Then I met a lot of other guys in jail who had stories like mine and that made it better. I wasn't any worse off than they were."

He looked at me and for a while didn't say anything. "But, Dick, as I got to thinking more, all the stories seemed to make no sense. At every turn there was a brick wall. I began thinking there must be some other way. I thought about my mother. She had high hopes for me. When she found out I was involved in gangs and killings she was really hurt. People expected her to put her head down, but she never did. She always held her head high."

Angelo looked at himself in captivity—the gang leader, powerful, daring, cunning, and in his moments of introspection he became increasingly troubled. What had he actually accomplished to satisfy his respect for his kind of people? His drive for dignity? For pride? His longing to prove his own worth? All of these basic urges had contributed to his rise in gangland. But what else?

"Anybody can pick up a gun and shoot," he said. "Anybody can rob and fight and be mean. But, you know, what does it prove?"

The street fighting, the acts of crime that had led to his dilemma—was this his only future? This is what he had done to prove his ability as a man, to obtain fulfillment, acceptance, and self-respect. But as he settled into his prison routine, his dreams and fantasies became less and less real, and without really understanding what he was doing to himself Angelo became more and more quiet, accepted his condition, and became eligible for transfer to a minimum-security institution.

"I knew a lot of the guys there, and that put me in pretty good. They had a kind of self-governing organization with a president and lieutenants. The president was a guy named Boone, a cousin of a friend of mine. Boone and myself got along pretty well and after about a year I became president.

"The prisoners were very segregated. If you walked across the line you would usually have to fight, and that caused a lot of cats to mess up. You see, it was not like in the streets. In jail somebody had control over your time, and when you got into fights it extended your time.

"We had about a thousand prisoners there, black, white, and Puerto Rican, but only about fifty of us were Puerto Ricans. We were the most respected because we could get along with both blacks and whites. We had to maintain our self-dignity and respect, especially in a minority group, so we took special care to make friends with the blacks and whites both."

Faced by the white-bastard, dirty-nigger mentality among prisoners, and seeing the disastrous results of fighting, Angelo, in his capacity as an inmate leader, proud of being Puerto Rican, found himself in a situation that for him was unique. Instead of acquiring status by fighting, he acquired status by preventing fights. Here was a new way to get what he wanted. Instead of building his self-image by striking out as he had in the streets at what he saw as a hostile society, he could now prove his ability as a man, gain acceptance and self-respect by reason and persuasion, by promoting human understanding, by being a peacemaker.

Those poor whites and blacks, trapped in their hatred. Why couldn't they be like the Puerto Ricans and see each other not as members of different races, but as human beings?

"Most Puerto Ricans are hospitable," he told me. "We have all colors among ourselves. We like to mingle and drink with different people. In jail I took advantage of that. Don't take sides, white or black. Just be Puerto Rican. So, I listened to both sides, and I found out they were all crazy. They were saying the same things but didn't know it. Man, they just didn't know each other so they were fighting and just hurting themselves."

According to Angelo's description, his was indeed a new attitude, certainly very different from that of a tough, arrogant gang leader.

"Aren't all men human individuals?" he said to me. "That ought to be enough reason for people to get along, to respect each other. What else could these black and white cats really want, except to understand and respect each other?"

I listened with fixed attention.

"So," he continued, "I started getting this idea of how things could be done. These guys were fighting each other just because they were different races, and I told them that didn't have to be so. I set up a line of communications between the whites and blacks. I got guys speaking to each other so they could understand what I was telling them.

"I was in the middle, a go-between, like, you know, a connection. Blacks and whites both would come to me. This gave me a bigger picture. And after a while everybody began to see that the man, the cops, the establishment, liked this scene. So my idea sort of grabbed on, and we said let us be the ones to change things."

He described an inmate disturbance which he said took place shortly after he had been recognized in this new role and which had reached the point where it seemed that a full-blown riot was in the making. He told me the assistant superintendent called him into his office and asked him to see if he could put a stop to the trouble.

Indignantly, Angelo recalled, "I told him he didn't have to call me in to ask me to do that. I was going to do it anyway."

Then he added, "I didn't want to see my brothers' heads broken."

Whatever life in a reformatory might be, whatever meanings it might hold to those who experience it, it was for Angelo an environment of varied forces and circumstances that appears to have met his personal needs in ways the environment of the streets had never done.

In this prison setting he seemed to have discovered and formulated a set of rules for getting ahead that were the exact reverse of those he had practiced in the streets, to have learned all over again what it was that could make him a leader.

"We sort of woke up to the idea that a few guys with their heads together, using some smarts, whites, blacks, and Puerto Ricans, could make it possible to make policies and rules for ourselves. And that's what we did."

According to Angelo, he was for the first time in his life serving others. Everybody, black, white, Puerto Rican—even the establishment, the prison officials—liked him. And he was getting all this, not by fighting or taking, but by being peaceful, by giving. He even felt moments of sorrow about the harm he had done to others, like the old Jewish guy in the elevator, like a lot of people he had hurt, like his mother and father, and as a result, he found a new way to use his talents.

"In jail," he told me, "I got the idea that when I got back on the outside, instead of busting heads and making crime, I would get people to work together. I figured there might still be some fighting, but then again, I figured that would be sort of natural. You can't change things overnight. But I figured that maybe after a while I could get the cats in the streets to see my ideas."

It was a strange and ambitious dream. Whether he would actually make it real, whether in the slum world he had known he could abandon his old ways and put his new dream into practice, remained to be seen. But Angelo Gonzales, now eighteen, decided to try.

On July 17, 1964, with two years off for good behavior, he was again free to roam the streets of New York City.

2

Chino

The same ghetto world that produced Angelo also produced Chino, a gang leader from the West Side who later moved to the Lower East Side and became one of Angelo's closest friends. Born in Puerto Rico, May 27, 1946, one of six children, Carlos Garcia, known as Chino, spent much of his early childhood in the care of his grandmother. His parents had gone to the industrial slums of Manhattan in search of advantages they had not found in the tropical slums of San Juan. As with many Puerto Ricans who had made this move, it was largely an illusionary search, but Chino's father was a determined man. He worked at various jobs, bricklayer, barber, waiter, whatever he could get. When Chino was five his parents brought him to New York, and within a short time his exposure to life in the streets began. His mother, deeply sensitive toward her children, tried to keep Chino in school, but under meager and crowded conditions, she had more burdens than she could effectively manage, and Chino adapted more easily to the streets than he did to the New York public school system.

In a number of respects he was a precocious youth. At an early age he grew to six feet and developed a large, muscular build. His rugged size, his dark complexion, his huge mop of black curly hair, and a ragged mustache gave him an impressive and formidable appearance, which from his mid-teens on caused him to seem years older than his actual age and made him something of a symbol of gang leadership. This, coupled with a generous supply of uninhibited emotional and biological drives, and an exceptional capacity for manipulation and physical action, provided him with ideal personal equipment for a leading role in the violence and adventure of the streets. There he was never at a loss. There he learned quickly the wiles of the hustler, the con man, the thief, the gang fighter, and with this expertise made his way into the world of gangland. By the time he reached his teenage years he had passed beyond parental control, and was well on his way to full independence.

As a practicing hoodlum, Chino matured rapidly, but this maturity was in sharp contrast to his growth in school. For him, as for others in the streets, school was an alien world far removed from the ghetto in which he had to survive, the only real world he knew anything about. School he simply did not comprehend. Its teachings, what it had to offer, and the ways its offerings were presented simply did not get through to him no matter how hard he tried. And he did try. But his effort was aimed more at satisfying his ego than it was at scholarly pursuit. Academically, it was a strained and futile effort, and the harder he tried, the more bitter was his failure. His teachers kept telling him he had the capacity to make it and each year passed him on to the next higher grade, but they never succeeded in causing him to see the relevance of what they were attempting to teach him. At each higher level he became increasingly lost. The subject matter became more and more vague, and the resentment he felt from not being able to learn what they kept telling him he should learn grew deeper and bigger. At the ninth grade, hopelessly mired in frustration, still unable to read or write English, his humiliation, his anger toward the system he had come to see as an enemy had pushed him to the limit of what he could endure. Meanwhile, his achievements in the streets, where he was free to express all the hostility building inside him, continued to increase and his personal status rose toward stardom. In the general scheme of his life situation, the school simply could not compete with the streets for his attention.

And so he quit school.

Several years later Chino and I talked at length about his life and his aspirations. Referring to his bitter experience with formal education, he frankly told me how he felt when he dropped out of high school.

"I had to make it my way. After I quit school I could spend all my time at what I had already started doing, running the streets, robbery, and gang fighting. I was about twelve when I began running with the gangs. I was one of the youngest to become a leader."

Chino built his reputation in a gang known as the Assassins.

"By the time I was fifteen," he said, "I was a leader of my division. Some divisions covered one block, others ten blocks. It's hard to establish the size of the Assassins because we had so many divisions."

Some of the gangs, known chiefly as fighting gangs, engaged in violence seemingly just for the fun of it, with various forms of theft as an interesting sideline. Others, known more as criminal or delinquent gangs, reversed this emphasis. Chino's special cadre was a combination of both. Operating mostly at night, armed and wielding raw, unrestrained force, this pack of young thugs roamed the streets and subways, mugging, burglarizing, and terrorizing. By day they slept in basement hideouts, vacant buildings, and freight yards, wherever they could find cover.

"We were a suicide division," he said. "We were the ones that took more chances with life. We used to go into another gang's territory and play knock-knock. We would go to a guy's door and knock, then shoot the cat that opened it. We did sniping from roof tops or from anywhere we could hide. That was some of the ways we took care of our enemies. We pulled robberies to make money. Mostly we did mugging. And we made money with whores and homosexuals. We gave them protection."

Gangland was a world in which Chino could actively apply his talents and give vent to his fierce craving for recognition and prestige. "Heart" was the important word. It meant a cat who had the guts to fight for himself and his friends, and who did not back down or say no to a daring adventure. That was what Chino had, heart. That was what he considered to be of basic value, an opportunity to test one's self. For those who met that test the gang provided a sense of power.

"Juvenile power," he said. "Most people don't realize the power of juveniles. In the gang it is a tremendous power."

Moreover, gang life was exciting.

"We had plenty of wine and plenty of girls. We smoked pot. We got drunk. We had a ball."

It was a world in which he felt free to do what he wanted to do. Yet gangland made powerful demands on his time, his behavior, and on his mental and physical energies.

"Everywhere we had enemies," he said to me. "We had to fight other gangs to protect a particular area we considered our territory, and the other gangs would protect theirs. We could walk freely in our area, but one block away could make a big difference, even across the street could be in another gang's territory. If we got in their area they would stomp us, knife us, or shoot us. We did the same to them if they came into our area. We knew there would be killings, and we never knew which one of us might get it. Even your mother could be hurt. Things like that were for revenge."

But the most feared of gangland activities were the gang wars. Known as "rumbles," these confrontations between rival gangs brought wild, screaming youths into riotous physical conflict, fighting with knives, iron pipes and chains, bottles and bricks, often with guns. In the fury of these violent melees, individual identities were often confused and it was not uncommon to be hit by both friend and foe. Many were hurt, often seriously, and sometimes somebody got killed. Even the gang leaders were afraid of these encounters. But gang war was part of gang life. To be respected, gang leaders had to talk tough and act tough. Proving themselves to themselves and to each other was a never-ending necessity, and with their predisposition to brag and threaten, a group of gang boys hanging around a corner could talk themselves into a frenzy, particularly when well plied with wine. In this state of self-induced madness and wild imagination, personal honor and a gang's reputation made rumbles inevitable. In an important sense, the rumble was a bizarre ritual, an extreme and deliberate means of acting out gang ways and gang beliefs after a period of wild threats and tough talk.

"A gang fight didn't mean anything personal," Chino told me. "It was a group thing. It was something the gangs did to establish themselves, to gain respect. Even after fighting each other two gangs might become friends. It was a seasonal thing. Like, maybe, winter— friends; summer—enemies. It didn't mean anything personal, even if you had to get revenge. That was to hold up your honor."

A rumble could draw large crowds of would-be participants, but in most instances only relatively small groups of the most belligerent did the actual fighting, carrying the assumed glory and prestige of themselves and their followers in personal combat. Essentially, it was an emotional orgy, a dramatic expression at the lowest primitive level, of the inner hostilities that seethed and boiled within roving bands of disturbed youths living in the streets amid the social wreckage of the slum. Then there was what they called "jitterbugging," sometimes "japping," a kind of guerrilla warfare in which a gang would invade another's territory, make a commando-type raid, and withdraw.

Reflecting on what it all meant, Chino said: "The gang structure was weird because it was very serious. It was organized to kill and protect, to gain respect. A street kid had to be in a gang for his own protection. He could be forced or drafted. Nearly everybody belonged to a gang. You just about had to. Many girls were in gangs and they would fight too."

For Chino the gang was the most important force in his ghetto world. It was his occupation, his way of life, his means of being the central figure in his environment. In his passion for self-importance and recognition it was essential for him to see himself as a person who made decisions, assumed initiative, and issued orders. Chino had to be a special kind of leader. He had to see himself as the protector, the guardian of his people, chieftain of his tribe, a model for others. He had to assume responsibility for those around him as a kind of benevolent patron. His manner was tough, wild, impulsive, and he looked like a gang leader. But Chino had a certain charm, a quality of personal warmth that made him very likable, and in time he de-

veloped a keen understanding of the possible disaster inherent in the
life he was living. As the years wore on he became increasingly aware
of the negative results of that life, and he began to experience moments of discomfort with what was happening to him and his kind of
people, with the direction they were headed. Gradually, as this
dimension to his character began to emerge, a sense of concern for
the well-being of himself and his friends was added to his backlog of
frustrations, and this concern began to infuse itself into his image of
himself as a leader.

"As I moved up in gang work I found myself gaining strength and
lots of friendships. People depended on me. My understanding was to
protect myself and my clique. That's what I believed, and I tried to
do what I believed. I always considered myself an honest cat. I liked
to do my own fighting, not gang up on a guy. I always made it clear
to my opponents that even if they got hurt or I got hurt, I was still
Chino. Some leaders would lose their respect and lose their leadership. I never lost my respect. I never lost my leadership. I said give a
guy a chance. Fight hard, but never kick a cat when he is down.
People followed me because they could trust me. As I got older I
thought more about people getting hurt, and, well, we were always
getting locked up in jail. I began thinking maybe we would be better
off if we did something else. In the gang you really get to a point
where you live in a fierce life. You are always hunted, especially
when you become known in the gang structure. People are always
challenging you. You really have to work to keep ahead."

Chino's moments of doubt began to come with increasing frequency. His moralizations became increasingly a part of his personal
code, his justification of himself. But like youth everywhere, his personal development was filled with conflicts and contradictions. The
irrational persisted with the rational. His explosive outbursts and
vindictive arrogance mixed with his milder self, and his fleeting
notions of a new direction were often confused and distorted. He was
an exceedingly proud human being, and could not afford to have
people think he was going soft. But circumstances gradually began to
bear in upon him.

"I was arrested many times," he told me. "A lot more than a dozen times. But even when I was locked in jail I kept fighting my case. I would not give in to the cops. They were out to get us, and we were out to get them. When I came out I went back to fighting in the streets, robbing, shooting up people. But I really wasn't getting too much out of the way we were living except trouble, and I figured hundreds of other cats must feel the same way. It got so my main interest was seriously to take to something else, even if it was an underworld type of movement."

Finally, Chino was jolted by the police into recognizing that for him the freedom of the streets was coming to an end. He began to see that he was losing his battle with the law, that its forces of constraint were being tightened around him. The game of being hunted ceased to be a lark. One night he went to his parents' house to get a change of clothes. The police had been there and talked to his mother. She was even more distraught than usual. She urged him to accept the alternative the police had offered: Leave the country, or else. And so in May 1963, far more grown than his age of seventeen would indicate, Chino Garcia went into temporary exile in Puerto Rico.

Out of personal pride this decision, coming as it did from a source outside himself, has been a matter that Chino has not always liked to talk about, but as events later proved, it was the best favor the police ever did for him.

He explained it to me this way: "I decided it was a good idea. Although to be honest, I didn't have too much choice. They would have actually busted me."

This change in environment was a major turning point in Chino's life. His self-image as a gang leader and protector of his friends, his fierce determination to maintain his independence, his defiance of the institutions he had come to look upon as enemies, had grown to tremendous proportions. The disturbing interludes he had begun to feel had allowed occasional openings for his other self, but the intensity of street life and its stream of corrupting events had always made it possible for him to get past these interludes. Now the major blockage to his impulse to seek another way was put aside.

In Puerto Rico he went to see an uncle, explained why he had come, and was welcomed with understanding. Chino was now in his native land, perhaps the one place in the world where he could discover who and what he was.

"I almost got into crime activities there in Puerto Rico," he told me. "But I kept trying something new to do. So I went to work for three or four months as a dishwasher, and saved some money. I figured I must find myself. I wanted to know what is Puerto Rico? What is a Puerto Rican? So I got a job with a moving-van company. That took me traveling to many places. Then I also went out on my own."

He drew unto himself Puerto Rico's tropical scenery, its sun and sea, its mountains and valleys and rain forests. In its villages and on its farms, in its cities and small towns he talked and listened to its people, learned what they were thinking, what they liked, and how they lived.

"I found out what Puerto Rico was. I began to feel that I knew my people. It was a nice feeling. I saw beautiful things about the people and their culture."

Puerto Rico was so much and so great, and it was his heritage. Chino discovered some of the answers to his questions about himself.

"I began to compare this to my past. In the gang I used to drink as high as eight pints of wine a day. I thought about the crime we were in. I began to see that I was destroying myself. Puerto Rico showed me a new light. I didn't become an angel overnight, but I knew I had to take a new step. Fighting, robbing, shooting, trouble with the cops, I was sick of all that."

He thought about his friends in the streets, in the basements, in freight terminals, and on the waterfront. It had been a year since he had seen them. He felt the magic of night in New York's slums. He wondered how his friends were doing. He decided to go find out.

"I didn't make any decision about anything. I just said to myself I will go back to New York. But I was thinking about helping people avoid so much misery. Puerto Rico changed me a lot."

3

The Fabulous Latin House

By the time Chino got back to New York in the early summer of 1964, the old gang days as he had known them were fading. The rumbles, which had been going out even before he left, were largely a thing of the past. The slum was still the same filthy, crowded world in which he had grown up. The noise, the polluted air, the poverty, the endless blocks of decaying buildings—all that was still there. Muggers, thieves, con men, prostitutes, pimps, winos still roamed the streets, and groups of idle youth on the prowl still hung on corners. But many of the street gangs, such as the Assassins and the Dragons, had either disbanded or were in the process of breaking up. Exactly why, nobody knew.

The gangs had been increasingly hard-pressed by the police. The New York City Youth Board and other agencies employing personnel called "detached workers" had stepped up their programs to reorient gang members away from violent activity and prevent or dissolve gang organization. And there had been a widespread increase in the availability and use of hard narcotics and hallucinogens, which meant that many gang members had been caught up in another form of "kicks." A clear break had been made in the nature of the gangland world in which Chino had grown up. In these changed conditions, fresh from his year of Puerto Rican discovery, he began the process of reformulating his role in the streets.

"My first thing was to visit my old friends to see how they were doing. Most of them had become junkies, or were selling heroin. I didn't like that, and I didn't take heroin. I didn't want anything to control me, girls or dope or anything else. I believe in individual freedom. I want to do things when I want. I talked to guys about these types of things, like, are we going to continue messing up? I told them we are all in the same bag, destroying ourselves. I could see this destruction by just looking in the mirror. I wanted us to do something else."

Chino was looked up to, and ghetto young people listened to him. But many of them didn't "dig" this new kind of talk. Moreover, he didn't quite know just what the "something else" was that he wanted to do.

About six weeks after Chino's return, Angelo Gonzales came back, and the two gang leaders began running together. They had been friends since the old days. Angelo had initiated Chino into the Dragons before Chino got into the Assassins. Occasionally, the two gangs had gotten into fights with each other, but primarily they had been allies.

"Our two gangs fought some," said Angelo, "but never Chino and me. Chino was always my friend. If I hadn't been in jail the Dragons would have never fought his gang."

After more than three years of forced separation, they discovered that each of them independently had decided to look for something new. On the basis of this common interest they set out together to see what new ways they might develop. Manhattan's Lower East Side, one of America's principal breeding grounds for criminals, was something less than an ideal environment in which two gang leaders might be expected to find a new way of life, but as partners they provided each other reinforcement.

"Chino and me spoke on the same terms," said Angelo. "We

wanted to work out a way for guys like us who had no chance to make a change. So we talked a lot to find ourselves a direction."

"We wanted a change thing," said Chino. "A new scene."

With this vague objective, they began their search by doing what came natural, roaming their old haunts, "rapping" with their friends, and dreaming the impossible. They spent endless hours lounging and talking and drinking. They smoked a little pot and imagined all kinds of crazy schemes. They went to dances, got high with their friends, had interludes with the girls, then got back to their fantasy world of talking and dreaming. Though their route of exploration was perfectly normal, considering the habits and past conditioning of the explorers, it was inefficient, uneven, and circuitous. Except for their amazing capacity to enjoy talking without reaching any definite conclusions, and their determination to keep looking for something that would satisfy their fierce pride and their obsession for independence, they didn't seem to be getting anywhere. At times they went off on tangents that gave reason to wonder what kind of new action they might finally evolve.

"We had offers from the Mafia to set up a dope and prostitution ring," Angelo told me. "We could have made big dough, and man, that kind of bread looked pretty good. I personally had a chance to be a Mafia lieutenant. But any way you looked at it, it all boiled down to the same thing, take orders from somebody else, jump when they snap their fingers. That wasn't the bag we wanted. It got pretty discouraging trying to get something going. We'd hear of friends dying from an overdose, cats out in the street shooting each other. Some of the most groovy cats we knew. We'd get to thinking, should we get out in the streets and raise hell too? We didn't like what we saw in the streets. Then again, maybe that was the only place for us. These were questions we asked ourselves."

But the more they kept talking, the more convinced they became that they could do something legal and hold on to their independence. Gradually, three or four old gang friends clustered around them, and they began referring to themselves as "our club," a new kind of street gang held together by self-admiration and the stimulation of exhilarating dreams and conversations about doing something new that would avoid run-ins with the police, enhance their independence, and make life better for them and their kind of people. The club, or gang, had no constitution or by-laws and no definite structure. It was simply taken for granted that Chino was president and Angelo vice-president, and the three or four other street youths rounded out the circle of friends—a group filled with enchantment and promise for something great and real and wonderful. Specifically what that something might be was for the moment unimportant. Its existence in the immediate present was enough. The mere act of being together and being inspired by Chino's and Angelo's talk of something new was exciting. That in itself, a self-contained society in its own special world with its own internal spirit and appeal, gave them plenty to talk about.

"We met in different places," Chino recalled. "Basements, rooftops, in the park, in the streets, the same as before, but for a different purpose, to talk about a different thing. We wanted to start something and we decided to call a meeting of as many cats as we could get to decide what we could do. It wasn't too easy to get a lot of guys because by 1964 we had a different kind of guys on the Lower East Side, junkies and that type of thing. We must have talked to a thousand people, but maybe fifty cats came to the meeting."

Whatever the number, all of the "cats" who did come talked, most of the time all at once. If all the outlandish suggestions they came up with could have been translated into reality, they would have started new business enterprises rivaling the largest firms in New York City. When the discussion reached the level of bedlam, Chino would shout, "Hold it! Hold it!" For a minute or two they would settle down to letting one person talk at a time. Then everybody would go back to talking at once. It was not a very organized meeting, but Chino and Angelo had already decided between themselves that the first thing they had to do was find a basement they could use for a clubhouse. With that, Angelo told them, they could throw dances, charge a dollar admission, and make money for the club. A night club. Their *own* night club. They would call it the Fabulous Latin House! Over the next several weeks Chino and Angelo and their small inner circle of confidants hustled a place in which to get started.

On East Ninth Street between Avenues B and C there was an old rundown, multistory brick building which housed a struggling social service known as the Bonitas Youth Hostel. In it a frustrated saint labored to provide food and lodging for homeless boys and keep them out of trouble in the streets. The basement had long since deteriorated into a dingy hole, but it was vacant. It could be entered from the street by a short stairway with an iron handrail, and in the fertile mind of Angelo Gonzales it could be easily converted into a night club. He and Chino, putting into practice their best street-tested salesmanship, talked the director of the hostel into letting them use it.

They cleaned up and painted up. With materials obtained from packing boxes and assorted pieces of lumber they built tables and chairs, and with candles and a few colored lights created a night-club decor.

"Our idea was to use it for building pride," said Angelo. "We said don't let nobody do nothin' for you that you can do yourself. So we built our own night club in this basement to prove that we could do like we said. After about three weeks' work, when we had our opening night everybody could see what we had done. Man, we was proud of ourselves."

From a financial standpoint it wasn't very fabulous. But to them, the Fabulous Latin House was the most swinging night club in New York City. Dances were held on Saturday nights, and as night-club manager, Angelo always insisted on the best band they could find. After expenses their maximum weekly profit from their dollar admission ranged from fifty to one hundred dollars, enough to get a few things for the club and provide spending money for parties, though hardly enough to build the major business enterprise which in their wilder moments of imagination they had dreamed about. But as a symbol of success, as a means of building the notion of personal advancement that Chino and Angelo kept talking about, it was a fabulous venture.

During the week the clubhouse was a kind of headquarters, a day and night hangout for anybody who wanted to come in and talk or just lounge around, mostly street youths who had a police record, and others who could easily get one.

"We made it a place where the cats could feel private," said Chino.

"Various gangs, like the Untouchables, would use our place," said Angelo. "It was our first project and we wanted it to be not just for our club, but a place other guys on the Lower East Side could see and use if they wanted to."

At times the two gang leaders took temporary jobs, but through the last six months of 1964 the Fabulous Latin House became their chief preoccupation.

"For a while I worked at a job that made me forty-five bucks a week," Angelo told me. "I gave twenty to my mother, and after expenses I had about ten for myself. My mother was proud of me, so I stayed on that job for a while because I didn't want to hurt her. My parents are great people. Some day I'm gonna buy them a house in Puerto Rico. This is one promise I made myself. But I had to make them understand I don't have to work in a factory or somewhere ten hours a day for forty-five dollars a week. That's nothing to be proud of. This country is big and beautiful enough so I don't have to live that way. That's one thing me and Chino decided to prove."

The partnership of Chino Garcia and Angelo Gonzales with their Fabulous Latin House held the potential of becoming an important new force on the Lower East Side.

Angelo told me many stories about his experiences, one of which was this: One afternoon while working as an electrician's helper on a job in an expensive New York residential district, he was out on the front sidewalk packing up the workmen's equipment when a fashionably dressed woman came up to him.

" 'Why don't you damn Puerto Ricans stay in your own dirty neighborhood?' she said to me. Normally, this would have made me ready to fight, but I looked at her and I said, 'Miss, I have feelings and you have feelings. Why do you want to put another person down like dirt? If you would respect all people as individuals you would be happier.' I was trying to show her how she could be better off."

I asked him what happened then.

"Well," he said, "some other people standing there started clappin' hands, and the woman just walked away. I was happy about what these people did, and went home and told my mother."

I asked him how, after such an insult, he was able to be so polite.

"In the old days we used to hurt people unnecessarily. But Chino and me decided it wasn't in us to hurt any more. When people degrade a minority group they're hurtin' somebody. Actually, they're hurtin' themselves. Even among rich people there's beautiful people, just mixed up like we were. What Chino and me wanted to do was get people to help each other."

Near the end of 1964 the new club suffered its first serious setback. One night in their Fabulous Latin House the boys got to partying and went on very late. When the liquor was gone somebody went out for another bottle. This was not the first time they had held parties in their clubhouse, but this one was a little louder and longer than usual. As a result, the Fabulous Latin House was closed.

"We had put so much sweat into it," Angelo said. "It was our one really big project and we had high hopes for it. Then the landlord told us we had to get out. We weren't in trouble with the police, but we had no liquor license. So we lost our Fabulous Latin House."

4

The Good Brothers

In addition to the small circle of street youths, Chino and Angelo attracted a number of persons from outside the ghetto whose participation became critically important to their development. Of these, the most devoted allies were the Good brothers—Michael A. Good, born October 13, 1942, and Frederic W. Good, born April 15, 1940, who became the group's chief counselor and advocate.

The early background of Mike and Fred was that of two children thoroughly spoiled by grandparents, growing up in highly sophisticated, intellectual surroundings, doing about as they pleased and getting away with it. They were born in America, but their family came from Belgium, where their great-grandfather founded an import business which their grandfather later sold to Texas oil interests, thus making himself head of the Belgian corporation of an international oil combine. In 1938 their parents moved to Pittsburgh. With America's entry into World War II, their father became an officer in the OSS, forerunner of the Central Intelligence Agency. After the war, following a series of moves about the country, he and the boys' mother established their home in Chestnut Hill, on the outskirts of Philadelphia, where Mr. Good later started a sheet-metal business. Each summer for a period of several years beginning in 1946, the boys visited with their grandparents near Antwerp and traveled in the cities of Europe.

From their family background and varied experiences, which gave them wide general knowledge, both Mike and Fred acquired delicate skill in the art of personal diplomacy, and a high capability for behavior befitting any setting or situation that seemed important to achieving their desired ends. Both were endowed with exceptional brilliance. Both developed a flair for adventure and an ability to excel at whatever struck them as worth doing, while at the same time being equally capable of ignoring or debunking that which they regarded as unimportant. They became extraordinarily determined, idealistic, self-reliant young men, keenly sensitive to social inequity and deeply resentful toward anything that to them was hypocritical. Both were extremely energetic and action-oriented. In these respects they grew into remarkably similar young men, though in other ways they were very different. Mike was never given to guilt feelings or self-abuse as was Fred. He tended to be methodical and businesslike, while Fred was inclined to be temperamental and poetic, and was more easily aroused to angry outbursts at people or situations he found distasteful. When Fred became irrational, Mike remained steady. When Fred plunged ahead, Mike examined the consequences. Fred was full of ideas, Mike worked out their practical application. They could argue vigorously, but they were held together by a bond of unity that made them a compatible and effective team.

As a child, Fred was frequently embroiled in emotional upheavals, and the process of growing up was often an exceptionally painful experience. He rebelled against authority, fluctuated between exultation and depression, and at times was withdrawn and fearful of imagined catastrophes. He was unhappy in school and disapproving of much that went on around him. Each year he anticipated the excitement of spending the summer in Europe where his grandparents allowed him almost unrestricted freedom. In Europe he felt relieved from the inhibitions and pressures that were so obnoxious to him during the balance of the year. Then in the fall he would return home to confront the humdrum circumstances of another term at school.

By the time he reached the ninth grade he had become so restless and unhappy that his father decided something special had to be done for the boy. So he was sent to Georgetown Prep School, the Jesuit institution near Washington. This opportunity to continue his schooling while living away from home contributed substantially to his personal development, but even then he did not apply himself academically until the last year, when he became the star of the debate team. He next entered Georgetown University, where he again failed to find anything that interested him, and for four years he was in constant conflict with both himself and his instructors. Although he never became a serious troublemaker, he frequently got himself into needless difficulty by deliberately provoking his professors. In a theology course, for example, he insisted on writing the word "religion" on his class papers only because he knew it annoyed the instructor, who repeatedly made it clear that the official course title was "theology." Fred twice flunked the course before he finally managed to talk his instructor into giving him a passing grade.

In June 1962 he was graduated from Georgetown University with a bachelor's degree. Thoroughly fed up with formal education and with his general life situation, he decided that at last he was free and would go back to Europe. During the previous summer he had the misfortune to fall in love with a girl named Isabelle, the daughter of an upper-class Belgian family, but she was too young then to get married, and her parents refused to grant their consent. Fred tried again during the summer of 1962, but it was of no use. That was the last time he ever saw her. In October of that year, even more discontented and unsettled than before, unable to forget his love for Isabelle, he returned to America and entered the United States Army.

Having been in the Reserve Training Corps while at Georgetown, he became a first lieutenant and served as a staff officer. But army life proved no more satisfying than university life, and although he managed to stay out of the guard house, he did everything he could get away with in his own way and never really tried to adjust to army customs. He bitterly detested the army's class system, cringed at the thought of being called "sir," and insisted on fraternizing with the enlisted men on a first-name basis. He violated regulations by wearing shoes that didn't match, and one day while standing at attention with the troops he snapped the trigger on his rifle, which was supposed to be unloaded, and the gun went off. He became adept at avoiding army red tape, but despite his ability to get things done, his unorthodox practices repeatedly made it necessary for him to devote extra time talking himself out of tight situations. Once during field maneuvers he managed somehow to open a private store selling beer and snacks to the troops. It became known as "Good's Goodies" and achieved such heights of popularity among the troops that the colonel decided to look the other way.

Even with all the problems he continuously brought on himself, Fred succeeded in bending the system at least a little bit to his own liking, and despite his obstinate ways, or perhaps on account of them, he enjoyed immense popularity, particularly with the enlisted men. In the army he did discover one thing that gave him contentment and a feeling of self-expression: oil painting. In all the off hours he could devote to it, painting became his preoccupation.

In October 1964, still in love, still thoroughly confused about what to do with his life, his tour of active duty in the army was ended. He drove to San Francisco in his white TR-4 sports car and spent about two thousand dollars—all the money he had—on two months of high living. He then returned to Philadelphia, went back to live temporarily with his parents, worked in his father's business, and spent his evenings avidly turning out paintings.

Mike's pattern of development was almost as checkered as Fred's, except that Mike was never quite as intense and was usually able to avoid the agony that seemed to plague his older brother. However, in spirit and outlook they were very close. Both were adventurous and restless and wanted to make the world a better place in which to live. Mike traveled extensively, as did Fred, and developed considerable understanding of the human enterprise. After going halfway through his junior year at Villanova, he became dissatisfied with academic life and decided to give it up. He became edgy living at home, so in May 1962, then nineteen, he went to New York for an indefinite stay to see what interests he might find. After a bit of drifting he wound up in the slums of the Lower East Side and discovered the Bonitas Youth Hostel. In exchange for room and board and what he felt would be valuable experience, he got himself accepted as an unpaid Bonitas staff man and worked in that capacity for almost two years, to him the most exciting liberal educational he could possibly have obtained. He learned firsthand the character of the Lower East Side. When the basement of the Bonitas building was converted into the Fabulous Latin House, he became a close friend and ally of Chino Garcia and Angelo Gonzales.

Angelo said: "Mike Good was a social worker, a sort of do-gooder, when we met him. But he was a groovy cat. When we were fixing up our clubhouse he took off his shirt and worked with us. He drank with us and became one of us."

"He was a good man for a rich kid," Chino recalled. "He helped us a lot, told us many things about the outside world and how the system worked. We were high school dropouts and didn't know about all this. And we helped Mike understand the ghetto."

Actually, Mike was not a rich kid, as he seemed to Chino and Angelo. There had been riches in his family background, and although both Mike and Fred had experienced the effect of those riches in their earlier years, their grandfather's wealth somehow never came through to their immediate family.

In fact, Mike finally got so hard up working at Bonitas for just experience and room and board that he took a temporary job as a substitute teacher in the New York public school system. In December 1964 he rented a cheap tenement apartment at 605 East Sixth Street, and in time it became one of the chief gathering places for Chino and Angelo and their little circle of friends. Mike bought paint and a few other things, and the boys worked with him to fix up the place.

One day during this period—early 1965—in one of their more inspirational moments the boys talked themselves into the notion that since fighting was the one thing they knew how to do best, they would start a military academy, organize a private army, and donate it to the United States government for an invasion of Cuba. Or if the government didn't want that, they would take it to Vietnam. They couldn't get into the U.S. Army because of their police records, but with an army of their own they could prove they were as good as anybody.

They tried out the new scheme on Mike. Though it did seem a little incredible, he could dream as much as they could and told them the plan was even more fabulous than the Fabulous Latin House. Night after night the partying at his apartment became wilder and louder and went on into the morning, Chino and Angelo and their friends coming in to drink beer, talk, philosophize, and expound on the future glories of their private military academy, for which they coined a name: the Spartican Army. But that wasn't all. As the talk grew, they could see themselves starting new businesses, rebuilding the neighborhood, leading the street youths of the Lower East Side away from crime and poverty, and becoming a vast, diversified, commercial operation. And they were going to do it all in their own way. Pride, recognition of all individuals as human beings, and "doing their own thing" on their own initiative became the central theme and steady refrain. Mike kept the beer coming, encouraged the brainstorming, kept telling them they could do anything, and was as wildly elated as anybody.

Meanwhile, his brother Fred, still working in his father's business near Philadelphia and devoting his evenings to painting, was getting anxious for another move. He remembered that in his senior year at Georgetown a representative from the Chase Manhattan Bank had told him during a job interview that if after leaving the service he was interested in international banking to come see him. Fred was fluent in French, and the thought of returning to Europe was a powerful lure. He wasn't much cut out for a banker, but then again, why not? Maybe Paris. He packed up and went to New York, thinking he would spend the night with Mike, call his friend at the bank and be on his way to a new career. It was late in the evening, about mid-April 1965, when he arrived at the Lower East Side tenement at 605 East Sixth Street. The apartment was a scene of jubilation. Smoke saturated the air and empty beer cans were strewn everywhere. Sitting on pads on a maroon-colored floor were five young men talking loudly, waving their arms, thoroughly engrossed and obviously having a wonderful time—Fred's brother Mike, a boy named Arthur, Chino, Angelo, and another gang leader who had become a member of the small inner-core group, named Armando Perez. A typical nightly session of Mike and his street friends was in full swing, and the Spartican Army was the big subject that had everybody's attention. Fred was completely fascinated.

The two brothers shouted greetings and engaged in boisterous handshaking and backslapping. Fred was quickly made acquainted, handed a beer, and invited to find a place on the floor. In letters and in visits home Mike had talked repeatedly about Chino and Angelo and what great guys they were. Now for the first time Fred was seeing them in person. He got comfortable on one of the pads, leaned against the wall, lit up a cigarette, started his beer, and listened as the conversation picked up again. Almost instantaneously it was rolling along as though there had been no interruption, and to a newcomer it was all very confusing.

"At first I didn't know what was going on, but it sounded exciting," he recalled to me. "They kept talking about something they called the Spartican Army and how they were going to get rid of poverty, make it possible for everybody to do anything he wanted, stop all racial conflict, do away with juvenile delinquency, create a beautiful and happy world, and take care of all the problems on the Lower East Side. It was wild, just a lot of crazy, wild talk. But they were serious. They were really unusual kids. They talked as though they could actually do all these things. I had never heard or seen anything like it."

The dreaming and free-wheeling went on unabated, and Fred soon felt as much a part of the group as though he had known them forever. Several hours and a lot of beers later he began singing and playing a guitar as the others made up lines.

"Poetry, man, real poetry," said one of them, as they all cheered. "How do you like that?"

Mike hauled out his tape recorder.

One thought of a line, Mike recorded, another filled in the next line, and Fred kept the rhythm going with his guitar. Everybody laughed and clapped. Mike gave them the playback, broke out another round of beers, and they all congratulated themselves for their creative genius.

> They rolled my aged body down to stoneland,
> They stood and watched the bones appear. . . .

"Somebody had died and they watched him taken to the graveyard and they all stood there and watched the body disintegrate," Fred recalled. "It was morbid, maybe didn't make any sense, but they kept making up lines, lines with tremendous imagery. It was really exciting, all this coming from kids who had always been pictured by the society I came from as bums, illiterate slum hoodlums, the dregs of humanity. But these guys were not the slum stereotype. It just wasn't true what my society had said about them. My society had no real feeling. These guys really had feeling. They were fabulous, creative, warm, human kids who wanted to solve all their life problems by their own efforts. I thought, God, people in suburbia don't know what real wealth there is in this country, they really don't."

Listening to the Spartican Army, being with them, being close to them, feeling the spirit they exuded, was to Fred the most thrilling experience of his life. Nothing like it had ever happened to him. He was almost delirious just reflecting on what he had found.

"I made a decision that night. To hell with business and banking. I took a pledge to myself to stay with these guys and help them in every way I could, and make their thing my way of life. They kept saying anybody can do anything he really wants to do if he makes up his mind to do it. I always believed that, but until then I never really had the guts to just do my own thing. I am a painter, I said to myself that night. I will stay here, work with them, and be a painter."

The party didn't break up until after two in the morning. Fred slept that night at the apartment. He never called Chase Manhattan. He had joined the Spartican Army.

It was a far cry from international banking, but Fred Good had at last started his career.

5

The Real Great Society

At the height of the beer drinking and self-adoration which climaxed in making up poetry and singing into a tape recorder that night at Mike's, Chino was moved to make an impromptu telephone call to a friend in New Jersey for whom he knew their great recording would have special appeal. This friend, Dr. Charles W. Slack, former Harvard professor, a genuine member of the *avant-garde* and an accomplished student of the internal workings of street gangs, was to become another key influence from outside the ghetto in shaping the course of the Spartican Army. Chino and Angelo and Mike had visited him only a week or so before and had received his wholehearted endorsement. Youthful, daring in spirit, well over six feet tall, and extremely articulate, Charlie Slack had a Ph.D. from Princeton, and the flamboyance and promotional flair of a Hollywood publicity agent. Chino had known him from the old Assassin days before his year in Puerto Rico when Charlie, then a research psychologist at Brooklyn College, had conducted an operation called SCORE, Street Corner Offense Reduction Experiment.

In that project Charlie became acquainted with numerous gang boys and won their acceptance. He persuaded a test group of thirty of them, including some of Chino's friends, to keep score on themselves to see how many days in succession they could stay out of trouble with the police, and he promised to reward them with special favors if they achieved a perfect month. The favors, which he financed out of private grants, included dinner and entertainment at posh supper clubs, pocket money, fancy clothes, riding around the city in expensive automobiles, trips out of town, whatever he could think of that would appeal to them and keep them off the streets.

"One of the first things I had to do," he explained to me, "was keep the gang members too busy to be out brushing with the police. It was typical for the police to come around and irritate them into starting something so they could arrest them. The police knew they had been committing crimes, robbing people on subways, knifing, fighting, throwing bricks. But they had to catch them at something to arrest them. So the kids would stand around on a corner, bothering people, and the cops would provoke them into doing something they could witness. Then the kids would show off to each other how tough they were by behaving in ways calculated to get the police to arrest them—you know, show how far they could go in provoking the police. So it was a mess, but to do any good I had to stop this kind of stuff."

He found they loved luxury and publicity, so he gave it to them. He obtained space in a church to use as a hangout, stocked it with free coffee and donuts, and developed what he called a "Theatre of the Streets." He built up their egoes by bringing in Broadway actors to help put on shows depicting dramatic episodes, such as gang wars, in which his SCORE boys became the performers.

He caused them to feel like celebrities by paying them to make tape recordings about themselves, by arranging newspaper stories on their activities, putting them on radio and television, and getting them invitations to appear before women's clubs and college groups billed as *West Side Story* boys telling how they had reformed. Whether or not all this was entirely factual was in Charlie Slack's mind unimportant. The publicity and personal appearances were major ingredients of his therapy.

"Whenever I put delinquents on the air," he told me, "they would always lie in the direction of conventional morality. The announcer would ask me, 'Dr. Slack, do you know how to reduce crime?' I would say, no I don't, but Sammy does. Sammy might be the worst crook in the bunch, but he would tell how he and the guys in his gang were reforming. Then for the next couple of days Sammy would be good.

"I had lots of invitations for them. Women's Clubs were especially interested. Bryn Mawr College wanted them. The girls there freaked out over the bizarre-colored gang sweaters the guys were wearing, and ordered some for themselves from the same sporting-goods store. When the gang kids found out the college girls were wearing their sweaters as a fad, they were kind of shocked. But it made them feel important, a chance to be recognized."

Part of Charlie's hypothesis was that the activities he provided had to compete with the glamor of gang life, be more rewarding, and at the time of day when gang life was the most active, at night. In his SCORE project he succeeded in doing just that, he actually brought about a reduction in the number of delinquent acts committed by the boys in his experiment. But it became an extremely difficult operation to maintain, and he was criticized by some of his professional colleagues on the grounds that he was simply paying the gang members to be good.

Finally, he tired of the constant pressure of trying to make the experiment work, and when the funds for his research ran out he went on to more lucrative activities. He became a public relations consultant and got interested in promoting teaching machines. After that some of his gang friends became junkies, and gradually he lost track of most of them. But he never quite got the lure of street life and gang boys out of his system, and when he was awakened at his home in New Jersey by Chino's late night call, the picture he envisioned of the Spartican Army and of what was going on in Mike Good's apartment was too enticing to resist.

The next afternoon Charlie Slack arrived at 605 East Sixth Street. As he listened to the dialogue and built on it with his own interpretations, all the excitement and interest he had felt in his previous work with the gangs came back to him.

"It was like a social worker's dream," he told me, recalling the experience. "Their values had done a 180-degree turn. They were talking about high purpose, high ideals, telling me the gang days had played out, that they were going to eliminate crime in the streets."

But he was no more impressed by them than they were by him.

"Charlie Slack was something else," Fred said to me. "He came in that afternoon really bubbling about the Spartican Army. His enthusiasm was so powerful we were all just absorbed by him. He was really a wild, crazy guy, really great. He agreed with everything Chino and Angelo and the rest of us said, then blew it up even higher. He made the street guys feel even more important than they felt already, and he turned me on even more than I already was. With Charlie Slack in the picture it became a really insane, Disneyland kind of framework. Nothing we said we could do seemed too big or impossible."

Fred made a trip to Philadelphia, got all his things including his paintings, and moved in with Mike. Charlie bragged on the improvement the boys had made in the apartment, making it sound like much more than they had actually done, and elaborated at great lengths on how fortunate they were to have an artist joining them. Art, he told them, could be one of their major works, and make their society beautiful. They could involve youths from all over the Lower East Side, some day open their own art gallery, attract nationwide attention, make big money, and have Fred as their chief artist in residence. To demonstrate his confidence he then and there bought two of Fred's paintings, one for $150, the other for $250. If Fred had harbored any doubts about his artistic ability, no such doubt remained now.

"I almost couldn't believe it," Fred recalled. "I wanted to be a painter. Now I was a painter. I didn't have to go to art school. All I had to do was paint."

Fred bought a stock of art supplies, and within a few days the apartment became an art studio. Street youths who had never painted began coming up for "paint-ins." Girls came in and did the cooking, and everybody had free conversation and beer. Fred sold more paintings, more than a thousand dollars' worth, at commercial galleries, and spent the money on the festivities of the Spartican Army. Charlie came often. He brought in musicians to play concerts on the apart-ment-house roof, and the tempo of partying and dreaming increased.

"It was a style of life we just invented as we went along," said Fred. "A style that said you just live, just do your thing, and to hell with everything else. It was like creating our own environment, one that we could all live in. We just ran around doing crazy things, having bull sessions, drinking beer, eating, painting, just living, and Charlie Slack kept coming in and reinforcing all the impossible dreams we kept dreaming."

As an informal social group evolving as it did out of the efforts of two gang leaders to find an alternative to crime, then being injected with the special flavoring of Mike and Fred Good, then Charlie Slack, the Spartican Army had become, to say the least, a hybrid combina-tion. A spirit of unconstrained pleasure and self-glorification became its central driving force, and its powers of imagination soared to heights unlimited.

At the time all this was going on, other forces were building up in the larger society outside that were to exert another powerful influ-ence on the group. In Washington, President Johnson was beginning his nationwide war on poverty. Special attention was being focused on the urban ghetto and the need for social change. Everywhere the once-silent poor were being organized to demand increased services from government, and a multitude of agencies was mobilizing ghetto residents for action. Hundreds of millions of federal dollars were being made available, and countless organizations—public and private—were engaged in a mad scramble to get in on the bonanza. Many private companies, including some of the nation's largest corporations, were entering into government contracts for the opera-tion of antipoverty programs, and were getting increasingly interested in ghetto youths such as those in the Spartican Army.

Charlie Slack was serving as a consultant to several private com-panies and organizations that were developing training projects for poverty-stricken young people, and he was in touch with professional antipoverty workers all over the country. When he entered into the activity at 605 East Sixth Street, it didn't take him long to recognize that it wouldn't be at all difficult, and would be a lot of fun, to build Chino and Angelo and their Lower East Side gang friends into hit performers in the professional circles with which he was familiar; he knew further that he would have no problem obtaining funds to put them on personal-appearance tours.

"In working with gang kids you have to move when the opportunity is ripe," Charlie said to me. "You can't get them to reform by telling them anything. You can put ideas into their heads, but the ideas have to become their ideas. Never try to tell them what to do. Watch for an opportunity to respond to them. Then you can expand on what they are already thinking, and when your timing is right you can suggest ideas that fit. Maybe you work around and create your opportunity. But when your opportunity comes you've got to move fast and begin dumping in whatever resources you have, but don't tell them. Just respond to them."

To a promoter and scholar of the caliber of Charlie Slack, the Spartican Army presented a rare opportunity for his special brand of response, and with the war on poverty then getting into full swing, the national climate for what he had in mind couldn't have been better. In his irrepressible style, pulling out all the stops from his old SCORE techniques, applying them now on an even grander scale, he went into action.

He called his friends at universities and other institutions across the country to tell them about the leaders of the Spartican Army and what a great idea it would be to set up speaking engagements so people interested in delinquency prevention and the antipoverty program could see and hear them. Meanwhile, he continue to condition the boys for the personal appearances he knew he could arrange. When they bragged on themselves and talked about how great they were, he encouraged them, and built their self-esteem even higher. When they dreamed about developing businesses of their own and doing away with poverty, he egged them on, expanded their dreams, and strengthened their notion that they could do anything. When they said they wanted no more trouble with the police, he picked up on the conversation and converted it into a city-wide crusade against crime. When they said they wanted to "do their thing" in their own way, he fortified their stand and elaborated on the notion that charity would ruin them. When they criticized the conventional social service agencies and their conventional social-work practices, he added his own disapproval and expanded the criticism, supporting their belief that a program of youth service wasn't any good unless it was youth-directed.

One night they got into an especially vigorous discussion about the federally supported antipoverty agencies on the Lower East Side, how little the government knew about the realities of life in the ghetto, and the Great Society of President Johnson. With Charlie leading them on, the criticism grew to a roar. In the heat of the conversation, Chino suddenly shouted out, "We are the *real* Great Society."

"That's it, that's it!" thundered Charlie, jumping to his feet. "The Real Great Society. That's what we are."

And so the Spartican Army became the Real Great Society. Then Charlie added another elaboration, which they adopted.

"Thomas Jefferson said, 'All men are created equal,' " he told them. "We in the Real Great Society should say all men are created great."

"They were really great kids. Working with them was a ball," he told me. "If you had been with them before and heard about all the crime and awful things they were doing, then to realize that something had turned them around and now they were talking like angels, it was really fabulous. From just talking and being with them I nearly went out of my mind."

Through his numerous business and professional associates, Charlie began scheduling their speaking engagements. He obtained a station wagon for their transportation, and Fred added to the gaiety by painting it with psychedelic colors and figures. In May 1965, only a short time after Charlie had entered the picture, the personal-appearance tours began.

In Syracuse, Chino and Angelo, accompanied by Charlie and Mike, visited a youth-development center that was being financed by a federal antipoverty grant. Their first move was to drop a bombshell by announcing that the center was of no value for fighting either poverty or delinquency. Charlie struck their dominant theme by pointing out that because the center was run by adults and offered young people no voice in planning and directing its program, there could be no real rapport between the center's staff and the poverty youth it was supposed to serve. Taking their cue from this, Chino and Angelo came on as the featured attractions before a crowd of several hundred howling youths and contrasted the inadequacy of the youth center in Syracuse with the superiority of the program they as formerly violent gang leaders were running on New York's Lower East Side by "doing their own thing."

Chino opened by telling his audience: "For a long time people have been saying all men are created equal. We of the Real Great Society say all men are created great!"

Then in vivid terms he and Angelo conveyed a picture of the Real Great Society as gang leaders and ex-convicts putting a stop to crime and violence, making friends with their old enemies the police, and on their own initiative, with no charity or government grant, creating their own great society in which tough street kids whose circumstances had been against them were developing dignity and pride and eliminating poverty.

Unrelenting criticism of any youth program not youth-directed, offering themselves as living proof that reformed gang leaders could create and direct their own programs with no help from the conventional agencies, became the thrust of their presentation, and it worked perfectly. They aroused their youthful audience to wild enthusiasm, then won immediate acceptance in additional appearances before university students, professors, and other professionals. Charlie put them on radio and television. The press raved about them. They promised to return and get the youth-development center on the right track, invited everybody to visit them in New York, then beaming from accolades, climbed into their psychedelic station wagon and rolled out of Syracuse.

Overnight they had become stars, and as their fame grew so did their stories.

In Pittsburgh, cast in the role of visiting experts, Charlie arranged for the gang leaders to appear at a Westinghouse research laboratory and witness a demonstration of teaching machines designed for antipoverty training programs. They charmed the technicians with their stories, made recordings for broadcast, and thrilled several seminar groups.

In Philadelphia they told a national convention of educators that they considered teaching machines so great they were going to buy one to use in educational programs for deprived youths on New York's Lower East Side, but insisted they didn't want any gifts. Whatever had to be done for purposes of education, they said they would do for themselves and in their own way.

Angelo made such a hit in Philadelphia that he was invited to speak at the Alabama State Prison, where he told the inmates about the futility of crime and the great new life they could build for themselves by respecting and helping each other as he and his ex-convict friends were doing in the Real Great Society.

Charlie Slack was so effective at lining up trips that in order to have at least one of his stars present, it was sometimes necessary for Chino and Angelo to separate and go in different directions. On May 10, 1965, Chino and Mike arrived in Albuquerque, New Mexico, where Charlie had arranged for them to visit another Westinghouse laboratory studying the use of teaching machines. For approximately two weeks they hung around the laboratory speaking to groups of workers in the war on poverty, exciting them about delinquency prevention and imaginative tales of how they were reforming New York's Lower East Side. They spoke at a high school assembly, appeared before the Junior Chamber of Commerce, and met with other civic leaders and officials. They made radio and television appearances, and had extensive press coverage. They had dreams of starting an organization among Albuquerque street gangs to become a New Mexico branch of the Real Great Society. They developed personal relationships and held meetings with some of the city's Spanish-American street youths. Temporarily, gang tempers were actually toned down, and for a short time it appeared that they were on the verge of establishing an operation to be known as SCORE, when an unfortunate mishap brought the project to an abrupt ending.

One night some of the Albuquerque street youths with whom they had been meeting were standing in front of a tavern making noise and having great fun tossing a stray cat into the air. A tipsy customer came out of the tavern and challenged them to try that on him. In short order a street-corner fight broke out and the police moved in. The arrests that followed made lively reading in the newspapers, which strengthened the position of some of the city fathers who had taken a dim view of the whole operation in the first place, and as Mike succinctly described it, "The support for a SCORE project in Albuquerque suddenly left."

Other appearances were scheduled in Washington, Chicago, and Milwaukee. At every stop the story of the Real Great Society became grander and bolder and more expansive, and their acclaim grew accordingly. At the University of Wisconsin they brought an audience of judges, probation officials, and police officers to its feet by citing the Real Great Society as a new plan for ending juvenile delinquency. Then, moved by their electrifying audience effect, Angelo announced that juvenile delinquency on New York's Lower East Side was a thing of the past! The Real Great Society, they said, had contracted with Westinghouse to buy a half-million-dollar teaching machine to be housed in a trailer which they would use to bring education to dropouts on the Lower East Side whom they said the school system had failed.

"An interesting aspect of the group," said Madison's *Wisconsin State Journal,* "is that it does not ask for money. It accepts investment money for a teaching machine, but promises to repay it with interest. During their stay on campus they haven't asked for a contribution."

In reality, they had no contract for a teaching machine and no source of funds with which to obtain one. But in the course of their travels their powers of imagination, stimulated by Charlie Slack, had grown to a half-million dollars, and they had become expert at picturing themselves as gang leaders now changing and reforming human life in a vast New York slum. Their audience, though somewhat skeptical, was wide-eyed and impressed.

Said the *Wisconsin State Journal:* "The group said it represents most of New York's Lower East Side, with the exception of dope addicts—whom they hope to incorporate into their group later."

Then in the closing line of its news story, the paper quoted Angelo's sweeping announcement, "Juvenile delinquency in New York is dead."

The personal appearances took on the attributes of the theatrical. They developed into productions bordering on extravaganzas which became more skilled, more polished, more grandiose with each performance. Each actor learned his role perfectly. Each learned when to pick up his cues. Each mastered the art of playing to the audience.

"It was a traveling road show," Charlie told me. "Full of heroics, way overblown, a terrific attention getter. And the guys got so they could really play it. They were natural-born actors anyway. They loved an audience. They loved attention. They were crazy about traveling. They had a ball, and I had a ball just being with them. You never knew what was going to happen next."

There was the night at a swank hotel when they were mistaken for a rock-and-roll band and people tried to get them to play. There were the times they lost one of their guys and had to drive back miles to find him. There were the girls who swarmed over them at every stop, and made them promise to return. There were the special dances given in their honor at university campuses, the singing, the free steaks at fancy dinner parties, and all they wanted to drink. There were the press conferences, the photographers, the hosting, and the special attention from local politicians.

"Nobody outside New York had ever seen a New York street-gang leader," Charlie explained. "That in itself made us an attraction. We could walk into a radio or television station anywhere, let the manager or program director know that Dr. Slack was there with a bunch of New York street-gang leaders, raise the question of what happened to the *West Side Story* boys, and we were on. At every meeting somebody would say, these kids ought to be heard by so-and-so. That would lead to another meeting with another local bigwig, another television appearance, more news stories, more picture taking. Then back to the motel and the girls from the town or the campus would come over and there would be another party.

"Getting expenses for the trips was no problem. I thought, for example, that if Westinghouse was going to run a Job Corps center, which they were planning to do, they should at least see some street kids. So Westinghouse would come up with expense money. The idea of New York street kids meeting with street kids in Pittsburgh or some other city was exciting. And I knew a few small foundations that kicked in a little money.

"Scheduling a trip was also no problem. I could usually make connections with an academic who would set up meetings for us at a university or with groups in town. So we would go on, give a seminar on social disorganization, criminology, or some such topic. A lot of academic criminologists, psychiatrists, sociologists—that type—had never seen the real thing. Our boys gave it to them. The appearances were a shotgun thing. I mean, when people would try to pin us down to specifics we would have a hard time, so the guys developed lines to avoid this. They would tell how they had organized all the street gangs in New York, you know, blow it way up. Then before they could get pinned down they would quote President Kennedy or President Johnson. They were expert at directing the action the way they could sense the people wanted it. They were skilled at snowing people, because they were experienced con men. That's one skill gang kids grow up with.

"Actually, they were just practicing the power of positive thinking. They would talk about themselves and how great they were—that was their basic subject—and the more they bragged, the more the people loved them. Then the middle-class and professional people we met would confirm how great they were. So the boys thought of themselves as a great success, as guys who could do anything. That all came natural to them, another carry-over from life in the street gangs, which are like tribes, a free, unstructured, open-ended way of living. On top of that these were swinging guys. They never acted hostile toward an audience, just charmed it.

"Most people went wild just listening to them. But the main thing for the guys, the really big thing for them, was just the act of going around. Traveling itself. Being accepted. Having fun. I have never known a gang kid who didn't go wild at the chance to travel."

In his efforts to promote the Real Great Society, Charlie could hardly contain himself. He extended his advertising to the top circles of government in Washington. And so, on May 12, 1965, he addressed a letter to Sargent Shriver, then director of the Office of Economic Opportunity, the central agency established by Congress to spearhead the war on poverty.

Here, in part, is what Dr. Charles W. Slack wrote to Mr. R. Sargent Shriver:

Dear Sargent Shriver:

The War on Poverty is being lost at Syracuse University in the so-called Youth Development Center there and is being won on the Lower East Side of Manhattan at 605 East 6th Street, Apartment 10.

Let me discuss the victory first. It began, as many great social movements, in prison. There Carlos Garcia (Big Chino) and Angelo Gonzales (Dragon) both street-gang leaders and accessories to murder, planned what they would do when they got out. Inspired by President Johnson's notion of A Great Society and by President Kennedy's statement, "Think not what your country can do for you, but what you can do for your country," the boys decided to establish a Great Society of their own. The entire purpose of their Great Society would be to eliminate poverty—*real* poverty in *real* time.

The boys believe in action *now*, not in too much talk. They set directly about the task of eliminating poverty in one concrete place to start.

They rented Apartment 10, 605 East 6th Street, and set about making it into a place of richness. The apartment was, to begin with, a terrible place. The toilet smelled, the floors were rotten, the walls dirty. The boys put five coats of maroon paint on the floor and ten coats of white paint on the walls. They fixed the plumbing and the windows. In this way they eliminated poverty of space.

Big Chino, the leader, said that a Great Society had to have both art and science. They decided to begin with art. The boys found themselves a successful painter, Fred Good. Good was so attracted to the beauty and the spirit of the place that he began to do his painting there. Soon boys and girls were painting along with him and, although no one taught anyone anything, the art that was produced was truly great. Hanging the paintings on the wall completed the task of eliminating poverty in that one apartment. . . .

No outside individuals or organizations have given any money to The Great Society. Specific activities at specific times have been supported by individuals and organizations interested in The Great Society. But The Society itself does *not* need money, and wants no grants of any kind. . . .

The spirit of The Great Society is something very tangible to those who are in it. We can see concrete evidence that poverty is being eliminated. The fact that The Society was started by former criminals and gang leaders makes it appear all the more remarkable. I myself go around in a daze, thinking how incredible it all is, since there was a time a few years back when most of these boys were participating in the bloodiest war that ever took place in the streets of New York.

But times have now changed on the Lower East Side and in the rest of the city. Although many problems, such as drug addiction, remain to plague the city, still the atmosphere has cleared. The leaders of The Great Society are the same leaders who led their young people into battle. Now that they have decided on peace, their will permeates the entire community and the threat of violence is removed.

The Great Society must be seen to be believed. In order to be seen it must be visited. As Angelo told a luncheon group of teachers and bureaucrats, "Jefferson said that all men are created equal, but nobody seems to be believing it. So now we say that in The Great Society all men are created great."

Puerto Rican street boys and girls, Philadelphia debutantes, great artists, musicians and scientists, industrial corporation representatives, advertising and promotion people—The Society has caught hold.

Yet I do not wish to try to describe The Society, but rather to point to one fact about it: namely, that it all began when a group of poor people—boys who would not even be allowed into the Job Corps—started to reduce poverty on their own by turning one small apartment into a truly beautiful place. . . .

What these boys and girls have done is all the more remarkable since they work under the most difficult conditions. They have tackled poverty at its worst. You see, every square foot in Apartment 10 must be used for four different purposes: someone sleeps on it, someone works on it, someone eats on it, and someone plays on it. Thus at the end of each activity the square foot must be prepared for the next activity. If people are friendly to each other and are cooperating with each other, that is, if they have the vision of their Society in mind, then they do not need as much space as they do when they are angry. This is the secret of The Great Society. As little Arthur says, "I like my life right here. Why do I need to go anywhere else?" The Great Society, then, has solved its own "problem of overcrowdedness." When people like each other, they don't *need* more space. When the conversation and the food are good, when people are having a great time together, they do not mind being crowded. Last night ten people slept in Apartment 10. There have been more. The atmosphere is very moral and no improper behavior ever goes on. People sleep on the floor, in sleeping bags which are rolled up during the day and stashed away to make room for activities.

Each person in The Great Society, including myself, has a plan for an even better way of life in the future. Each plan is worked out concretely through discussion with other members of The Society. Thus one person may want to become a carpenter, another a lawyer, a third a politician. Within our Society a youngster who wants to become a lawyer can be a lawyer now. A girl who wants to be a dress designer or an interior decorator can be one this minute. The Great Society is invaluable in helping its members prepare for "The Complex Society."

One of the most poverty-stricken places in the Complex Society is the Youth Development Center at Syracuse University in Syracuse, New York. The Youth Development Center is almost entirely supported by the Government and large foundations. It is supposed to be a place where the War on Poverty is being directed and fought. . . .

Referring to their visit to the Syracuse center, and to what he called a lack of understanding on the part of certain staff members, Charlie then proceeded to contrast their "cold and professional manner" with the personal and informal atmosphere at Mike's apartment. He referred to the center's "poverty of spirit," and mentioned "dull beat-nik-type" drawings and perverted jokes which he said were "scribbled on the walls." He referred to a "professor of poverty," said the center's leaders were "imitating the beatniks," and that while they thought it was smart to act that way and show hostility toward the police, the friendly attitude of the boys in "The Great Society" was transforming New York's Lower East Side into "a place of smiling cops." He said the boys had volunteered to return to Syracuse and eliminate poverty at the center by doing a clean-up, paint-up job, and hanging great art on its walls. He closed by inviting Sargent Shriver to "Visit us soon at Apartment 10." Then with an extra dash of brashness, he sent copies of the letter to a list of corporation executives, newspaper editors, members of Congress, and his friends at Syracuse—including those he had singled out as targets for his attack.

Charlie Slack was not unconscious of reality, nor a person who operated in an uncalculated manner. He was a shrewd and practical psychologist, a talented promoter, and an advertising genius. No one knew more intimately than he did how extravagantly his letter to Shriver amplified the truth. But for the purpose of building a public image for the Real Great Society, furthering its own internal feeling of greatness, and presenting it as a thrilling innovation, Charlie knew very well that his letter to the national director of the war on poverty was a masterpiece.

Charlie not only reinforced dreams of the impossible, he supplied an ingredient that transformed the here and now into a fantasy world, an enchanting state of affairs built up from certain basic truths and pyramided to dreamland proportion, a combination of achievements and conditions that were largely nonexistent.

And so a great myth came into being. The media elaborated on the myth, and it became increasingly difficult to say where reality ended and mythology began. By the time Charlie Slack dropped from the scene in the late summer of 1965, the Real Great Society had an incredible public image.

6

Myth and Reality

In the summer of 1965 the Real Great Society acquired a fabulous reputation that surged way beyond its actual achievements. The acquiring of that reputation solidified a powerful feeling of pride and self-respect, and increased the group's commitment to the idea that the best route to progress was through self-help and constructive works. It provided a kind of advance credit for achievements yet to be accomplished. With this sudden public acclaim the group was thoroughly convinced that society was not only willing to accept it, but to lavish it with rewards.

This raised a number of questions. Would the group, now basking in glory, be able to make good its claims? Would it be able to see that although it deserved enthusiastic recognition for the break it had made with the past, it was being recognized for much more than it actually was? Would it be able to see that unless this deficiency were corrected, the inflated portion of its reputation would inevitably collapse? It also raised another, even more serious question: Had the group's level of expectations been heightened to such an extent that no matter how effective its work might become, some of its hopes were so overly glamorized as to be unattainable—at least in the foreseeable future? Unless satisfactory answers were made to questions such as these there was the strong possibility that the group would be faced by eventual disappointment so deep as to trigger old feelings of hostility, or it could become so impressed by its own importance as to reassert the old arrogance of the gang, or it could simply burn up its energy in grandiloquent talk. No serious consideration was being given to these questions.

The harsh reality was that while the traveling and personal appearances reached sensational proportions, this activity was built primarily around four individuals: Chino and Angelo as the star performers, Mike as a working associate, and Charlie as tour manager and public relations director. Beyond these leading characters there were only six street youths who alternately went along on some of the trips in supporting roles, and during the summer three of them dropped by the wayside. Charlie was there only temporarily, and while on the New Mexico trip Mike got interested in developing a small business with two needy youths and stayed on for several weeks in Albuquerque. After that he became involved in other activities and moved away from New York, leaving his Lower East Side apartment to his brother Fred.

What actually existed at this point was a small group of highly enthusiastic gang youths, all emotionally charged, living with inflated notions of what they were doing to reduce crime and poverty on New York's Lower East Side, earning a little money from temporary jobs, and traveling, dreaming, and living high.

At this point in time the best description of the Real Great Society was perhaps that given by Fred: "A wonderful state of mind embodied in the physical presence of Chino and Angelo."

The Real Great Society—which gradually came to be referred to by those engaged in its activity simply as RGS—was limited to the small group of gang youths, Chino and Angelo and three or four of their street-gang friends, and in a sense, their close ally, Fred. This was a priceless group of human beings. From the standpoint of ideology, they had come through a very real period of growth. But their potential for applying that ideology to actual program development was yet to be realized, and if they were to make good on their newly acquired reputation there was still a great deal of growing to be done.

As a newcomer to the Lower East Side and to ghetto life in general, Fred occupied a unique position at this stage of the group's development. He inherited not only Mike's apartment, but also his brother's former role as the group's in-house confidant. He was not really a member of the group but his possible contribution toward the group's further development was significant. He did not participate in any substantial way in the tours that were promoted by Charlie Slack. His role during the summer of 1965 was more that of a novitiate earning the acceptance of the order, a period of discovering his ghetto environs, and of working out "his thing" within the context of a deliriously happy life, which had thoroughly captivated him. When the traveling began in early May, Fred chose to stay behind painting and exploring his adopted neighborhood. Youths from the streets and a wide assortment of visitors from outside the ghetto came to the apartment for parties and bull sessions, and as the accepted "artist-in-residence," Fred acted as host. In the publicity, these affairs—which often spilled out onto the roof of the building—were referred to as "cross-cultural meetings."

The flow of outsiders brought musicians, businessmen, teachers, academicians, college students, and war-on-poverty professionals, all of whom contributed to the development of the group's image. Most of the outsiders, only temporary visitors who faded out almost as rapidly as they appeared, went away raving about their remarkable discovery.

Other than Mike and Charlie, Fred was the only outsider during this period who really became an insider, and by the end of the summer he was the one upon whom the group depended for advice. He, like the RGS youths themselves, was having a wonderful time, and accepted without question the free style of living from event to event, never knowing what new experiences the next event would bring, but willing to let nature take its course, to believe that if they just kept talking about great ideas the future would somehow open. It was a commitment to the notion that everyone should "do his own thing" unencumbered by the inhibitions of middle-class society, or by not being able to see in detail just how their great ideas were going to work out. It was a willingness to live experimentally, and to learn from direct, personal experience—a value that was not commonly accepted in the world in which Fred had grown up.

As a consequence of this frame of mind, Fred entered into an experiment early that summer which resulted in one of the major crises of his life. On the eleventh day of June, barely two months after his entry into the group, while engaged in conversation with a stranger in front of a tavern a few blocks from the apartment, he was offered a small cube of sugar on which a drop of lysergic acid diethylamide had been placed, and in the mood for exploration he was then going through, he decided to give it a try.

He walked back to the apartment, and in his words, "I started going out of my head."

As he parted company with his last remnants of self-control, he began knocking things onto the floor, then throwing them. Then gripped in a spell of hallucination, he reduced the apartment to a shambles. He fought with Chino, who just happened in, threw an iron rod through a window, ran into the hallway, down the stairs to a floor below, out onto the fire escape on the front of the building, stood there a few moments shouting and waving his arms, then jumped, falling three flights to the street below. He landed on top of a parked automobile, thus breaking his fall, then rolled onto the sidewalk amidst a crowd that had been attracted by the exhibition.

His last words before losing consciousness were: "The Real Great Society has conquered the world!"

He was rushed to a hospital with a cracked vertebra, two broken ribs, and numerous cuts and abrasions. For ten days he lay in critical condition. He almost died.

"It was the greatest utopia I had ever been in," he told me. "Chino understood and tried to keep me from hurting myself even though I was being nasty to him. But I felt no concern for anything. I became completely irrational and just acted out the wild, unrestrained way I felt. It really was a bad scene."

He was expected to be in the hospital at least two months, but when he could walk, two of his RGS friends helped him sneak out of the hospital and took him back to the apartment to finish recovering from his private "trip."

That was his first and last experiment with LSD.

The period of hallucination may have been "utopia," as Fred described it, but the sobering aftermath over the next several weeks was seriously disquieting. As a result of his near tragedy and its jolting effect on his ability to function, he was afforded some long moments alone in which to think. He took repeated hard looks at himself. He thought about how much his street friends had come to mean to him. Over and over he reviewed all the extravagant things that were being said about what they were doing. He pondered the difference between this and what was actually going on, and remembered his own declaration about having conquered the world which he had proclaimed that day on the sidewalk before losing consciousness. In this state of reflection he was confronted by the myth that was being created.

"It was a horrible thought," he said to me. "Suddenly, I realized that it was all just a game, a huge, fantastic promotional trick. I began feeling depressed about the gap between this wild, crazy myth—this public image of gang leaders reforming the Lower East Side—and the real thing. With all this attention, the guys were getting notions of what they were doing that were all out of proportion with reality. They were building up hopes that could never be realized. Sooner or later the bubble would explode. I didn't even want to face it. I was as responsible for the myth as anybody."

To Fred, RGS was the greatest group of people and symbolized the greatest way of life he had ever encountered. In his mind his experiment with LSD had vividly demonstrated the place that he, Fred, had attained in the group and the deep, personal attachments he had come to feel to its members. Through his period of recovery in the hospital, then back at the apartment, Chino and Angelo and the others in the inner circle comforted and assisted him.

"We were down pretty low," said Angelo. "It hurt us so bad because he had got to be one of us. He was a cat that learned fast and got accepted fast. He worked like a nut. He showed us he really believed in us. He picked us up a lot of times when we were falling. He helped us in a lot of ways to understand things. We sort of loved the guy. So seeing him in the bad shape he was in was pretty hard on us."

"Fred was one of our most important guys," Chino told me. "It would have been bad to lose him."

Never in any other group of people had Fred experienced deeper emotion. Never had he felt closer ties of friendship. In any event, after his experience with LSD, Fred's determination to help develop RGS into an effective service to itself and to all ghetto youths on the Lower East Side grew to a personal crusade.

Charlie Slack put it succinctly: "Fred became a lay monk."

But this renewal of dedication to the development of the group, along with his perception of the myth, brought Fred into painful conflict with himself. Cold reasoning had forced him to examine objectively the group's actual potential as an instrument of social change and community service, and to consider in the context of reality the practical development of that potential. Until now no one had really done that.

"It was a lot of fun," he recalled, "going to Milwaukee and all these other places, throwing wild parties in the motels, thrilling the audiences, and going on television with all these crazy stories of the impossible things we were supposedly doing. The problem was that it was all in our imagination, just a big publicity stunt."

Fred was still excited by the great ideas they were all talking about, and by the fact that a very unique social group had come into being. He did not minimize these values. But he had been hit by the unpleasant recognition that this was about all that had happened, and the need to make certain that reality kept pace with the myth produced in him an anxiety that he could barely contain.

"The only thing that was real about the myth," he told me, "was the fact of their going out and creating it. Charlie Slack was thrilled by the mere fact of their doing that, and he had every right to be. It was therapeutic. It was a way of creating and firming up ideas. But what started bothering me was that if the guys got themselves enough

sold on the notion that they were doing things they really weren't doing, they could get their kicks from just that. They would never go any
further than drinking beer. After they repeated these stories often
enough, they really became very convincing, not only to the audience,
but to themselves."

To Fred, the purpose of RGS was to create on the Lower East Side
a framework of activities and opportunities within which all people of
all races could develop in healthy and constructive ways their individual talents in accordance with their own ambitions and desires.
This was his interpretation of the group's often repeated belief that
every individual should be free to "do his own thing." He saw RGS as
a vehicle for working with the people and materials at hand to create
an environment in which the development of individuals would no
longer be restricted, an environment in which people could fashion by
their own efforts what they as human beings needed and wanted.

"But the only thing that actually produces buildings is builders,"
he told me. "To be real and great RGS had to produce builders,
people who didn't just talk, but who could take real action. We had
the ideas. We just had to become what we kept telling ourselves we
already were. We had to actually develop the kind of a society we
kept talking about as a living, breathing human community on the
Lower East Side. And we weren't doing that. We were just talking
about doing it, then being publicized for what we were saying. We
were beginning to believe our own publicity."

But the direction they were moving was established. The image
jelled. The performance as it had been set in motion was too exciting
and too well developed to change, and despite its hazards, Fred was
as caught up as anybody. He was in love with a group of people, an
idea, a way of life, and could not accept what his inner reflections
were saying. So he worked out a rationale. It was not the group itself
that disturbed him, only its public image. The group could do whatever it said it could do. The only danger was being smothered in
illusion. But even illusion could come true. At least that is what he
told himself. He was not uncomfortable with the idea of doing the
impossible.

Perhaps, he decided, the creation of the fantasy was in itself a legitimate process of development—a process of creativity in which the very act of envisioning an end product would in itself generate the necessary action to actually result in that product. Perhaps they were real inventors. Unlike conventional society, they were engaged in a genuinely creative method of planning, out of which action could flow naturally. What means of program development could be more daring? How, after all, could anything be more valid? What other method could better accommodate the normal life style of this particular group? By means of this rationalization he resolved his inner conflict, at least temporarily, suppressed his concern about the gap between myth and reality, and continued to swing with the action.

The personal-appearance tours grew, and the boys even began collecting speakers' fees. Some of the visitors to the apartment held informal instruction sessions to help prepare dropouts for high school equivalency tests. Chino worked part time as a trainee at one of the city's manpower-development training centers, and began to read and write English. Between trips the group made a little money by doing various odd jobs, and on several weekends they held dances in a nearby church. It was a very busy summer.

Then as the summer came to an end the intensity of the activity began to run down. Fred took a temporary job so he could pay the rent. Most of the visitors stopped coming. Most of the street youths drifted away, and the gatherings at the apartment became less frequent.

But the inner-core group of which RGS was comprised, with Fred as a loyal ally and chief adviser, was still there.

7

Nothin' for Nothin'

In the fall of 1965, RGS, still cocky with optimism, took a new turn in its development.

On numerous occasions the group had vowed not to accept any form of financial aid that would detract from its freedom of movement. This theme was constantly supported by Charlie Slack, and the boys used it repeatedly in their public appearances.

"Nothin' for nothin'," said Angelo.

That was their slogan. And always it elicited enthusiastic audience approval.

"The Real Great Society does not accept charity," said one of its press releases. "Charity, we have learned, tends to eliminate human initiative and self-respect. A man may accept something for nothing, but seems usually to lose in the long run. He often comes to feel himself a burden to himself and to the society in which he lives. He loses respect for himself and for those who have given him charity. He no longer feels the real joy of succeeding on his own merits and because of his own efforts."

Said Angelo: "RGS was great because we respected ourselves. We did things our way. We'd work out our own operation. We became attractive to a lot of people because we believed in doing our own thing. We said these cats that take money from the government are working for the man, the establishment. They have to do what they're told."

It was a brand of rugged individualism that had a ring from the American pioneer past, but in the midst of exploding support for the myriad programs then building up in the war on poverty it was inevitable that the Real Great Society would sooner or later find reason to depart from that policy. Some of the visitors who had joined in the summer activities at Fred's apartment, and who were professionally engaged in the government's programs, were urging the group to apply for a grant from the government's chief antipoverty agency, the Office of Economic Opportunity (OEO). Several experts in federal grantsmanship were standing by to write the grant proposal.

RGS clung stubbornly to its policy of independence, but as talk grew about the possibility of Washington support, the visions of federal dollars grew more alluring. That fall the group began holding evening meetings with some of the visitors at Fred's apartment to decide what should be done about it.

Up to this time no one in the group, including Fred, had any idea what OEO was, although fighting poverty had been one of their prime subjects of conversation. Without their realizing it, OEO had been an indirect source of support for much of their traveling. They listened intently as the visitors explained OEO and the possibility of a federally supported program. Their immediate reaction was, they weren't interested. It would violate their principles. The last thing they wanted was government bureaucrats putting strings on them, telling them what they could do, how they should operate. They were revolted by the very thought. Then again, think what they could do with all that money! Maybe they ought to talk about it some more.

Under the prodding of their outside counselors, a rationale developed that would allow them to accept a government grant without compromising their principles, and the group gave in.

The rationale went something like this: During the summer there had been so much overcrowding at Fred's apartment that many of the street youths who had been drawn into the activities had left. If RGS had the money to get adequate physical facilities on a long-term basis it could get large numbers of street youths involved in something constructive. Many volunteers from outside the ghetto were willing to come in and work with them. Further, RGS, because it was made up of gang leaders, could bring street youths together with professional personnel far more effectively than could the established agencies. It was long-accepted practice, they agreed, for social programs such as educational services to be publicly supported, and if RGS offered such programs the ultimate benefit to taxpayers would be many times greater than the cost of supporting them. On that basis they could look upon a government grant as a loan. Certainly, that wasn't charity. That wasn't "nothin' for nothin'." RGS would only be selling its services for the public's benefit. Moreover, this would be a program in which poor people would be deciding for themselves what they needed. If RGS couldn't make its own decisions, it wouldn't accept the money.

On the basis of that rationale the gang leaders agreed to apply for an OEO "community-action demonstration grant," and egged on by their visitors, who saw them as an effective means of reaching ghetto youth, they decided to make it big. To cover them during the first year they would ask the government for a million dollars.

Off and on for nearly six months they talked about what they could do with a million dollars to help young people on the Lower East Side rise out of poverty. The program that finally evolved was mostly the work of the professionals who actually wrote the project proposal. Especially active in readying the proposal were the representatives of a private company that was to serve as a contractor to RGS if federal funds were obtained. The grant-supported program was to offer remedial basic education, vocational training and job placement, small-business development, an instructional-materials center, a storefront library, and a day-care center that would provide a wide range of services to preschool children. A board of directors headed by Chino as president and Angelo as vice-president was to provide overall direction, and a slate of business and professional people was drawn up as an advisory committee. The written proposal, with a letter signed by Chino, was submitted to OEO in March 1966. It came to 124 pages. The overall program was projected over two years and carried a final cost estimate of $2,450,000.

On May 11, 1966, an assistant director of OEO wrote from Washington:

> Dear Chino:
> I am sorry that I did not have an earlier opportunity to acknowledge receipt of your proposal and your letter. I have finally gotten a chance to look at it and I find it of great interest. I know that it is now being reviewed by the experts around here. No matter what may happen to this particular project—and I have no way of knowing at this point—I have no doubt but that the work that has gone into producing this proposal will pay off and that you and your associates will be helped somehow in reaching the objectives that you have so correctly set for yourselves. I appreciate having this opportunity to look at your proposal. If I should have any information which might be of interest to you, I will be in further touch with you.

For months efforts were made to get OEO approval, but the proposal was never approved. In Washington several OEO officials said privately they thought it was great, but that it could never have been funded at that time.

The effect was not as disturbing to the group's morale as it might have been because the matter was dragged out over so long a period of time the blow was largely discounted before it became clear they were not going to get the money. Moreover, the mere fact of being an applicant for a government grant added a new dimension to the group's feelings of self-importance. Now a whole new horizon had been opened. Now they were ready to hustle major outside financial support.

"This really made our reputation at OEO," said Fred. "Imagine, a bunch of New York gang kids asking the government for two and a half million dollars."

They continued the usual partying and brainstorming, and continued to feel that what they had going was the greatest. Also, they never got the excitement of travel out of their blood, and became inveterate peripatetics. Sometimes they made junkets on their own, hitchhiking and making new contacts as they went. Often they traveled by invitation, appearing at student gatherings on university campuses, picking up expense money and consulting fees. They made appearances on educational television, and the magic of their appeal as gang leaders engaged in reform and self-help continued to build.

One hindrance they had hoped to correct with the government grant was the lack of a suitable headquarters. At the Sixth Street apartment Fred had to put up with constant complaints from the landlord, and on top of that annoyance, the place was repeatedly robbed while he was away at work. In addition to these irritations, Fred was becoming increasingly unhappy with his job, which was routine office work, and by February 1966 he decided he had to make a change. He took a job with the city's Neighborhood Youth Corps and moved to an apartment on West 78th Street close to his new place of work in uptown Manhattan. That was a long way from the Lower East Side, but RGS had become such a traveling group anyway that one place was about as good as another, and Fred's West 78th Street apartment became its new headquarters. There street youths drawn from widely separated parts of the city, college students, and the usual variety of other outside visitors came in, and through the summer of 1966 they repeated the same pattern of activity that had gone on in Fred's apartment the summer before.

Among these visitors was a student named Bill Watman. Bill, then approaching his mid-twenties and about to graduate from George Washington University, was completely taken by the RGS free style of living and its lack of inhibitions about rebuilding the world. Had he not been married he would probably have thrown in with the group immediately as Fred had done when he was first exposed. Vicariously, however, Bill did just about that. He made a trip to Warrenton, Virginia, for a job interview with an OEO-supported antipoverty agency. Borrowing on RGS technique, he described in glowing terms what the New York gang leaders were supposedly accomplishing, and allowed the board of the Warrenton agency to think he had been responsible for it. The board was so impressed it invited him to be the agency's youth director. Bill took the job and did everything possible to pattern his work in Warrenton after his interpretation of RGS.

Within a few weeks he built up a highly active organization of some two hundred young people, using stories of gang leaders he had met in New York as his main inspirational theme. With this appeal he succeeded in attracting to the youth center in Warrenton the toughest kids in the area, including many with police records who normally would never have come near the place. Then he formed a committee of five hard-core poverty blacks to drive with him to New York to see the Real Great Society for themselves and report their experience to the others at the youth center when they got back to Virginia.

They arrived in New York in July 1966 and threw a huge party with all the right people, including Chino and Angelo, in Fred's West 78th Street apartment. Everything clicked just as Bill had suspected it would. The Warrenton organization would become the RGS southern branch. They would set up an exchange. The New York guys would visit Warrenton, and the Warrenton guys would visit New York. From their two bases of operation they would spread all over the North and the South. They would organize RGS from coast to coast. Ghetto youth would take over the country. It all fit beautifully the fantasy that already had been created, and with imaginations soaring they all zoomed upward and outward.

Through connections he had in Washington, Bill got federal money to pay RGS travel costs, and on August 27, 1966, Chino, Angelo, and a couple of others arrived in Warrenton.

Said Warrenton's newspaper, the *Fauquier Democrat:*

FORMER STREET FIGHTERS URGE RESPECT FOR LAW

Out of a meeting last Saturday afternoon between Warrenton teenagers and New York City ex-gang leaders has come a plan for a cultural exchange program for young people. . . .

Garcia, Gonzales and friends have a strong appeal: Forty-five kids from Warrenton and environs sat enrapt last Saturday for an hour-and-a-half as the soft spoken ex-toughs told them they counted for something in the world but would have to prove it with continual self-betterment. "No one will do it for you," said Chino Garcia. "You must do something, and do it now."

Impressed by Garcia's words the youngsters called a meeting, kicked
about thoughts of a do-it-yourself program, and out came the idea for
the New York–Warrenton cultural exchange program. Remembering
that they must pay their own way, the young people hit upon the idea
of a football team.

The team will play other local teams, and admission charged will pay
the way to New York—and perhaps considerably beyond.

Chino and Angelo did their usual effective performance, but the
southern branch was very short-lived.

"After this big rousing meeting," Bill Watman recalled, "we got
drunk and carried on pretty late. We began talking about holding the
first national conference of the Real Great Society, and when that
word got around in the community the chief of police came in and
told me I had better be careful."

At the Warrenton youth center a split had already begun between
what Bill referred to as the "good kids" and the "bad kids." With the
RGS appeal, increasing numbers of the "bad kids" began coming to
the center and most of the "good kids" left.

Bill summed up the situation: "The good kids' parents began to
object to what we were doing, and we had a problem with bootleg
liquor. One night a white girl's father came to the center and saw her
dancing with a black guy. He was furious. He loaded her into the car
and took her home. Then the situation began falling apart. It grew
into a confrontation between the good families and the bad families,
and I was in real hot water. The county fathers didn't like me
bringing in foreigners, Puerto Ricans from New York, big-city gang
leaders. I became persona non grata in spades."

The cultural exchange between Warrenton, Virginia, and New
York City continued for a short while, but the disapproval of the
Virginia community leaders became so intense that Bill had to get
out. That was the end of the southern branch, and for the time being,
the scheme to organize ghetto youth across the United States. But as
a consequence of this episode, Bill and his wife moved to New York,
where Bill teamed up with Fred and added his promotional talent to
the Real Great Society.

By the time Bill arrived in the city on Thanksgiving Day, 1966, the
major interest of the group was in raising money. All around them a

host of private and public agencies were getting money to operate antipoverty programs, and in the opinion of RGS none was doing the job that it could do.

They were itching to get into business: A leather-goods shop, a photography shop, a night club—the reopening of their Fabulous Latin House—a child-care center, a learning center for school dropouts. Their idea was that the new businesses would make regular employment and the profits could be used to support the social services.

Fred had taken a new job with the New York City Youth Board, where he had become familiar with a list of private foundations that were putting money into youth activities. So he sent a proposal extolling the virtues of the group to twenty of these foundations. It was short, specific, and to the point. RGS wanted $150,000 to start three new businesses, and the neighborhood child-care center. Fred received a letter from the Vincent Astor Foundation indicating interest, and in December 1966 got an invitation to bring Chino and Angelo to the foundation's Park Avenue offices.

The prime area of interest of the Astor Foundation at that time was delinquency prevention. Allan Betts, its chief executive officer, had long been convinced that the professional social-work institutions were not equal to the task of coping with the problems of urban slum neighborhoods, that new solutions would have to be found, and that these new solutions would have to come from inside the ghetto. But as he discussed the RGS proposal with Fred, Chino, and Angelo it became apparent that most of the $150,000 was to be used to put people on the payroll, and that relatively little was to go into the actual development of their proposed ghetto businesses.

"They seemed to have the idea," he told me, "that all you had to do was set up a business and the profits would flow in and would be sufficient to support all sorts of social projects."

He explained the importance of investing earnings back into the business, and other requirements of a successful operation. He persuaded them that they would be more likely to succeed by starting small, then building up as their business growth allowed. On this basis they agreed that a grant of fifteen thousand would be enough to get started.

"It was obvious they knew nothing about business," he told me. "But I was attracted to them because of their sincerity, their enthusiasm, and their self-confidence. I felt that they might learn, at least they would have a valuable experience. This was the first time I had seen ghetto people like them, really wanting to make good, and I was deeply impressed."

Betts recommended the grant, and the foundation trustees approved.

On Tuesday evening, January 3, 1967, Fred came into one of the group's strategy sessions, waited for a break in the conversation, then holding up a piece of paper calmly announced that they had received a check for fifteen thousand dollars.

The meeting became an uproar. Everybody wanted to touch this piece of paper worth more money than any of them had ever seen. They celebrated far into the night. The next day RGS, then more than two years old, was faced by an enormous task. They had done a lot of talking about what they would do if the Astor grant came through. Now they had to translate their words into operations.

How much money should go into each project? Which project should start first? How would they handle the accounts? These and a hundred other questions had to be answered. Fred had already been working with a lawyer to get the group incorporated as a nonprofit social service organization, but questions had been raised by state welfare officials over incorporation papers for an organization that was headed by former hoodlums.

"I was scared as hell," said Fred. "Here we were with fifteen thousand dollars, and legally we were nobody. We had to get all this cleared up and get our tax-exemption certificate from the Internal Revenue Service."

After much frenzy, a new nonprofit, tax-exempt organization was born, the Real Great Society, Incorporated, ". . . to be instrumental in the elimination of poverty and delinquency and in the development of dialogue between young people of all backgrounds and culture. . . ."

Now they had a formal structure and official sanction. A board of directors was elected: Chino, president; Angelo, vice-president. A bank account was opened with Fred designated to sign checks and keep track of the money. Each business was to be an independent enterprise. Each would receive a loan repayable to the corporation when the business could afford it, and pay a percentage of its profits into the corporate treasury, thus creating a revolving fund for the development of social services and more businesses. The idea was that the corporation would serve as a funding and promotional body from which various projects would be spun off as autonomous community operations. As later events were to prove, the scheme didn't actually work out that way.

Chino described the idea to me this way: "RGS should not develop into a big structure. It should be just a spark in a body of activities, a way of thinking."

Out of the Astor grant, nine thousand dollars went for a new Fabulous Latin House on East Fourteenth Street. It featured live bands and Latin music, and on its opening night, April 1, 1967, grossed $850.

"We told Astor we wanted to do things our way or not at all," said Angelo. "So we put in a night club. Whoever heard of a foundation giving money for a night club!"

Three thousand dollars went into a business known as The Leather Bag, which sold leather skirts, belts, sandals, handbags, and other leather goods.

Another three thousand dollars went to establish the neighborhood child-care service in a storefront on East Tenth Street. Known as the Visiting Mothers, this service was to organize working mothers to provide baby-sitting for each other on an exchange basis and make it possible for unwed mothers to keep their babies.

That ate up the fifteen thousand dollars.

Within about a year all of these projects were out of business.

The Fabulous Latin House had no liquor license. The place was in violation of city building codes. It was dirty, overcrowded, and poorly ventilated. The plumbing was inadequate. Its income was up and down and its expenses were too high. The Leather Bag became unprofitable, and the Visiting Mothers fell into a state of disorganization. Inexperience, lack of training, mismanagement, miscalculation were the basic problems of the group's ventures into business, and the revolving fund which was to be used for more businesses never developed.

But as a result of starting these projects and receiving a foundation grant, the press reports sounded better than ever and the RGS reputation accelerated rapidly. Shortly after the grant had been received the group spent several days at Harvard University, where it was virtually idolized. In a feature story *The Boston Sunday Herald* pictured them as ex-delinquents setting the pace for social reform. They were covered by the *Harvard Crimson* in a story headlined, "Ex-Gangsters Plan Poverty War For 'Real Great Society.'" They appeared before more than two hundred Harvard students and faculty members, were featured guests in a round of seminars, and partied and danced with the girls at Radcliffe. The group's reputation as a movement of gang leaders reforming and developing the Lower East Side continued to expand.

8

The University of the Streets

Early in 1967 Fred Good and Bill Watman got jobs as consultants at a Job Corps camp in New Jersey, just outside New York City, and conceived the idea of an educational center in a Manhattan hotel where youths coming out of the Job Corps would spend one or two weeks in discussion sessions with the RGS gang leaders before going on to their home communities. The notion of renting a Manhattan hotel failed to win official acceptance of the Job Corps so Fred and Bill decided to bring RGS to the camp in New Jersey.

As Bill put it: "The Job Corps kids really got turned on."

In fact, they got so turned on that camp officials became alarmed and put a stop to the visits.

Out of this experience came the idea that RGS could start a school in which the ghetto and the city at large would learn from each other by developing free discussion groups on any topic of their choosing.

Fred had become acquainted with Robert Theobald, a well-known British economist then living in New York who was interested in what he referred to as nonauthoritarian education. Briefly, this meant a situation in which small groups of discussants organized themselves with resource people, selected their own subjects of discussion, and learned by interacting with each other. This form of education fit perfectly with the belief that everybody should "do his own thing," which Fred, Chino, Angelo, and the others had always talked about, and to which Bill had so eagerly responded. Taking various procedural techniques from Theobald, Fred and Bill kept talking about a "massive program of education" on the Lower East Side under the aegis of RGS.

The idea was still not really crystallized, but Fred decided it was time for another call to the Vincent Astor Foundation. The first three projects for which the foundation had granted the fifteen thousand were at this point still in operation, and according to the publicity were all going great. Fred began with the premise that with this to its credit, RGS was now eligible for another grant. He presented enough possibilities for a summer educational program to add up to something in the vicinity of two hundred thousand dollars, but on Betts's advice scaled down the request to twenty-five thousand. The agreement was virtually made on the telephone. Fred was told not to bother with a formal document but to come in with the budget in writing, and to make it soon because a meeting of the foundation's trustees was imminent. Fred did that. And a few days later the budget was approved. As of June 1, 1967, RGS had twenty-five thousand dollars, enough to start what was to become its largest and most important project—the University of the Streets.

Thoroughly experimental, it was to be open to all persons of all ages, races, and educational backgrounds, including preschool children, high school dropouts, and holders of college degrees. But its prime focus was to provide Lower East Side street youths with a new challenge for learning and self-development.

The first department of the University of the Streets to go into operation was a School of Martial Arts—a program of karate training and character building—not because that was a part of the original idea but because the person who developed this department happened along at the right time and wanted to start it.

Owen Watson, a Mongolian, then twenty-five, was a trained karate

expert, a blackbelt, had won many championships, and knew intimately the ways of the streets. He grew up in a Bronx slum, later
lived in the ghetto in East Harlem, and in his earlier years was
probably an even tougher street fighter than the RGS gang leaders.
Certainly, none of them was a better hustler than Owen or more
rugged or more competitive.

"When I got back from the Navy," he told me, "I saw that people
had all kinds of hang-ups and were at each other's throats. It was
black, white, Puerto Rican. A racial thing. Everybody was preju-
diced. Kids were pushing drugs, pimping, stealing, always in trouble.
I wanted to help the kids get over that, cut out this racial shit. I said
when guys bleed they all bleed red. But nobody seemed to give a
damn. Then I met these RGS guys and dropped in on a couple of
their meetings at Fred's place."

That was in the spring of 1967, not long before Fred got the
twenty-five thousand dollars. To Owen most of the talk at the apartment was a waste of time. He had no patience for impractical dreaming. But he listened long enough to see if they were really going to do
anything, and when it looked like they might, he offered to start a
karate school without pay.

"I had no time to just sit around talking," he said.

So when the Astor grant came through he and Fred went to the
Lower East Side to look for a place to build the karate school. At the
corner of Avenue A and East Seventh Street, across from Tompkins
Square Park, then a haven for the East Village hippie colony, they
spotted a furniture store vacating space in a seven-story building.
They made a fast inspection of the premises and found a large room
on the second floor that Owen said would work. They rushed off to
find the building owner and learned that they could get the space
Owen wanted for two hundred dollars a month. But they also learned
that they could get about half of the space on each of five floors—the
first, second, third, fourth, and seventh—most of the basement, and
the roof of the building, including a small penthouse, for $1,350 per
month.

There was just one catch. They would have to sign a two-year
lease. With the expenses anticipated for the total program, including
a small staff, Fred knew they had only enough money to carry the

building through the summer. It had been assumed originally that the University of the Streets would start in a storefront. But with this building they would have a storefront, plus all that additional space. Instead of starting small they could start big. Why not? They would find the money. So they agreed to the lease. Fred wrote a check for the first month's rent and everybody was overjoyed.

"We had to take chances like that or we never would have gotten anywhere," he said.

In a letter to a friend shortly afterward he wrote: "I've just signed a lease on a five-story building, and I don't have the money to pay for it after the end of August. But I'm not worried. By that time we'll have turned on every poor kid in the neighborhood, and we'll have the power to be convincing to either the Mayor of New York or the people in our local community that the facilities ought to continue to be financed. The secret is to say yes to everyone."

For three days and nights Owen and Fred labored at converting the large second-floor room into a karate gymnasium, or dojo, and on June 15, 1967, Owen opened the School of Martial Arts with two street youths as his first students.

At the beginning this was the only specific class the University of the Streets had to offer.

The major part of its program was to be based on the idea that Fred and Bill had talked about with Theobald, a variety of informal learning groups to study whatever people wanted to study. The only advance planning necessary to get these groups started was a simple procedure that would make it possible for people to get together and begin. Thus, the main operation of the university, which might be called its "Department of Miscellaneous Studies," was to be allowed to develop from day to day in whatever direction it might take as people came in and developed it. This way of developing an educational program was loose and haphazard by conventional standards, but in this university that is the way it was supposed to be. This was to be a program that would evolve freely out of the streets in accordance with the individual feelings, interests, and life style of those who came in from the streets. Nothing was to be imposed from the top down.

There was to be no formal structure, none of the academic paraphernalia, such as grades, credits, prerequisites, examinations, or requirements for graduation. In fact, no graduation. A person could attend as often or for as long as he wished. In the usual sense of the words this part of the program was to be made up, not of students, teachers, and classes, but of learners, resource persons, and workshops—or meetings of various interest groups. The participants in these groups could invite in people they might wish to ask who had special information to offer. They could read, listen to recordings, or view films. But the basic idea was that they would learn from each other, by exchanging ideas, by mixing the experiences and values of life in the ghetto with experiences and values from outside the ghetto.

People could volunteer as group leaders on whatever subject they might know something about. Learning groups were to be formed by matching people on the basis of mutual interests. This was to be done by taking names from sign-up sheets and posting them on a bulletin board under desired topic headings. When as many as six or eight people expressed interest in a given subject and a volunteer teacher, or leader, was obtained, they would be notified. Then they were to agree among themselves on time, place, and frequency of their "class sessions" and get organized. This was to enable everybody to "do his own thing," or as one of the slogans of the program put it: "What people want to learn is what is taught."

Young people came from all over the city to serve as volunteer workers. Second-hand sofas and chairs, old desks, tables, lamps, filing cabinets, typewriters, blackboards, a mimeograph machine, and miscellaneous other pieces of equipment were hauled in, and in the large glass display windows on the street floor of the building brightly lettered posters announced to passers-by: "The Real Great Society— University of the Streets—Come in and Register—Be a Student or a Teacher—It's All Free—Give Your Time and Effort to Help Your Community—Learn, Teach, Learn."

Mimeographed notices were circulated and news stories appeared in both the neighborhood and metropolitan press. Doors were open for registration beginning June 15, the same day Owen Watson started his School of Martial Arts. Volunteer teachers came from just about everywhere, including such practical experts as a top executive from Macy's department store. Within a few days the street-floor display area which only a short time before had been a furniture store became a scene of chatter and confusion. People milling in and out, clustered in groups sitting on sofas and chairs and on the floor, typewriters and a mimeograph machine going incessantly, bulletin boards loaded with announcements, stacks of donated books and pamphlets piled here and there, coffee cups everywhere, ash trays overflowing, and the air a haze of smoke. Six days a week all day and half the night, the University of the Streets became one of the most lively social centers on the Lower East Side.

Within three weeks eight hundred people signed up, and during the summer its enrollment grew to more than 1,600 persons from widely different backgrounds and social and economic levels—white, black, Puerto Rican—teenagers to adults in their forties. Classes ranged from preparation for high school equivalency tests to literature and philosophy, language, social problems, black and Puerto Rican history, and radio and television repair.

Open as it was to whatever anybody who was interested and willing to work wanted to do, the university became a product of those who were attracted to it, most of them by chance.

Leroy Bostic, a tall, handsome black in his late twenties, was an accomplished painter who specialized in African and primitive art. He also liked to teach. Leroy came in to help develop the university. That summer he and another artist, Eddie Marrero, conducted an arts and crafts workshop on the seventh floor of the building for between thirty and forty children ranging from four years of age to early teens. Leroy developed an art gallery, and in doing this made a major improvement in the whole university operation. In the first-floor display room which served as the information and registration center, as the university office, and as a general hangout, the congestion had become overwhelming. Leroy helped move the office to the fourth floor. Then he and Fred cleaned out the display room, and Leroy built large fiberboard screens to divide it into two functional areas, one for information and registration, the other for his art gallery. With this facility, which he named the Tompkins Square Gallery, he offered neighborhood artists a commercial outlet for their works. Any aspiring artist could display his works and join others in the formation of art classes. The gallery collected a percentage of the proceeds from the works sold and these funds were used to help develop the program. With the gallery, Leroy gradually developed what became known as the Art Department.

The university had a Drama Department because one day a talented and sensitive black playwright named Arnold Johnson, a man in his middle thirties, walked in from the street and said he would like to start it. Fred provided him with space on the third floor, and that summer Arnold started an acting workshop which he called "total theatre education." It included acting, directing, lighting, set design, and playwriting.

Arnold Johnson was a dedicated humanist, intense and demanding in his instruction, and his students loved it. He had a warm and affable disposition, but could turn harsh immediately toward anyone who interrupted or interfered in any way with his work. He knew exactly what he was doing and asked nothing more than to be left alone to develop his department. He worked on the principle that the neighborhood itself was a living drama and that by developing plays out of that actual life situation people could gain new insight into themselves and turn the emotions of the streets into a constructive human force.

"In my classes," he said, "I try to channel the emotions of love and hate into creative form. I want to destroy by creating something which will bring us above what we had before. There is love and hate on the Lower East Side—and there is more emphasis on hate. The neighborhood itself leads to hate which becomes violence and destruction. I am trying to offset this by teaching. My student actors are beginning to see that they may have a chance at a better way of life and they are influencing others to believe this. This can be accomplished through creative drama. If we don't do this our young people are likely to explode, because this neighborhood in which we are living is not organized to survive."

A brilliant young musician named Bill Dixon who taught part time at Columbia came in and developed a music workshop which later became the university's Music Department.

The small penthouse above the seventh floor of the building was used as living quarters for several homeless youths who were to pay for their keep by helping with the janitor work.

The basement space, which had a convenient outside entrance, was used for meetings. Eventually, it was planned to make this space into a coffee house.

One of the university's most popular activities that summer was a series of bus trips which Fred arranged to take some two hundred street youths to the world's fair, Expo 67, then being held in Montreal. These trips enabled the youths to see and learn about an outside world of which they had hardly dreamed, and with Owen Watson's karate team, a group of musicians, and Arnold Johnson's acting students, they put on several performances at the Expo 67 Youth Pavilion.

Of all the unique features of the University of the Streets, perhaps the most unique was its system of administration. This was unique because, in effect, there was no system. And in accordance with the whole university idea, it was that way by intent. A committee, known as the council, made up of the inner-core group of RGS gang leaders, university department heads, instructors, and others who served as staff members, supposedly acted in an overall coordinating capacity. But the council was very loosely organized. It met weekly, more or less, and its meetings were open to anybody who wanted to attend. These meetings were not much more than bull sessions in which anybody could gripe about whatever might be on his mind, and they almost never produced any definite decisions or administrative actions. In practice, the department heads, instructors, and various staff workers went ahead on their own, handling their respective parts of the operation, making decisions, and doing their work with little or no regard for what was said in the meetings of the council.

An example of this was Owen Watson's personal development of the karate program. It is highly doubtful that anybody other than Owen and his students really understood what he was doing. He rarely saw fit to tell anybody and few ever asked. The School of Martial Arts was not just a place to get instruction in self-defense as most people thought. It was a "temple of learning," devoted to the coordinated development of what Owen referred to as "the three bodies of the arts"—mental, physical, and spiritual.

He explained it to me this way: "If your mind tells your body you can't do something, you can't. If you think negative your reactions will be negative. If you are physically weak your spirit will be weak, and the other way around. So I develop all three. This applies to everything a kid does in his life, his school work, everything."

Owen taught his students to meditate, to concentrate, to relax, and to practice self-discipline. If a student was a dropout from the public schools, he had to get reinstated. If his grades were below a B average, he had to bring them up, and to prove his performance, he was required to bring in his report card signed by his parents for Owen's personal inspection. If he was using drugs, he had to get clean. If he was engaged in any other delinquent activities, he had to get out of those activities.

"My students include every race and every kind of kid in the street," he told me. "My aim is to condition them to function properly in life. I don't fool around, and I don't allow anybody to tell me how to run my school. These are my kids. I'm working only for them, nobody else."

He taught his students eleven virtues of character:

> We shall be proud to be Karate K,
> We shall always practice and study,
> We shall be quick to seize opportunity,
> We shall always practice patience,
> We shall always keep the fighting spirit of Nisei Goju, which is our system and style,
> We shall block soft and hit hard,
> We shall always believe that nothing is impossible,
> We shall always discard the bad,
> We shall always keep the good,
> We shall always be loyal to ourselves, Karate, and Country,
> We shall always be aware.

When the karate program started, the RGS gang leaders decided it could be a source of income for the corporate treasury. Karate students were to pay a fifteen-dollar monthly fee, and Owen was to collect additional funds by selling supplies and equipment. He was given an advance of eight hundred dollars to get the program established and was to make repayment within three months. But privately, Owen had no intention of complying with these requirements. He charged only what he thought his students could afford. For those who couldn't afford to pay anything he waived the fee entirely. Karate became one of the most popular departments in the university, and Owen used all the income he took in to develop his program and buy additional supplies and equipment. He kept detailed accounting records and for a long while said nothing about what he was doing.

"The University of the Streets was supposed to be a place where everybody could do their thing, so I decided to pull my little thing," he told me.

"I kept reading all this shit about gang leaders and what they were supposed to be doing, and I wasn't impressed. I wouldn't allow them to interfere in my program in any way whatsoever. I stayed away from them because all they did was mouthe and waste time. I had to hustle to build my program. So when I had my thing all set I took my records and showed these RGS cats what I was doing with the money. The University of the Streets was all free, except karate. I told them from now on that was free too. So they approved my proposal. What else could they do?"

But Owen Watson was no more independent in building his department than Arnold Johnson or any other staff member was in building his. The miscellaneous learning groups which comprised the bulk of the university operated so independently that it was impossible for any one person, let alone a "coordinating council," to know even when or where they were meeting.

There was no director, no clearly defined lines of responsibility. Everybody made a little bit of policy. Everybody did a little bit of almost everything.

"The whole thing was spontaneous," said Fred. "We would dream up an idea for something we thought ought to be done, then forge ahead. When we got the twenty-five thousand dollars from Astor we just started. We had no administrative organization. I had no title, I didn't want one. I took care of the money, that is, I wrote the checks.

I didn't even try to do any real accounting or bookkeeping. I am no good at that. And we weren't interested in anything like fiscal control. This wasn't supposed to be like a formal agency. We wanted people to be free of that kind of restraint. Somebody would come in and say he needed some money, so I just wrote out a check. That's how we operated."

This lack of planning and of definite lines of responsibility gave rise to frustration, disharmony, and confusion among the staff and volunteer workers. But this in no way dimmed their devotion or their output of effort. On the contrary, it seemed only to make them more excited.

In light of the origin and evolution of RGS and its associated activities, a more orderly pattern of management in the University of the Streets would have been abnormal. Had an effort been made at the beginning to develop a carefully structured system of organization and planning, it is unlikely that the project would ever have gotten started. Technically, the university was a project of a corporation—the Real Great Society, Inc.—chartered under the laws of the state of New York. In compliance with these laws the corporation had a board of directors and a slate of officers. But that was only a formality that Fred had gotten worked out because it was a legal necessity in obtaining foundation grants. Actually, the corporation was a small group of free-wheeling gang leaders, an informal society of friends who traveled over the country "doing their thing," making startling speeches, having a wild time, and basking in publicity. Under the corporate name various energetic individuals, most of them young, all of them idealistic, were attracted to the activity at the university and came in and developed it as a labor of love. This is what got it started. Any move toward tight accountability or systematic direction would have killed the initiative. Fueled by this unrestrained energy, the University of the Streets grew rapidly into a bold and imaginative experiment which offered infinite opportunities for community service and development. But as a practical matter, there was a large gap between this potential and the actual level of performance, and before that gap could be closed at least two problems, much more basic than this early lack of structure, had to be solved.

First, the basic assumption underlying the whole project was not working. This assumption was that the RGS gang leaders were in a strategic position to appeal to the indigenous youths of the neighborhood and get them engaged in self-help activities that would result in constructive social change. This group, it had been said, was far more able than any professional social worker or outsider to contact youths in the street and provide a connecting link between them and those outside the ghetto who were prepared to support and assist them. It sounded valid. But in practice this group played a minor role in the actual development and operations of the University of the Streets. Many still looked upon RGS as just another gang. Others, like Owen Watson, who knew what was going on, were unimpressed. What was needed inside the neighborhood was actual work, an application of the group's knowledge of ghetto life, a real effort to go into the street, get the youth organized and inspired to get involved in self-help action. But at no time did RGS make a concerted effort at recruitment.

RGS had become so absorbed in its public image that only a minor fraction of its energy was available for leadership in the streets. Much of the time its leaders weren't even on the Lower East Side. The lure of travel, the thrill of being honored guests at academic and professional gatherings had become irresistible. Summer trips were made all over the country, and the publicity mounted. Even *Life* was preparing a story. Against this background of acclaim the mere opening of the University of the Streets was all RGS needed to further its sense of importance. The mere advertising of the university's enrollment figures, the mere fact that it was being represented as the work of a group of gang leaders out to mobilize the young people on Manhattan's Lower East Side for a private war on poverty and delinquency was in itself enough to feed the group's acquired taste for fame. The mechanics of day-to-day operations, the actual building of a program to make the myth come true, were not necessary. These actions called for unglamorous, laborious work that offered no attraction to celebrities.

In lieu of a solution to this basic problem it was virtually impossible to solve a second basic problem which faced the university that summer. This had to do with the make-up of its student body.

Located as it was across the street from Tompkins Square Park, a hangout for the East Village hippie colony, the University of the Streets was virtually swamped by this transient middle-class population. Probably eighty percent or more of the university's enrollment that summer was made up of young people who had come in from outside the neighborhood, largely from suburbia, searching for adventure and stimulation. Most had no understanding of the Lower East Side or of the street youths who lived there. They brought to the university an orientation and combination of interests that did not mesh with the more earthy interests of the street youths for whom the university was primarily intended.

As a consequence of this, and the permissive method of allowing the university to develop according to the wishes of its students, most of its classes—or learning groups—took on a coloring and emphasis that had little appeal to local young people. These youths were attracted to Owen Watson and his karate program, to Arnold Johnson and his drama workshop, and to Leroy Bostic with his art activities. Preparation for high school equivalency classes, photography, music, and some of the vocational activities had local appeal. The bus trips to Montreal that Fred organized were a major attraction. But for purposes of reaching street youths the largest activity, the "Department of Miscellaneous Studies," was almost a total loss. Although the impressive size of the enrollment made the press, nothing was ever said about its composition, or about the influx of hippies. But to those who were seriously attempting to serve indigenous neighborhood youth, this was a perplexing problem.

9

The Junior Echelon

In the fall of 1967 most of the hippies left Tompkins Square Park and moved on. Graduate students and teachers returned from summer vacation to their normal pursuits, and the enrollment and volunteer work force at the University of the Streets suffered a drastic setback. From the summer peak of approximately 1,600, the number of people involved in the project declined to less than two hundred. This exodus had a serious effect on staff and worker morale. It became forcibly clear that after all the excitement and publicity the overwhelming portion of the summer activity had contributed little to the basic purpose of the project.

In the absence of any overall direction other than the loosely organized council—which didn't really direct anything—the numerous details of leadership concerning the total operation fell chiefly to Fred Good or Bill Watman. This was in part because they had certain qualifications that were in demand, such as the ability to write press releases and other promotional materials, handle correspondence, make outside business contacts, and develop proposals for additional

funding. Partly it was because both of them were personally interested in anything that related to RGS, but mainly it was because no
one else was available to assume this overall responsibility.

Despite their personal commitment to the cause, Fred and Bill
were not legitimate street types. Their connection with RGS provided
them with a romantic story to sell when dealing with prospective
donors and people in positions of influence outside the neighborhood.
But inside the neighborhood that connection was not enough to
qualify them to go foraging on their own for youths in the streets.
They could earn these credentials only by becoming widely accepted
in their own right. Until that happened they were seriously handi-
capped in dealing with the neighborhood itself. All through the
summer indigenous youths had walked into the university's information center, been greeted by hippies whom they didn't "dig," and
walked out again. The only other people available to respond to their
questions were usually Fred or Bill, quite obviously not Lower East
Side street people.

Bill often traveled with the gang leaders, which meant that he too
was gone a good deal of the time. He had an exceptionally imaginative mind, and for him, RGS was a fantastic lark, an opportunity to be
in on a wild adventure in social change. It was an experience which
could have strategic value to his career; it was one of the most fun
things he had ever promoted. And Bill was a high-powered promoter.
He was smooth, smart, and skilled in the art of persuasion.

Fred's attachment was more a form of personal devotion. He was
bothered at times when confronted by facts that didn't square with
the myth he was helping to create, but his intense admiration for the
group suppressed these moments of concern. He loved the group. He
loved the environment in which he found himself, and all the people
who were a part of that environment. In this free style of living he
found personal values which he very much wanted to make his own.
Having become a person *in* the streets, he wanted to become a person
of the streets. He wanted to know the neighborhood and be fully
accepted by it. To him a university had always existed in the streets,
all he was doing now was discovering it. For him this voyage of
discovery was a kind of religion, requiring nothing less than total
commitment.

By the end of the summer the second Astor grant was practically gone, and with salaries and expenses approaching ten thousand dollars a month, money was rapidly becoming the leading cause of concern. Through various influential individuals Fred and Bill had managed to bring in an additional six thousand dollars. But by September they were frantically searching for more and the pressure of economic necessity was growing increasingly stringent.

"It reached the point," said Bill, "where Fred and I had to put in so much energy just keeping the operation alive, paying the rent, the phone bill—which was a killer—buying supplies, meeting the payroll, that about all we had time for was fund raising. We never planned ahead. We were about ready to blow our stacks. We even started getting on each other's nerves. Then I found out that with what we had going and the RGS image we could probably get money from the government."

On one of his trips to Washington late that summer Bill was introduced to an official at OEO who suggested that RGS apply for an OEO grant for the University of the Streets. After their previous negative experience with OEO the gang leaders were a bit cool to this suggestion. Also, there was the old question of what would happen to their independence if they accepted money from the government. Bill had reason to believe that OEO was ready to move. The RGS image had by this time acquired a considerable reputation at OEO, and the idea of using a street gang as an agent in the war on poverty was gaining Washington acceptance. After wrangling over how to avoid any more strings than utterly necessary, and a lot of talk about the possibilities of going broke, RGS decided it would be happy to accept the government's money.

Bill then began spending his time in Washington working with friends who knew their way around the bureaucracy, including several employees in OEO itself, putting together an official proposal that would bring in something between a quarter and a half million dollars. Over the next several months Bill and Fred managed to solicit from the city government, from various small foundations, and from private companies and individuals approximately thirty thousand dollars, which more or less met current expenses while Bill continued to push the negotiations in Washington.

Despite the pressure of fund-raising Fred still managed to devote long hours in the neighborhood and at the university. Working almost around the clock, often to the point of exhaustion, he applied himself to every aspect of the operation—program development, recruitment, public relations, fund-raising, even sweeping the floor. He became the one to whom others most often turned for advice. He was the one who ran from crisis to crisis, serving as troubleshooter, answering questions, doing the paper work, handling the details nobody else took care of.

He was passionately determined to reach out and bring in indigenous young people from the streets. As a result of organizing the bus trips to Montreal he had substantially enlarged his acquaintances with neighborhood youth and was moving steadily to extend the university's service to the local community by every means available to him. He took an apartment about three blocks from the university, involved himself with other neighborhood organizations, and made himself increasingly active in the streets. He helped arrange neighborhood social affairs. He visited youths in jail, obtained bail bonds, helped them find jobs, and got to know their parents. He promoted scholarships, organized committees to assist neighborhood projects that needed political support, and became a storehouse of confidential information. From this kind of personal involvement, Fred gradually earned his credentials and became well known and well liked by numerous Lower East Side street youths outside the small RGS inner circle.

One of these youths, José Feliciano, age twenty when Fred began to know him, was known in the neighborhood as Pee Wee. He had lived there all his life, and though he had grown to average height, he never lost the nickname he had acquired in his earlier years. Pee Wee was active in all kinds of things, good and bad, and had a seemingly unlimited capacity to go either way. He had been in and out of jail more times than he could remember. He was the leader of the Untouchables, which used to fight Chino's old gang, the Assassins, as well as most other gangs in the area. In time it took over many of them, enlarged its turf, and became one of the largest and most powerful gangs on the Lower East Side.

"We had connections with the Mafia," Pee Wee told me. "They hired us to do their things, like blow up their club competition. We stole cars, cut 'em up and sold the parts, pulled robberies, hustled. We had plenty of ways to make money."

Gradually, he led his followers in a more peaceful direction, though many of the Untouchables continued to have frequent troubles with the police. Many of them became heroin addicts, as did Pee Wee, and—as they say in the streets—he was "strung out" much of the time, often using as many as five or six bags of heroin a day. It was an expensive habit, but when he was off drugs and his natural self was free to function he proved that he could be as constructive a neighborhood force as he had been destructive.

In the summer of 1967 the New York City Youth Board opened a temporary storefront center about a block from the University of the Streets and hired Pee Wee, along with a number of other neighborhood youths, to organize youth activities and help prevent rioting. Both the weather and the people's tempers were hot, and on several occasions neighborhood disturbances almost ended in riots. Pee Wee so successfully demonstrated his ability as a leader in cooling wrought-up emotions that he was recognized by city officials as a major element in preventing several riots. That fall the storefront center was closed and the summer youth employees were dropped from the city payroll.

Pee Wee was still off drugs. He had saved his summer earnings, rented an apartment, and was preparing to get married. Then about two days later he was arrested, accused of holding up a Jordanian student with a knife and robbing him of his watch and one dollar. The Jordanian was said to have followed him, hailed a police cruiser, and pointed out Pee Wee as his assailant. Pee Wee swore he was innocent, a victim of mistaken identity. But he had a long record of previous arrests, and the Jordanian stuck to his complaint. Pee Wee was charged with the crime and released on bail.

Fred had known Pee Wee from his work in riot prevention, and the two became close friends, visiting frequently in the streets, in Fred's apartment, and at the university. Pee Wee even took Fred to meet his parents, and Fred and Mr. Feliciano became friends.

Pee Wee was virtually a human magnet for street youths. He was always in the streets and was one of the neighborhood's most influential natural leaders. Under his leadership a large group of teenagers— more than fifty of them—took over the basement of the university building, which Fred told Pee Wee he could have. They cleaned it out, painted and decorated, installed psychedelic lighting, brought in tables and chairs, put in a record player, and developed an attractive neighborhood social center, which became known as the Community Clubhouse. By the spring of 1968, Pee Wee and his followers built it to a membership of well over three hundred, and the clubhouse became an important means of channeling street youths into the university.

That spring, still out on bail awaiting trial, Pee Wee organized a five-team baseball league, successfully arbitrated peace among street gangs on the Lower East Side and in other parts of the city, was personally responsible for getting numerous youths into treatment for the drug habit, organized an improvement association among the residents on his block, developed a storefront recreation center as an extension of the Community Clubhouse, and managed to find jobs for about a dozen youths.

Of all his operations perhaps the most ingenious was his approach to the problem of job finding. For youths experienced in taking apart stolen automobiles he sought jobs in garages. Those skilled at injecting drugs were adept at learning to take blood samples. For those experienced in breaking into buildings and moving out furniture he solicited the furniture stores. Whatever a gang youth had learned to do illegally, Pee Wee figured was the basis for a legitimate job. And the amazing thing was he made his theory work.

"These cats that know how to steal furniture are fast at handling the stuff," he told me. "In every store where I got jobs for them they were great."

In people such as Pee Wee, Fred began to find answers to the university's recruitment and leadership problems.

"Our project is not substantive, it's just there," said Fred. "It is the people who meet each other, interact with each other, do things to each other, learn from each other, and in the process become what they are capable of becoming. Our results can't be determined by any standard prescription or by conventional job descriptions. How, for instance, would we define a community organizer? We would have to begin by defining Pee Wee. The job flows out of the person. That's the meaning of the university."

Pee Wee was an example of what this experiment was intended to offer young people on the Lower East Side, whether they were delinquents in need of redirection, or merely poor and in need of opportunity.

Fred was determined to keep Pee Wee free on probation so he could continue his work in the community. He accumulated evidence to help counter the charge, worked with the defense attorney in preparing the case, and from city officials, neighborhood residents, clergymen, and business leaders obtained letters testifying to Pee Wee's value to the community and to the change he appeared to be making in himself. But Pee Wee was charged with a felony, and his earlier reputation was very much against him. If he were to plead not guilty, then be found guilty by a jury, he could be sentenced to five to forty years. Basically, it was his word against the Jordanian student's word, and it was the attorney's opinion that the jury would believe the Jordanian. He therefore advised Pee Wee to plead guilty to a lesser charge, which could be arranged, and thus risk a lesser sentence. Pee Wee accepted the lawyer's advice, and was sentenced to one day to three years. Fred then went to work to get him paroled.

During the time interval between his arrest and conviction Pee Wee had been married. Upon receiving word that his wife was going to have a baby, he wrote Fred from prison: "I would like you to baptize my son or daughter . . . no one but you, because you being a good friend to me I would like you to be part of my family. That is why I want you to baptize my son or daughter."

This was the kind of attachment Fred acquired on the Lower East Side.

Alvin King was another youth who had run with the gangs. He was the leader of the Falcons, and was eighteen when he met Fred and became interested in the University of the Streets. Shortly after they got to know each other a form letter came to the university from

Senator Javits's office announcing a scholarship from the American Institute for Foreign Studies for an outstanding young man from a poverty area for a European tour and six weeks' study at the University of North Wales. Two such scholarships were to be awarded in New York, one by Senator Javits, the other by Mayor Lindsay. With Alvin's permission, Fred presented his name for the award to be made by Senator Javits and with characteristic vigor went to work to convince the senator's office that his candidate should be selected.

Alvin won the award.

A city hall press conference was scheduled at which Senator Javits was to present the award to Alvin, and Mayor Lindsay was to present the award to his candidate. While waiting for this special day to arrive, Alvin was working with Fred at the university and from this association had become engrossed in the effort to keep Pee Wee out of jail. Then about two weeks before the scheduled ceremony at city hall, Fred got a call telling him Alvin was in jail.

According to Alvin, a friend had offered him an army bayonet that had been given to him by another friend who had stolen it from the army. Alvin said he had gone to his friend's house after dark, picked up the bayonet, tucked it under his shirt, and on coming out into the street encountered a group of youths having a fight. Knowing the combatants, Alvin said he thought he could stop the fight and for that reason ran into the melee. About one minute later the police arrived, found the bayonet in Alvin's shirt, and locked him up. It was a complicated situation: Senator Javits's outstanding young man about to be awarded a scholarship for European study and travel, now in jail charged with attempt to do bodily harm with a deadly weapon, and his only defense a story that almost nobody could be expected to believe. Except for the matter of the award, this was routine on the Lower East Side. He was released on bail, and on the same day Pee Wee was sent to prison appeared before the news media at City Hall with the Senator, the Mayor, and distinguished guests to be publicly awarded his scholarship.

Senator Javits and Mayor Lindsay presented their awards and made statements for the press. A reporter asked Alvin for his reaction. Addressing the press and assembled dignitaries, Alvin told them he thought it was very nice. Then taking out of his pocket a mimeographed paper Fred had prepared, he said: "But my main interest in being here is to speak about Pee Wee's case."

The audience listened while Alvin explained Pee Wee's importance to the community and asked that the Senator and the Mayor use their influence to get him out of jail. Alvin handed out copies of the mimeographed paper, and that was the end of the ceremony. He was taking full advantage of what seemed to be an opportunity to help his friend.

About three weeks later Alvin had to appear in court on his own behalf. He was sentenced to three months in the custody of the Vera Institute of Justice, a court referral agency engaged in working with delinquents. That kept him out of jail, but his scheduled departure for Europe was only a few days away. With Fred's help he was granted permission to postpone his sessions at Vera and was allowed to leave for his new experience—foreign travel and studies in English literature, archeology, architecture, and "Great Britain Today." He became one of the best-liked students at the University of North Wales, made a B average, returned to the Lower East Side, completed his assignment at Vera, and became one of the most valuable workers at the University of the Streets—bringing in scores of young people who previously had not been reached.

Fred arranged with the city's Neighborhood Youth Corps for a summer job program to employ forty youths in the university, and brought in Alvin's younger brother Michael, age fifteen, who was failing the ninth grade, to manage the operation. Later Fred recommended him for a scholarship, and a friend of the university, Frank Vorkink, worked it out at Solebury Prep School in New Hope, Pennsylvania, where Michael became an honor student. While there Michael wrote back: "When I am through with my education I plan to work for the university as a lawyer . . . the university has been a big part of my life."

In addition to Michael, Alvin King had an older brother in the Marine Corps, and three younger sisters. Their mother, who was born in Puerto Rico, was a deeply civic-minded woman. She worked steady for a small income and managed to support her family, struggling constantly against heavy odds to make her influence on her children compete with the influence of the streets. Fred helped get her appointed as a community aide with the Mayor's Urban Task Force on the Lower East Side, and with the Kings the University of the Streets became a family affair.

"I am separated and must look after my children," Mrs. King said to me. "When I first heard about this university I was concerned. Is this just another gang? I was worried. But my kids kept telling me it was a good thing. Then Fred came to visit at our home. So I decided to go see for myself. I liked what I saw. It kept the kids out of the streets. I even saw them doing their homework, something unusual. I saw no drugs. They even began getting books from the library. So I told Fred I wanted to be involved in the program.

"When Alvin told me Fred was getting him a scholarship and that he was going to travel in Europe, I didn't believe him. I told him, sure, I travel every day, in my dreams. But sure enough, it really happened. Then in a little while Fred got Michael a scholarship. I didn't get a high school diploma, but I don't want my kids to not have one. I want them to go to college. That's what the University of the Streets means to my family."

Into the summer of 1968, Fred worked in the streets every hour he could take away from his multitude of other chores, encouraging Pee Wee, Alvin, Michael, and dozens of other youths in similar situations; through them a new group of street youths began coming into the university, a kind of junior echelon that began to deepen and broaden its influence in the neighborhood.

Bobo Ortiz, who had been a street-gang warlord, turned his energies to organizing a cooperative called the Thirteenth Street Block Association.

Norman Wright, a young black, one of the most conscientious persons I have met, collected two file drawers of information on housing for the university's use, then developed an art workshop for thirty teenagers.

Wayne Edwards, another black youth, whom Fred took in to live with him, wrote a résumé for employment which began: "Since the age of fourteen I have been the leader of two street gangs, a mugging and robbery ring, a marijuana salesman, a numbers runner, and the leader of a group of young people who scared and assaulted people for a price." With Fred's help, Wayne organized a storefront education center as an extension of the University of the Streets in Brooklyn's Bedford-Stuyvesant.

A boy just thirteen and very bright had already begun experimenting with drugs, including heroin. His father was dead and he hadn't lived with his mother since he was seven. He and three younger brothers lived with an elder brother and his family in a crowded apartment, but most of the time he ran the streets. He had no police record, but it seemed inevitable that he soon would. The junior echelon got him into the Community Clubhouse and from there into art classes.

"He's an exceptional kid," said Fred. "His brother's family loves him, he now has good friends, and he has found his alternative to the streets. Our job is to help him along in that alternative."

Johnny, Cucho, Everett, Thomas, Vernon—black, white, Puerto Rican, Chinese—and girls like Kelly, Vesta, and Jerry came in from the streets and found their alternatives, and Fred made every effort possible to expand those alternatives.

An illustration of this effort was an arrangement he worked out with Kenyon & Eckhardt, a leading New York advertising agency. Its president, E. L. Timberman, Jr., saw the problem of the ghetto as an infinite number of smaller problems, many of which he believed could be attacked as simply a matter of good business.

> I am pessimistic about the ability of the federal government or the fifty largest corporations in the country to make these problems disappear [Timberman told me].
>
> Many smaller companies have a part to play and to prevent them from copping out we've got to show that it can be done on a practical business basis. For example, in the advertising business we have an endless need for talented people, and a college degree doesn't necessarily tell you anything about talent. I began thinking that in ghetto minority groups there must be many young people who don't have college degrees, but who do have the native talent we need. If we could get these people and help them develop their talent it would not only be

good for them and good for society, it would be good for business. But the question is, how do you find this talent in the ghetto?

That was where Fred and his junior echelon came in.

Timberman had read of RGS and the University of the Streets and had gotten in touch with Fred. Together they worked out a plan. Fred knew the people who could find the talented street youths. Kenyon & Eckhardt would hire and train them. Timberman looked through his company's budget and carved out enough money to pay four extra employees until they could gain sufficient skill to justify their inclusion in the regular payroll. Alvin King became the chief talent finder, and four youths who had no experience or college degree were pulled out of the streets and placed in jobs that would enable them to learn advertising.

This was not charity. Kenyon & Eckhardt expected them to do a job the company would be willing to pay for.

And they did.

This opened other possibilities. Kenyon & Eckhardt was only one of many advertising agencies. So they conceived the idea of an employment agency to specialize in supplying talent from the ghetto to advertising firms, to be owned and operated by a Lower East Side youth. Alvin would find the youth. Kenyon & Eckhardt would get him trained and supply enough credit and follow-up consultation to see him through to success.

Alvin went to the streets and found his man, Douglas Boozer, a twenty-two-year-old black who lived with his mother and sister and hadn't seen his father since 1951. He had a high school diploma, had worked around at odd jobs, and was unemployed. His work experience had no apparent relationship to the advertising business, but he was excited over the idea and Alvin insisted he had the talent. After talking all night, Alvin took Douglas to Fred's apartment at five o'clock in the morning and the three of them talked until almost noon. Fred made an appointment for Douglas to see the personnel director at Kenyon & Eckhardt.

"All I need is training," Douglas said to me. "I already know the streets and which cats can draw or do this or that. Plenty of them have the talent. All they need is a chance and somebody to show them where to find it."

I went with Fred, Alvin, and Douglas to Kenyon & Eckhardt, just trailed along and listened. The firm was located in well-appointed quarters in the Pan American Building, 200 Park Avenue. All four of us were wearing wash slacks and open-neck shirts and were quite different in appearance from the neatly attired people we met inside. But my three companions were totally unconcerned. They approached their interview as though they were taking over the place. We stopped long enough to visit the four youths from the University of the Streets who were already in training at Kenyon & Eckhardt and found that one of them was thinking of leaving because through the people he had met there he had received a higher salary offer.

When we were ushered into the personnel director's office, he looked at us, took off his jacket, and loosened his tie.

"With you guys I feel like I ought to take off my shoes," he said.

He asked if Douglas could do the job.

Sure, he could do the job, Fred and Alvin assured him. Douglas confidently agreed.

Why? Because, they explained, they knew Douglas like street people know street people.

"Our knowledge of him is real," said Fred. "Not artificial like the information you get from application blanks and these conventional screening devices."

The meeting was as friendly and casual as if they were having a beer in a Lower East Side tavern. The personnel director seemed satisfied, and after a short talk with Douglas alone while the rest of us waited in the outer office, agreed that he could do the job.

Later, in discussing the project with Timberman, the personnel director said to me:

"Don't get me wrong. We aren't going into this on a bleeding-heart basis. We aren't going to throw company money into this thing without watching it. We've got to select the right kid, but we can't do that by applying our usual standards of measurement. We've got to trust Fred and his friends."

"Amazing," I remarked.

Then he added: "Two different cultures are meeting in this project. We must let them operate in their style. I think their judgment as to who has a certain talent is reliable. If we do our part and let them do their part we can come together and make it work. There are a lot of reformers and dreamers who want to take care of the problems of the ghetto overnight, but who never get down to work and follow through the specific details. What we need is more Fred Goods."

This was a sample of what the University of the Streets could do in one field: employment and job development. There were also other fields.

"We are working with a lot of great possibilities," said Fred. "But we can't promise kids anything. We have to make sure they have a real alternative; with Douglas it's a real alternative because it's a real opportunity, not a fake opportunity."

"I can be a force that helps guys," Alvin added, "if I can have my own thing, you know, be able to find my own groove so I can operate the way I know how. Then I can be a vehicle that others can move through."

"That's it," Fred said, excitedly. "That's what the University of the Streets does. The university is an environment, an environment for action made up of guys like Alvin that both causes and allows people to learn by doing what they want to do. If it ever evolved into a structure that restricted that kind of movement it would lose its value."

Gradually, the University of the Streets was taking a new turn. It still had serious internal problems of leadership and organization. It had yet to resolve its financial difficulties. But its enrollment of indigenous neighborhood youth was beginning to increase, and it was beginning to demonstrate its potential as an instrument of development.

10

RGS Expands to East Harlem

The decisions and actions that shaped the course of RGS were due largely to influence from outside the group itself and to a series of events that occurred by happenstance.

Frank Ferguson was a tall, slow-talking but exceptionally bright and articulate young man who became a specialist in a variety of fields ranging from computer science to the workings of the federal bureaucracy. During 1965 he and his wife lived in a cheap apartment on the Lower East Side because at that time Frank was going to graduate school, he had just become a father, and he was broke. A tough gang kid used to sit on the steps outside the Fergusons' first-floor window and keep them awake at night playing bongo drums. People would pound on the door at all hours wanting some kind of help. One night about 4 A.M. it was a black girl from the apartment next door, her face bleeding and splattered with broken glass from the screen of a television set somebody had thrown at her. Family fights, screaming, and bleeding were commonplace. Prostitutes and their customers roamed in and out of the building. Junkies idling in the hallways, drunks lying in the street were part of the daily routine. Repeatedly, the Ferguson apartment was robbed.

"This was really abject poverty," Frank said to me. "I just hadn't known that people actually lived that way."

Then through Charlie Slack, whom he had known from college days, he met Chino and Fred. He joined many of the sessions at Fred's, and like virtually everyone else who witnessed these sessions, became enamored with RGS. Often in their rounds of the streets the gang leaders would drop in at Ferguson's, usually at dinner time, and Laura, Frank's wife, would dish up more beans.

"She finally got kind of upset about our feeding the neighborhood when we could barely afford to feed ourselves," Frank told me.

But that was how Frank Ferguson got involved.

After that he worked for various organizations dealing with poverty problems, including a scientific company where he put together a massive plan that ultimately evolved into the Model Cities Program of the Department of Housing and Urban Development. Later he wound up as a planner for the Job Corps in the Office of Economic Opportunity, and eventually became the president of a successful business in Silver Springs, Maryland, specializing in the use of programmed teaching materials, Basic Education Computers, Inc. Wherever he went he continued to keep in touch with RGS, often visiting Fred in New York. It was Frank's work that supplied many of the ideas for the group's first government proposal that got lost in Washington. He was instrumental in getting Fred and Bill hired as consultants at the New Jersey Job Corps camp and putting them in touch with Robert Theobald, all of which led to the University of the Streets. In these and many other ways Frank Ferguson, working always behind the scenes, became a strategic mover for RGS, opening many doors leading to funds for it.

In May 1967, in Washington, Frank met a man named C. McKenzie Lewis. He was in his mid-fifties, a distinguished tax attorney by profession, well established in influential middle- and upper-class circles. He lived comfortably in an expensive home on the outskirts of Washington, and had an uncanny ability to put odd assortments of people and institutions together in ways that caused actions and events to occur that he believed ought to happen for the benefit of society.

Deeply influenced by the challenge of President Kennedy, he took a substantial reduction in income to join the New Frontier, accepted a position in the Agency for International Development, and became interested in the agonizing poverty of urban slums in Latin America. But for Mac Lewis the response of the foreign-aid bureaucracy was too limited and too slow, so he took to traveling at his own expense between Washington, New York, and South America, and involved himself in various private efforts to organize social change by motivating action among the slum dwellers themselves.

On meeting Frank Ferguson he was immediately taken by Ferguson's quick mind and ability to perceive the failings of the federal antipoverty program in the United States, and for that reason invited Frank to accompany him to Santiago for a look at possible programs in the slums of the Chilean capital. The next day Frank found himself aboard a flight with Mac Lewis bound for South America at Mac's expense. In Santiago, Mac was fascinated by the possibility of slum youth gangs as vehicles for social change, and expressed the feeling that it was unfortunate there weren't such groups in the United States.

"Up to that point," Frank told me, "I had carefully avoided telling Mac about RGS because I thought it would be too scary and wild for a man of his propriety. But in Santiago when I did tell him, he acted as though he didn't believe me. So after we got back from South America I arranged through Fred Good for him to meet the guys in New York and have a look for himself."

Meanwhile, another former street fighter named Angelo Giordani, known as Papo, a close friend of Angelo Gonzales, had become a member of the RGS inner-core group and had made himself one of its principal leaders. Medium height, slender build, black wavy hair, he lived in Spanish East Harlem, one of the most crowded and poverty-ridden slums in New York. Endowed with high native intelligence, Papo was extremely shrewd in the ways of the streets, and was determined to become equally shrewd in the ways of conventional society. He was intensely Puerto Rican, had an engaging smile, and was a born politician. With help from Fred he was offered a scholarship at

Harvard, but turned it down because at the time he wanted to stay in New York. Later he graduated from New York's Pace College and decided to go after a law degree. Ultimately, he had his eye on becoming a spokesman for East Harlem in New York political and economic circles.

One of Papo's first ambitions was to expand RGS to East Harlem, and he was able to get a portion of the twenty-five-thousand-dollar Astor grant for the University of the Streets set aside for that purpose.

To get started in East Harlem, they rented for three hundred dollars a month a loft space on Madison Avenue just above 111th Street and began a remedial-education center for high school dropouts. Papo and a few of his East Harlem friends recruited twenty-four dropouts, and several East Harlem college students volunteered as summer instructors. Fred and Bill arranged to get additional help from the city's Neighborhood Youth Corps and talked the Job Corps out of six thousand dollars' worth of curriculum materials for the new center. Papo then became RGS vice-president for East Harlem. Thus, the inner-core group was now enlarged to include a half-dozen more members in an uptown wing which came to be referred to as RGS/Uptown, or RGS/East Harlem.

It was late in July 1967, only a few weeks after this new extension of the group had started, that Mac Lewis got his introduction to the organization. The weather was hot and humid. East Harlem had just been through three nights of rioting which started when a young Puerto Rican reported to be wielding a knife was killed by a policeman, and pent-up neighborhood emotions exploded. As fire bombs and snipers' bullets punctuated the destruction, the Tactical Patrol Force, New York's elite emergency police, moved in. Three more people were killed, scores injured. Mayor Lindsay tried personally to calm the violence by walking the streets, shaking hands, and making speeches. But each night until their ardor was quelled by rain, the rioters were back in the streets.

"It was the last day of the East Harlem riots," Mac recalled. "Everybody was running around like chickens with their heads off. They all had circles under their eyes, and literally were exhausted, having been out all night trying to calm the riot. The Real Great Society wanted to load several hundred kids on buses and take them out of town for a couple of days. I thought that was an excellent idea, and they asked me if I could help. The city had offered the buses, but they had no place to go where a large group could be fed and stay overnight."

Mac called several friends, checked every possibility he could think of, and got nowhere.

"There was an iron ring around the white surburbs that these ghetto kids simply could not get through," he exclaimed.

He tried National Guard camps, small outlying colleges, and summer youth camps. Everybody said no. Either the project was too expensive or facilities were already booked, some for as much as two years.

Finally, in exasperation, and more determined than ever to get action, he went to Columbia University. This was at a time when Columbia was becoming increasingly involved in community service and urban planning, and efforts were being made to get professors and businessmen to relate to ghetto problems together, the professors contributing their scientific knowledge, and the businessmen their practical management capabilities. Mac Lewis suggested that a third element—ghetto youth groups, such as RGS—should be added to that combination, and in discussing this suggestion with Columbia's planners he parlayed the original notion of a bus trip into a plan for a weekend East Harlem youth conference to be held on Columbia's Morningside Campus.

The Division of Urban Planning of Columbia's School of Architecture obtained private financial support to help pay the costs, including meals, and helped work out a conference agenda. The youths who attended were to be in complete control of the proceedings so they could feel free to say whatever they felt like saying. RGS/East Harlem was billed as the conference sponsor, with Papo slated as chairman. For two days beginning August 12, 1967, more than two hundred ghetto teenagers and young adults who had never dreamed of getting free room and board at Columbia University, including many who had engaged in the rioting, moved into Columbia dormitories for what was called "The First East Harlem Youth Conference."

It started with a general assembly, then divided into five topical committees: "Why do riots start in areas like ours and what can be done to prevent them? What are the needs of the community? How do we organize to meet the needs of our community? What's wrong with our antipoverty programs, and how do we improve them? How do we stand with the police and how do we improve our relations with them?"

Columbia invited a blue-chip list of corporation executives to sit in with the professors to hear what the East Harlem youths had on their minds and what they thought private business and the university should do to help them, and the youths took full advantage of the opportunity. Most of them arrived for the conference still seething with the same bitterness they had felt during the riot, except that now they were an assembly, not a mob, and instead of throwing bottles and bricks they threw only words.

But their words were angry words. The opening session moved quickly into a contentious mood, hands waving for recognition. Amidst assertions of black power and Puerto Rican power, a barrage of accusations was hurled against university faculty members, businessmen, city officials, and everybody in general who was not black, Puerto Rican, or poor. To the accompaniment of loud applause, the recriminations rose in tempo, and everybody, including the professors and the corporate executives who had come to listen, became thoroughly and completely absorbed.

Merle A. Gulick, vice-president of the Equitable Life Assurance Society of the United States, one of the business executives who attended the conference, described to me his impressions:

"It was a very confusing picture for the businessmen. There were all these youngsters ranging from fifteen to thirty or so, Puerto Ricans, Negroes, and a few whites. There was a long delay in opening the meeting, but we learned later that this was normal. Then in all this confusion a Puerto Rican in an open shirt and leather jacket stood up and yelled, 'cool it,' and they came to order just like at a corporate board meeting. They talked about the groovy speakers, and referred to each other as cats. Somebody said they had to get down to the nitty gritty. One of them said you couldn't trust the honkies, which we realized meant us. Then one of them said all this was nonsense, that all people were human beings, and that the real problem was not to fight but to get along.

"They referred to us as the observers from the establishment, told us where we could sit and told us to keep our mouths shut. So we did what they said. The whole thing was so fascinating I called my wife and one of the other businessmen called his, and they both came. I had to leave for a luncheon appointment but my wife stayed and ate with them in the cafeteria. At one of the tables she asked if she could join them. Then after telling her she could sit there if she wanted to they all got up and left. So she tried another table. That group was just as belligerent, but they did let her sit with them. They asked her where she lived and if she was ashamed, or was she afraid they would burn her house? She told them where she lived and that she wasn't ashamed or afraid. Then they asked if she was going to talk with them a little while and become an authority on the ghetto. It was very obvious they didn't trust us."

Afterward the Gulicks did take time to get acquainted and made themselves an important source of both moral and financial support.

As it became clear that the youths were free to voice whatever feelings were in them and that at least some people were listening, the venom that had accumulated from their feelings of being kicked and looked down upon, of being trapped at the bottom of society by forces too overwhelming to conquer by peaceful means, was at least for the moment partially expelled, and the conference moved to a more moderate tone.

As to the cause of riots? The list was long: Rioting was the only way to get attention; slum conditions, houses for which they had to pay rent but which weren't fit to live in; having to compete for jobs that didn't pay enough for a decent living because better jobs weren't open to them; the lack of opportunities for an education; being drafted to fight for a country in which they were treated unjustly; city officials who made promises that were never kept; politicians who sent "flunkies" to pacify the ghetto when life became so intolerable its residents could no longer be peaceful; bickering among antipoverty agencies whose programs didn't make any real difference anyway. Prejudice. Discrimination.

How can riots be stopped? By eliminating the conditions that breed riots, they said. But of more importance, by allowing them—the youth of East Harlem—to plan and operate their own programs. They were adamant in their demands for outside support, but they were equally adamant in making it known that they expected to receive this support with no strings attached and with no outside interference. They couldn't expect any real change, they asserted, unless they made it, unless their demands were met on their terms. And for that purpose, they said, they had to have power. They had to get organized and assert themselves.

"We've made our first step in really grooving," said Papo. "I mean really getting active."

With that declaration of self-confidence the conference adjourned.

It had been a great experience—the angry outbursts of racial pride, the demands for power and organization in East Harlem, the freedom of self-expression. It had been exhilarating talk. It had been a moment of triumph, an act of standing on the establishment's own grounds and forcing it to listen. The public flexing of muscle, the emotional satisfaction of being in control had provided a psychology of strength and a determination to be even stronger.

For those who had come to listen, the sounds of rebellion in a conference setting on Columbia's Morningside Campus, coming as it did in the wake of three days of rioting, was in refreshing contrast to the agony of death that had come from the riot.

Thus, RGS/Uptown emerged from the conference with a substantial new following of important advocates and allies. It had Columbia University, the support of some of the top executives in the city's business community, and it had an expanded corps of aggressive young adults in East Harlem.

The shock caused by the riot, coupled with the stimulus of the conference, triggered the formation of two new organizations: Young Citizens for Progress, made up of high school dropouts interested in getting more education; and the East Harlem College Society, a group of college students who wanted to help young people obtain college degrees, then return to the neighborhood and apply their talents to its improvement. The combined membership of these new organizations was not more than two dozen youths, but they brought together some of the sharpest young people in East Harlem to join forces with the East Harlem wing of RGS.

East Harlem was Columbia's neighbor. The university was heavily committed to public service, and was already engaged in programs that dealt with East Harlem problems. Columbia helped with fund-raising. It held numerous meetings with the street leaders. Thirty East Harlem Puerto Rican youths were taken into Columbia's Foreign Students Center for cost-free training in English as a second language, and two scholarships were provided for training in community relations.

Columbia created a special planning studio which provided a means by which the university and East Harlem young people could join together in an ongoing mutual effort. During the 1968 spring term the planning studio was formally established as a graduate-studies project in the School of Architecture, with eighteen students and a professor of urban planning. A representative of the RGS East Harlem branch was designated to act as an official liaison person between the university and the group, and Columbia provided the cost of an East Harlem storefront center so that the work of the studio could actually take place in the community. The graduate students were to conduct studies of community problems and design plans aimed at their solution. The uptown members of RGS and their allied groups were to function as teammates with the students, show them the community, explain its life patterns and activities, tell them what improvements they felt were needed, react to recommended project designs, and organize essential follow-up action. That was the general scheme.

With this assistance, plans were made to expand the previously started remedial-education program into what became known as the East Harlem Education Center. The plans called for special study rooms for the use of East Harlem youth who had no place to study at home, a tutorial and counseling service to assist high school students, an instructional service to help dropouts prepare for high school equivalency examinations, a library to include Puerto Rican and black studies materials, job-placement services, and recreational activities.

To finance this proposed center, a request was submitted to the Astor Foundation. Largely because of Columbia's involvement in the planning and the foundation's previous relations with Fred and RGS on the Lower East Side, it responded in January 1968 with a grant of fifty thousand dollars. The Real Great Society, Inc., was designated as the legal corporate body to receive the grant, but all of the funds were to be used in East Harlem. The East Harlem wing of the RGS inner-core group was to have administrative control, and the East Harlem College Society and Young Citizens for Progress were to supply leaders for program operations.

The loft space that had been rented earlier for the remedial-education program was looked upon as only a place in which the proposed new center could get started. At the Columbia conference it had been recommended that a townhouse be developed for a neighborhood youth center to be owned and managed by the youths themselves. Two old adjoining five-story brownstones owned by the city on East 110th Street had been selected for acquisition. One of these buildings had been damaged by fire and was vacant. The other was partially occupied by residential tenants. Both of them would require extensive and costly renovation before they could be put to use. Now with fifty thousand dollars from the Astor Foundation the uptown leaders were prepared to make the city an offer for the property.

City officials were reluctant to deal with a street organization headed by gang leaders, but Columbia prevailed upon an influential attorney and real estate dealer to intercede on their behalf. After describing to the city officials the purpose of the proposed project and telling them that the Columbia School of Architecture "is banking on us to deliver the buildings," the attorney persuaded them to schedule the property for public auction and accept the Real Great Society, Inc., as an eligible bidder. He also suggested that at the auction RGS be identified as a neighborhood charitable organization, thus making a subtle appeal to any other bidders who might attend to let their bids be governed by their consciences.

The auction was held on March 19, 1968, at the Roosevelt Hotel in midtown Manhattan, with RGS competing against two other bidders.

Papo opened with a bid of $5,300, carefully making clear that he was representing a nonprofit, tax-exempt, charitable organization.

Another bidder offered $5,400.

"Going once, going twice. . . ."

Papo raised his bid to six thousand.

$6,100 was offered.

Papo came back with $6,300, again, for a nonprofit, tax-exempt, charitable organization.

The bid went to $6,600.

Papo offered $6,700, again making his appeal for charity, and it worked.

The other bidders, offering only token resistance, remained silent. The auctioneer came down with his gavel, and the uptown leaders, cheering wildly, found themselves in possession of two five-story buildings in East Harlem.

For RGS/Uptown this was an enormous success. It fed hungry egos and lifted to lofty heights the self-esteem of those who made up this new extension of the group. They had risen out of the streets of East Harlem's ghetto to become property owners. A Columbia sociologist conducted special studies in the neighborhood to help design the reconstruction of the buildings to meet local needs. Expertise in social planning, architecture, law, and business finance came in to work on the plan, and with this flow of talent emanating from the connection with Columbia University, started by C. McKenzie Lewis, a highly professional design for the future development of the townhouses was put together.

Architectural plans provided for converting the upper three floors of the buildings into low-income housing: six two-bedroom apartments and six three-bedroom apartments. The two lower floors were to be devoted to neighborhood services, including technical planning services. The wall between the two buildings at the street-floor level was to be removed, thus creating a large area to be divided into a general reception lobby, a separate lobby for access to the apartments, an assembly hall for large meetings and social events, an art workshop, a recreation room, and a café. The second floors were to provide three classrooms, a center for individual and group study, a library containing materials in both English and Spanish, and space for offices and the headquarters of RGS/East Harlem. A vacant lot adjacent to the townhouse was to be converted into a vest-pocket recreational park. Construction costs were estimated at $102,000 for the three residential floors, plus $75,000 for the two lower floors and the vest-pocket park. The housing costs were to be financed by a mortgage to be obtained from the New York City Municipal Loan Program, and the construction on the two lower floors was to be financed by contributions from foundations and other private sources.

The relationship with Columbia which led to this kind of professional planning was looked upon by both the university and the uptown branch of RGS as highly desirable, but it was not without problems. In the course of time, elements of stress and misunderstanding began to creep into the association. In its original conception the Columbia planning studio was to have been a mutual effort by street youths and graduate students, backed up by experienced professionals at the university and private business executives. But as the graduate students and technicians began work it became increasingly difficult for them to get any meaningful participation from the street leaders. The people at the university began to feel that the uptown leaders were becoming overly ambitious, expecting too much too soon, and were falling down on their end of the bargain to supply the co-workers from the streets who were needed to achieve the goals of the planning studio and make effective use of Columbia's resources. Plans were put together that sounded great on paper, but RGS was preoccupied with grandiose schemes for the future; the graduate students, working largely alone in the absence of the teammates they had expected from the streets, were bogged down in research and planning that led to no definite action. Whether these two old brownstones will actually be converted into the townhouse planned so enthusiastically would be pure conjecture. In any event, actual development never matched the output of paper work.

One of the professionals at Columbia who was deeply interested in helping the uptown leaders said to me: "Their emotional commitment was greater than their time and work commitment, that is, their willingness to settle down to learn what we had to teach and get on with actual project development."

The uptown street leaders were not content to be merely co-workers or learners in a joint enterprise with Columbia. They wanted to be in command. They wanted Columbia to work *for* them, not *with* them.

One of the uptown leaders put it to me this way: "The Rand Corporation has a think tank for the U.S. Government. That's what we want to have for East Harlem."

They were shrewd enough to know that if their organization could become the owner and director of a neighborhood "think tank"—or planning studio—in which they could place technicians, including personnel from Columbia University, working under their control, then RGS/Uptown could attain pre-eminence. Other residents and organizations in the community would have to turn to them for assistance. They could have their own power base.

As these ambitions grew, the uptown leaders laid down conditions under which they would be willing to continue their relationship with Columbia. The conditions would have the effect of putting the planners and students, who were to have been the leaders' co-workers, under their control, giving the leaders final decision-making power over what work Columbia's people would perform and what projects they would undertake. Columbia would not accept these conditions. It was interested in seeing its graduate students get practical planning experience and in extending technical assistance to community groups in East Harlem, including the East Harlem branch of RGS. But it was not willing to have its work limited to any one group or to grant to RGS the power to distribute Columbia's resources in the community. As a result, Columbia phased out its East Harlem planning studio with RGS. However, the university continued to offer assistance on mutually agreed-upon projects, and to help the group with fund-raising.

Despite these difficulties the overall relationship with Columbia University made a significant impact on the East Harlem branch of

RGS. Its leaders, several of whom attended college themselves, were sensitized to urban-planning techniques, corporate-business procedures, and formal program development. They adopted some of Columbia's style, its approach to planning, its ways of operating within the framework of conventional society.

They learned a bit of capitalism, they made contacts that enabled them to get funds, and they brought into their organization professional personnel. After the Columbia studio ceased operating, they set up their own planning studio, and because Columbia was still willing to cooperate with them on a project-by-project basis, they continued to get the assistance of graduate students. They obtained the part-time services of a leading architect who taught courses at Columbia, which made their planning studio acceptable to the university as a place in which students could work on projects for university credit; and from Columbia's urban center, established with a fund of ten million dollars from the Ford Foundation, they later obtained a grant of forty-five thousand dollars.

From a technical point of view their relationship with Columbia was altered so that they were no longer a client of the School of Architecture, and therefore were no longer subject to the reponsibility of a mutual effort. But with Columbia's assistance, which began with the East Harlem youth conference, they succeeded in large part in getting the power they were after.

By adding skills from conventional society to the raw skills of survival learned in the streets, the uptown leaders developed a potent brand of sophistication, and RGS/East Harlem took on a very different pattern of development from that which characterized the original wing of the organization.

On the Lower East Side, RGS started as a small group of ghetto gang youths who wanted no more trouble with the police, and in their own unorthodox manner set out to find something different. They banded together and dreamed of great and wonderful things. They had no knowledge of urban planning or program development. They simply lived from day to day, moving with unbounded optimism and enjoyment as the flow of events and circumstances dictated. With simple idealism and a good deal of personal warmth, they charmed and fascinated almost everyone they encountered and attracted a stream of admirers. As they were extolled and publicized, their powers of imagination were extended. They acquired a fabulous reputation of creating and leading a great enterprise of social reform, and with that as their calling card they went out over the country preaching their gospel: Ghetto youths must look to themselves to solve their problems, respect each other regardless of race or social background, and can do anything they want to do.

The East Harlem extension of RGS was started by people who had grown up in the streets the same as the gang leaders on the Lower East Side and were equally experienced in the art of manipulation. But they also had something else. They were better educated, more sophisticated, much colder and more calculating in going after what they wanted, and they knew a good thing when they saw it. By early 1967, when they became a part of the inner-core group, RGS already had its famous reputation. It was incorporated and was getting foundation money. It was ready-made. It was an organization the uptown leaders could use, and eventually control, just as they sought to control a piece of Columbia University.

The idealism that characterized the Lower East Side wing of the organization was also present in the East Harlem wing, but was expressed in very different ways. The uptown portion of the group was much more intense in its drive for power and influence, more deliberate, more hard-line, more structured, and less imaginative. By comparison with the University of the Streets, the operation in East Harlem was prosaic and standardized. But in terms of method and style and purpose, it was far more revolutionary, more conscious of race and Puerto Rican nationalism, and much more attuned to the militance of current minority revolt.

Some of the street leaders who became involved with the uptown branch were among those who helped carry out the East Harlem riot, and the revolutionary feeling of that violent episode was clearly expressed in the angry tone of the Columbia conference which fueled the development of RGS in East Harlem.

Later several of the leaders who attended that conference and became active in the expanded organizational effort that followed made clear to me how they felt.

"The conference got me turned on. That was the first time I had heard Puerto Rican talk that was meaningful. Now, man, we're making that kind of talk louder, and we intend to keep on making it louder until the establishment hears what we're saying."

"We intend to control our own education."

"We don't want to be branded with words like 'militant,' but we are militant because we've got to be powerful to get what we want. We think political power, economic power, every other kind of power, should be divvied up, and we're demanding our share. It has something to do with manhood, with respect. The word is organization. With that we can apply pressure in the right places. So we're organized."

"Nobody in the establishment is going to push us around or control us. We've got our own sense of direction. We know where we're going. We know where we're headed. That's how we intend to keep it."

With the East Harlem members of RGS this belligerence was not mere idle talk.

In July 1968, when they felt the city was putting less antipoverty money into East Harlem than the area deserved, they decided to organize a demonstration. Every day for three days in accordance with a carefully worked-out strategy, youths holding hands, singing, and shouting formed human barricades across busy intersections at peak rush hours in First, Third, and Fifth avenues and created massive traffic jams.

"On First Avenue the cops moved in and pushed us off the street," one of them said to me. "So we talked to a truck driver in Spanish and got him to stall his truck. One of our cats reached in another truck and snatched the keys. Man, we really stalled a lot of traffic."

After the third day some of the leaders began thinking that while the demonstration was a good idea, it was not too smart for them to be in the forefront.

"Cops were coming into our place bothering us on all kinds of pretexts. Once they said they were looking for a stolen typewriter, so we decided to withdraw and let the community take over. The community kept working it for two more days. Then all of a sudden a million more dollars came from Lindsay's office for summer jobs in East Harlem."

One of the leaders described to me in simple language the goals of RGS in East Harlem: "To educate, to make self-sufficient, to build power."

When the uptown branch got its start in June 1967, it was almost totally dependent upon the Lower East Side portion of the organization. It was a product of the effort spearheaded by Fred Good and Bill Watman which resulted in creating the University of the Streets. Indeed, it was in the context of that effort that the initial move toward extending RGS into East Harlem was born. The money, the curriculum materials, the support from the city's Neighborhood Youth Corps that went into starting the uptown branch all came out of that effort. The uptown branch was dependent upon the treasury, the legal corporation, and the reputation which the Lower East Side wing already had. Virtually every outside influence that led to the development of the uptown portion of the group, including the initial connection with Mac Lewis and Columbia University, resulted from RGS on the Lower East Side and its friends and supporters.

But if the uptown leaders ever felt any such dependency, it was not reflected in their actions. From the very outset they were on the offensive. Accepting without hesitation anything they could get from whatever the organization had to offer, and always wanting more, they asserted complete autonomy in East Harlem and moved relentlessly toward control of the affairs of the total organization, including its main operation and prime instrument of financial support—the University of the Streets.

The orientation toward Puerto Rican power that emerged in East Harlem and was increasingly pressed on the Lower East Side led to heated arguments between the two wings of the organization. With the advantages obtained from the Lower East Side, RGS/Uptown had by early 1968 obtained the fifty-thousand-dollar Astor grant for its own exclusive use, had its own pipelines into sources of influence, and had become the recipient of a free flow of professional assistance. With these assets, and with feelings of superiority and expectations almost without limit, its power struggle with the leadership on the Lower East Side became so intense that the two wings of RGS almost split.

The principal targets of the East Harlem attack were Fred Good and Bill Watman. Their leadership, it was argued, was not needed. They were outsiders. They had too much say in the policy of the organization, and were an obstruction to the Puerto Rican leadership. At first the gang leaders on the Lower East Side refused to accept that argument. Fred and Bill were their friends. No one had been more loyal to them or done more to help them. But as the uptown leaders continued to push their demands, the Lower East Side leaders began to yield; to prevent the organization from breaking apart, they agreed to a compromise. Fred and Bill would remain, but the Puerto Rican leaders who made up the inner-core group—including those in East Harlem—would assume a more active role in the control of the University of the Streets. The council which had served as the university's nominal governing body, and in which both Fred and Bill held membership, was abolished. Henceforth the final authority over the university was to be vested in the RGS board of directors. There the East Harlem branch exercised significant influence.

11

Youth Organizations United

To Mac Lewis the Real Great Society gave substance to his conviction that ghetto street gangs—which he carefully referred to as "youth groups"—were a powerful vehicle for social change in urban America. In New York and at the Lewis family cottage on Cape Cod he engaged in lengthy conversations with Fred Good and Bill Watman. He became extremely friendly with Chino, Angelo, Papo, and the others. He entered into a close alliance with Frank Ferguson in Washington. He contributed generous cash donations, enlarged and enhanced the group's following of middle- and upper-class admirers by dropping the right words in the right places, and made possible much of the fund-raising for the University of the Streets. He had a compulsion to remain in the background, feeling this was his proper role, and always credited the gang leaders themselves with whatever was achieved, including such things as the East Harlem youth conference, which would never have occurred without his personal maneuvering.

"After he had seen the group and been impressed," said Frank, "Mac added a new dimension to its activities. He felt that it was necessary to build a community of such groups throughout the whole country, and he saw the Real Great Society as the instrument for getting that accomplished."

This notion of expanding nationwide had been dreamed about by the group itself during the summer of 1966, when Bill arranged the ill-fated exchange trips between RGS and the youth organization at Warrenton, Virginia. In press releases and other public statements it was often claimed that the organization was actually forming new groups, or branches of itself, in cities across the country. But this claim was applied to about every gathering in which the group was involved during its many travels, and was like many other claims that over time were embellished and worked into the fantasy. It was not until Mac Lewis entered the scene that this kind of talk took on real meaning.

Mac was concerned with what would happen when the gang leaders got older. He wondered how much longer RGS would continue to exist. Could it effect the transfer of leadership that some day would be necessary? Where was it headed eventually? How could the idea it represented be spread to other cities?

Looking at the group within the context of the total urban crisis, Mac envisioned a nationwide ghetto-youth leadership seasoned by gang life and streetcorner organization growing into a vast human force aimed at correcting the ills of the social order. It was a concept totally revolutionary in scope, to be applied not only nationally but ultimately, he hoped, internationally, especially in Latin America. To start such a mobilization of youth power, he felt it was first necessary to search out from coast to coast other gang leaders similar to those in RGS, and create an opportunity for them to set up a nationwide network of communications. Then they could exchange ideas and speak with a voice that could be heard by the establishment every-where—especially in Washington.

"This was Mac's vision," Frank said to me. "But he didn't know where these other leaders or other gangs might be, and he was in no position to go out on his own to find them. So he hunted for leads in newspapers and magazines, and I hunted through OEO in Washington."

Early in October, Mac found his lead, an article in *Time* featuring a black man named Jesse James, a thirty-nine-year-old ex-convict who wound up in the high-crime Mission District of San Francisco, got himself ordained as a minister, and was instrumental in starting an organization of tough street kids known as the Mission Rebels in Action, which had the same type of reputation as RGS. Chino and his gang friends, only the month before, had been featured in *Life*. Mac saw the perfect connection. Elated by his discovery, he immediately put Chino Garcia on the East Coast in touch with Jesse James on the West Coast.

Moving quickly to capitalize on this opportunity to hold a national conference, Mac flew to New York and began pushing through Fred for immediate follow-up. Frank telephoned a New York official of the Episcopal Church, explained the idea of the conference, and asked for money. The church gave seven hundred dollars. Mac made up the difference between that and what was needed. Merle Gulick arranged for them to use the conference facilities at Equitable Life on the Avenue of the Americas. Invitations went out—air travel and other expenses to be paid by the conference.

RGS acted as host, and the conference took place on October 28 and 29, 1967. Twenty-four ghetto street leaders were there, most from New York, but several from Washington, Milwaukee, and San Francisco, including Jesse James. Of course Mac Lewis and Frank Ferguson were there.

Fred opened on Saturday afternoon by introducing Chino, who as usual had just returned from a trip. The agenda, which Mac had helped work out in advance, was largely forgotten. The entire first session was devoted to a show of threatening verbal aggression, with each conferee showing off his own toughness and invincibility, and probing for weak spots in the others. In voices full of suspicion and anger, they wanted certain answers before going any further. What was the angle? What was somebody trying to pull? Most of them had never been in conference quarters quite like Equitable's, and they wanted to know what was somebody trying to get out of this? Who was paying the bills, and why? Who were these white dudes, Mac Lewis and Frank Ferguson? What was their bag? Could black people and Puerto Rican people trust these honkies? Could they trust anybody from the establishment? For that matter, could they even trust each other?

Gradually, the atmosphere began to clear for them to start talking about problems in their home cities and what their respective organizations were doing. All of them were accustomed to slum conditions, had at one time or another been in jail, and had all lived through similar experiences. All of them had about the same demands. All of them insisted on doings things their way, and all felt equally belligerent in wanting money with no strings attached. All of them wanted their own power base, and all agreed that they had to jar the establishment into meeting their demands.

Then the conference moved on to a party at Fred's apartment, and there got down to issues. Before the night was over, they were so much on the same wavelength that when one started an idea, the others, all shouting at once, would jump in and finish it.

"That night," said Fred, "we really got together."

It was all working out just as Mac had hoped.

The second and final session got under way with an *esprit de corps* that carried through to the last farewell. Definitely, they agreed, they wanted to keep in touch, but also that they were too few in number to make final decisions about the shape and form of a national organization. They needed to get more groups, then call another conference.

In the meantime, to keep the idea alive and sell it nationally, they decided to form an interim organization to be known as Youth Organizations United (YOU) and elected Chino and Jesse, along with Ken Addison, a black community organizer from Milwaukee, as a three-man national organizing committee. These three were to travel throughout the country, locate other groups, find out what they were doing, what they considered relevant to ghetto youth, see how they reacted to the idea of having a YOU, and—assuming they liked it—invite them to send delegates to the next national conference, to be called within six months. There it would be decided whether YOU was to be continued, and if yes, all details, including an election of officers and directors, would be worked out. The purpose: To develop a nationwide system of communications among ghetto youth groups, set up a headquarters in Washington to represent their demands with other national organizations—especially the government—raise money, and help all member groups in whatever ways they wanted to be helped. Chino would travel the eastern states, Jesse the western states, Ken the central states.

At Mac's suggestion, it was also decided that each traveler would carry a tape recorder with which to make detailed on-the-spot recordings about the ideas and operations of each group contacted. These recordings would be put into a national information bank for the exchange of ideas, and be used as the basis for planning the next national conference in accordance with the stated interests of the groups the travelers interviewed.

Mac and Frank would start a fund-raising campaign and temporarily act as the YOU Washington staff.

With this much settled the meeting ended, and Bill Watman issued a press release announcing the formation of a new national federation of "grass-roots youth organizations" which was to be "a vital and dynamic force in the alleviation of poverty and the prevention of further 'long hot summers.' "

According to the publicity and the word-of-mouth advertising, all this had been accomplished on the spontaneous initiative of the gang leaders, whose insights made them recognize the importance of getting together and for that reason had taken it upon themselves to call this New York meeting "the first national conference of Youth Organizations United." No mention was made of Mac Lewis or Frank Ferguson, or anyone other than the gang leaders themselves. RGS emerged as the chief initiator of YOU, with Chino as the leading figure in the action. With Jesse James and Ken Addison on the national committee, and with Mac and Frank operating in the background, Chino and his RGS gang friends now found themselves in an exciting new national adventure with shrewd, high-powered company.

Mac took up the promotion of YOU with the fervor of a convert. At his own expense he opened a YOU Washington office, and devoted himself untiringly to making connections aimed at raising funds for the travelers to begin the nationwide search for additional groups, get together for strategy sessions, and pay for the next national conference. Beyond raising funds for these purposes, he felt an urgent necessity to obtain much larger funding commitments so that upon holding the big organizing conference, hopefully no later than mid-April 1968, there would be an immediate outside response to the organization's demands, thus enabling YOU to become fully operational before the onset of hot weather.

Almost weekly he traveled between Washington and New York selling YOU, using RGS as his prime case example. Numerous letters were sent out to business and communications executives, religious leaders, prominent socialites, educators, union heads, and foundation and government officials. He brought Chino and his friends to Washington for consultations, arranged meetings for them with people of influence in both Washington and New York, and cocktails and dinner at the best places in town became standard practice. In promoting his case for YOU, bringing in the RGS leaders to give it the flavor that made it convincing, he spared no effort. He visited in San Francisco, went out with the Mission Rebels, and brought Jesse James into Washington to join Chino in the meetings with important people. Heavy use was made of long-distance telephone. To Mac, YOU was the most important single enterprise on the horizon.

To facilitate the receipt and handling of money, the national committee, on Mac's advice, decided that YOU had to be incorporated. So he arranged through his Washington attorney to create Youth Organizations United, Inc., a District of Columbia, nonprofit, tax-exempt corporation. Mac, Frank, and the attorney were listed as the corporate directors. Officers were: Chino, president; Jesse, first vice-president; Ken, second vice-president; Mac, treasurer; and the attorney, secretary. This action was completed early in January 1968, but was taken with the understanding that the delegates at the national organizing conference would still be entitled to the final decision about going ahead, could amend the by-laws as they wished, and elect the directors and officers.

Later that month in Washington, the President's Council on Youth Opportunities, chaired by Vice-President Humphrey, convened a national conference with a White House mandate to devise plans for dealing with the needs of poverty youth to help forestall the mounting threat of ghetto violence. Some fifty of the nation's mayors, with members of their staffs, were in attendance. High-level federal and state officials, private consultants, and academicians were there. And YOU was there, Chino and Jesse, Mac and Frank, along with several other ghetto-youth leaders.

The conference droned on. Many who were present found nothing to get very excited about, as the federal officials explained what the municipal governments should be doing.

"It was pretty dull stuff," said one of the younger officials. "Fuzzy bureaucrats putting out meaningless garbage and explaining that we had to be satisfied with limited funding because Congress was putting screws on the President's budget."

On the second afternoon a youth who described himself as one of those the conference was about expressed the opinion that the methods being discussed weren't relevant to ghetto young people. Then Chino came on with a blast that sounded like revolt. Identifying himself as president of the Real Great Society and of Youth Organizations United, he told the conference his people were tired of being studied, tired of tokenism, tired of having strings put on them, that instead of cutting back, summer youth funds should be increased, and that any program not planned and directed by youth groups themselves would fail. Then Jesse delivered his blast. With this injection of anger the conference came alive.

Rising to quell the disturbance, one of Humphrey's aides said that such opinions from the young people themselves were exactly what the Vice-President wanted, and suggested that the youths hold a meeting of their own to formulate their recommendations. Without waiting for any further signal, about ten of them led by Chino and Jesse walked out to caucus. They met until two-thirty in the morning, then came in the next day with a resolution that said about what Chino had said in the first place—Congress should add another $275 million to the proposed budget for summer youth programs, and youth groups should be included in their planning and direction. Failure to act on this resolution, they said, could result in "serious consequences." Then they demanded a private meeting with the Vice-President and left to see him. Following that, Humphrey himself came in and addressed the conference. He said he had met with the youth leaders and agreed totally with their position. Suddenly, youth participation and control became the popular theme. Chino and Jesse had stolen the conference, and YOU became a hot item around Washington.

That night Chino and Jesse, accompanied by Mac Lewis, were the center of attention at a private Washington cocktail party where they charmed a group of young bureaucrats in the war on poverty, and further deepened and expanded their connections.

A few days later, they became acquainted with the Coalition for Youth Action in the Department of Labor. Then only a few weeks old, made up of bright young men and women recently out of college, armed with broad authority, and three hundred thousand dollars of federal grant money to start with, the Coalition was eager to cut red tape, experiment with bold new ideas, and was looking for ghetto youth groups through which to develop antipoverty projects.

In starting these young federal employees on their assignment, Secretary W. Willard Wirtz summed up the general purpose of the Coalition: "Young people have ideas and energies which they seemingly are dying to expend. The government has resources. I am willing to put them together and see if the mix produces worthwhile results. It is a risk on my part and yours. Be aware of that and good luck."

On meeting the Coalition officials, Chino said, "I can't believe you're for real. You're from heaven, very beautiful people."

But the Coalition for Youth Action was no less enthusiastic about RGS and YOU. Here it saw an entree to ghetto youth groups nationwide, and a valuable source of information. The Coalition was especially interested in the tape recordings that were to be made by the travelers as they searched out groups for their national alliance.

A proposed one-year YOU budget was developed. After a period of negotiations it finally settled down to $33,525 for three months— to cover travel, salaries, and miscellany. Further funding, it was understood, would be worked out later. It seemed fairly certain that this three-month grant would be forthcoming, but details still had to be processed through the Department of Labor. Meanwhile, a tentative commitment for fifteen thousand dollars in private money was being developed with the Stern Family Fund in New York, thus bringing the total expected funding for the three-month period up to $48,525.

But none of these funds were yet available, and Mac Lewis was getting extremely anxious. They were now well into February. Hot weather was not more than three months away. If YOU was to get organized and become an operating force before summer, there wasn't much time. Despite the absence of cash on hand, the search for more gangs—or youth groups—had to get started, and soon. The recordings which Mac regarded as essential to the conference planning, and which were of special interest to Labor's Coalition for Youth Action, had to be taped, transcribed, and analyzed. That alone was an enormous job. Then the organizing conference itself had to be held, and to make the time pressure even greater, it had now been tentatively decided that before holding the national conference they should first have three regional conferences—East, Central, and West—then the national conference, the delegates for which would be selected at each of the three regional conferences. This, Mac believed, would allow better planning, make it possible for street leaders in each region to get to know each other before coming together nationally, and make for smoother organizational procedure. Later it was decided to divide the central region into northern and southern areas, thus making four regional conferences prior to the national conference.

As these plans evolved it became clear to Mac that the three members of the national committee could not accomplish all the traveling themselves in time for YOU to be firmed up before summer. Then the pressure was further increased because it began to appear that illness and a heavy load of graduate studies would make it necessary for Ken Addison to drop out, and Jesse James was beginning to have doubts as to how much travel he would be able to do. Chino was reluctant to delegate the committee's authority but Mac pushed hard concerning the time squeeze, and it was decided to add more travelers.

Chino would bring in some of his RGS people from New York,

and get some gang leaders from Chicago to cover the north central region. Jesse would get some of his group in San Francisco to cover the West. They would all gather at Ken's place in Milwaukee, roughly halfway between, hold a final strategy session, and the traveling would begin.

Mac was extremely enthusiastic.

Ken arranged to hold the meeting at Northcott Neighborhood House, a Methodist-supported social service agency in a Milwaukee ghetto. The dates: Friday through Sunday, February 16–18, 1968. Mac arranged to buy airline tickets on credit and agreed to advance the other expenses pending receipt of the expected Coalition and Stern money.

On the sixteenth Chino and Angelo, with three others from New York, flew to Milwaukee. At the last minute it developed that Jesse couldn't make it, but he sent two others from the West Coast, including a representative of a San Francisco Chinatown group, and Mac flew out from Washington. All eight of them checked in at the Sheraton Schroeder in downtown Milwaukee, where Mac had made reservations.

I had agreed to handle the transcription and analysis of the tape recordings, and was there as an observer. This was my first meeting with the group since my visits in New York and Washington in late November 1967, at the time I was first informed of the activity.

Leaders from the Conservative Vice Lords, a street gang on Chicago's West Side, were to have been there, but never showed up. Also, leaders from a well-known gang on Chicago's South Side, the Blackstone Rangers, which had agreed to be one of the cosponsors of YOU, were to have been there. They didn't arrive because of what was described to me as a "bum rap" said to have been framed by the Chicago police. Months later I learned more precisely the nature of the Rangers' problem. At the time of the Milwaukee meeting their president, then twenty-four, was being held on suspicion of soliciting several younger members of the gang, age fourteen to sixteen, to commit murder, a charge for which he was later sentenced to five to fifteen years in the Illinois State Penitentiary.

I had expected the Milwaukee meeting to get under way promptly on the evening of the sixteenth. I checked in at the hotel in the late afternoon, received a message that the travelers were already assembled in a room upstairs, and lost no time getting there.

I was greeted by what was in most respects a typical conference scene—air thick with tobacco, dresser covered with bottles, mixers, and ice buckets, men sitting on every chair, the bed, the windowsill, and a wastebasket turned upside down, all talking in loud voices, telling jokes, and laughing. Other than that the scene was not very typical, because these people were not typical conference-goers. I asked when the meeting would start, seeing that it very obviously was not about to start any time soon. Mac smiled, shrugged his shoulders, and offered me a drink. Somebody else told me the meeting would start tomorrow. That night they were celebrating.

After a couple of hours, they were hungry, so we moved down to the main bar and dining room. Not everybody met the requirement of a coat and tie, but after looking us over, apparently the maitre d' decided it might be just as well not to resist too much, so we went in. Moving toward a select corner of the room as though we were some kind of privileged characters who didn't particularly care about Sheraton house rules or what anybody might think of us, we attracted considerable attention and stood out in sharp contrast to other groups of youths who were there for a state DeMolay sweetheart convention. We ordered several rounds of drinks, ate lobster tails and strip sirloins, finished off with after-dinner liqueurs, and gave the tab to Mac.

After that the group went out to continue celebrating, and Mac and I stayed at the hotel. I thought he was one of the most committed individuals I had ever met. Certainly, he was by all odds one of the most patient. There seemed to be only one way to work with this bunch—their way, and at their convenience. At least, that was Mac's philosophy. Efficiency didn't seem to apply, just as a good many other conventional standards didn't seem to apply.

However, the group did have a good many similarities to other conference-goers. They awakened other guests in the hotel with loud singing and yelling, and went to bed some time after daylight, still in good spirits and apparently with no serious mishaps. Around noon they gathered for breakfast, several of them still accompanied by girl friends they had picked up during the events of the night.

Around one o'clock in the afternoon Chino herded them together in front of the hotel, and performing like a dispatcher, loaded them into taxicabs with instructions to the drivers to take them to North-cott Neighborhood House. There he switched them onto business with the deftness of a top sergeant. He sketched in the purpose of the meeting, told them they had to start traveling, find up to 150 groups, get prepared for the conferences—regional and national—before April, and reminded them that the United States covered thousands of miles of territory.

With that introduction, they went into a point-by-point reading of the YOU incorporation papers that Mac had brought from Washington, and haggled over every provision and by-law. Their central theme was that YOU was not to rob any group of its independence, was not to be a policy-making body—only a means of communication and service—but was to speak with a commanding voice to the establishment. Nothing was accepted on faith. Every line that had been written into the YOU corporate papers by Mac and his Washington attorney was called into question. By the time they finished this exercise it was around seven o'clock, and we all went out to a fancy restaurant. Another round of celebrating, and that wiped out Saturday. Mac had supplied them with a single-spaced, five-page agenda covering items he thought they should consider in planning the traveling and the regional conferences. But again he had to be patient. They didn't understand written agendas too well anyway. It would just have to wait.

Sunday morning was bright and crisp. Breakfast at noon, and a new batch of girl friends. Where all the girls came from I never knew, but this group was not lacking in nighttime resourcefulness. The second business session began about two that afternoon.

After numerous diversions—including an hour or so of unexpected interruption by six militant street youths representing an organization called BAD (Black, Active, and Determined), who came in drinking wine and demanding an explanation of everybody's "bag"—Mac finally eased the meeting into taking up the agenda.

The five pages of material were read aloud and Mac struggled from the sidelines to keep the conversation from wandering. The agenda placed heavy emphasis on the type of groups the travelers were to look for, supplied written criteria by which to identify them—including such qualities as "leadership, imagination, energy, sense of accomplishment"—and stressed the importance of the tape recordings that were to be made—five hundred hours or more—as the essential means of reporting the activities and interests of each group the travelers located.

It was a long, restless afternoon. Quite obviously they knew what they were looking for, and it didn't include Boy Scout troops. They were after their kind of "cats," ghetto kids—many of whom were no longer kids—who operated in the twilight world of the streets but wanted to do "something positive." Like Mac, the travelers never used the term "street gangs," always "youth groups" or "youth organizations." But the terms weren't too important. They didn't need any written criteria, and it was also obvious that they had no intention of asking too many questions. They thought of a police record as normal, distrusted society in general, were harsh in their demands, and exceedingly bold. And there were thousands like them in the nation's ghettos.

Chino cut the map of the United States into four areas and handed out travel assignments. They still didn't have enough travelers. But they would figure that out later.

On one agenda item Mac had no trouble holding their attention: money. They still didn't have any, but it was expected that any day they would be getting their grants from the Labor Department and the Stern Family Fund.

"We better," said Angelo. "I don't like hustling in a strange town without bread."

Mac explained how they could obtain cash as soon as the money came in, and the importance of turning in receipts for plane tickets. Hotels and meals were to be covered by a flat per diem, and beyond that each traveler was to be paid a hundred-dollar weekly fee. Chino, of all people, admonished them to be careful about how much they spent.

They talked about where to hold the national conference and decided it should be in a city that would be interesting—San Francisco, or maybe San Juan, Puerto Rico.

By the time it began getting dark it was clear that the limits of their attention had been more than reached, and the meeting started breaking up. Several said they had to leave. For the others the hour for celebrating was again at hand. Everybody was to keep in touch by telephone, mail in their tape recordings from each city visited, and call Mac in Washington if they wanted anything.

It had been almost seven months since Frank Ferguson introduced Mac Lewis to RGS. From the East Harlem youth conference to the Milwaukee strategy session he had become deeply involved and very influential. Where it would all lead no one really knew.

12

The Affair at East St. Louis

Symbolically, and in many respects as a matter of fact, the Real Great Society had become the springboard for the building of a coast-to-coast association of street gangs with a Washington-based headquarters. But while it was never openly acknowledged, and if asked, he would deny it, the major responsibility fell to Mac Lewis—with the active assistance of Frank Ferguson. Mac meticulously respected the authority of the gang leaders and explained his position to outsiders as simply that of an interested party who offered advice when asked. But despite his efforts to make it appear that he was only a minor functionary, he was in fact the master architect and builder, the prime mover behind the action.

This divergence of leadership often led to resentment from the gang leaders. Mac's businesslike procedure, his formality and attention to detail, his prodigious output of mimeographed documents—routine among most Americans who form national organizations—was a drastic and mysterious departure from the accustomed ways of the gang leaders, whose mode of planning was on a day-to-day basis, and who zealously insisted on complete control over the effort that was being engineered on their behalf. It was a strange mix of vastly different types symbolized by Chino as the gang leader and Mac as the empathic social reformist, neither quite understanding the other, but neither of whom could have started the action without the other.

To RGS, YOU offered new luster for its already lustrous position. To Mac, it offered the possibility of a nationwide indigenous effort from inside the ghetto which he saw as the basis for an equal partnership between the grass roots and the upper levels of the social order that would result in a general advancement of democracy and urban problem solving. It is highly doubtful that the street youths ever fully grasped this concept, and it is equally doubtful that Mac ever came to terms in a wholly realistic way with the odds against its accomplishment. However, he was an exceedingly formidable and determined person, equipped with rare ability to accept personal abuse and overlook or attribute to environmental causes any action or behavior that deviated from the goals he envisioned. Mac left the Milwaukee strategy session full of hope. RGS left full of ebullience.

In March the expected grants came in from Labor's Coalition for Youth Action and the Stern Family Fund, but by that time the middle of April—which Mac had set as the deadline for the regional and national conferences—was only a month away, and the street leaders were showing no great enthusiasm for actually getting to work. En route home from Milwaukee, the two travelers from San Francisco visited two street gangs in the Los Angeles area, and about a week later met with several groups in the Bay Area. But with a month having already passed since the Milwaukee strategy session, that was about the extent of the field work. There were still no travelers for the southern or central states, and most of the work in the East had yet to be done.

It had been agreed at Milwaukee that on their way home the RGS leaders would stop in Chicago to recruit travelers for the Midwest, but in the course of celebrating, then being in a hurry to get back to New York, that stopover never materialized. So a few weeks later

Chino flew back to Chicago. The Blackstone Rangers were still too involved with their own problems to devote time traveling for YOU, so he went to the city's West Side to make a deal with the leaders of the Conservative Vice Lords. They agreed to think about it, and to let him know later what they decided. After waiting about two weeks and still not having heard from them, Frank Ferguson discovered one day that they were in Washington looking for grants, invited them to stop in at Mac's YOU office, and telephoned Chino to fly down immediately from New York.

What happened was typical of the maneuvering Mac and Frank went through in their efforts to get YOU organized. The Vice Lords leaders arrived at the office before Chino got in from New York and neither Mac nor Frank was able to sell them on the travel assignment, or get them to wait for Chino. Nor were they able to get them to leave a Washington address or phone number where they could be reached when Chino did get in. The Vice Lords left saying they would call back, but when they did Chino still hadn't arrived. However, this time they consented to leaving their number, saying that if he got in soon enough he could join them for dinner. Then when he finally did arrive and learned what was happening, he turned aloof. Why should he go out of his way for them? This kind of sparring was perfectly normal in the streets, but to Mac and Frank, time was wasting.

"The whole thing was getting pretty frustrating," Frank said to me. "These were the kind of guys YOU needed, because we knew they could get the traveling done in the central states if we could get them to believe that YOU had something to offer them. But they were plainly skeptical of us. We weren't their types. Our only hope was to get them and Chino together."

Pressed by Frank, Chino finally let down enough to return the phone call, but the dinner meeting fell through. Frank kept on persisting and later that evening he and Chino went to the Vice Lords' hotel room.

"It was a very interesting meeting," Frank recalled. "They and Chino were doing all the talking. The conversation kept going off on tangents and the Chicago guys kept testing me by trying to scare me with how tough they were—which they were. I figured that was just part of the game, but I was getting worried because we weren't getting anywhere."

After considerable haggling over money, with the Conservative Vice Lords making it clear that YOU could forget about them unless they were paid in advance and given a free hand to do the job as they saw fit, Frank reached in his pocket, took out $250 in bills, and tossed it on the bed, saying they could be assured that any travelers they sent out would be paid for their services.

"I was afraid for a while I had overplayed my hand with Chino," Frank said to me. "He reached over and picked up the money and sounded as though he wasn't going to release it to them. But after more arguing he finally consented to give them the money and let them run the operation in the Midwest with no controls from Washington or New York. Otherwise, they weren't interested."

The Vice Lord leaders said that while they were too busy to do the traveling themselves, they would make travelers available and guarantee results, pointing out that they personally reviewed whatever was done by any of their people. To head the job, they suggested Warren Gilmore, a black, then thirty-six, who a few months previously had become a member of their organization, and whom Chino had already met in Chicago where Gilmore was operating a small art shop.

Gilmore was contacted by long-distance telephone, and the next day, with a YOU airplane ticket and expense money, flew into Washington for a briefing with Mac and Frank, then went on to New York to meet with Chino. By that time there were only five days left in March, and most of the nationwide search for street gangs had yet to begin.

Tall and impressive in appearance, Gilmore was all business. No celebrating, no fooling around, no sleeping through the morning. After visiting with RGS in New York, he returned to Chicago, organized a team of travelers, and in the course of several weeks they made trips into Illinois, Indiana, Ohio, Wisconsin, Minnesota, Missouri, Kansas, and Kentucky. Total cost: about nine thousand dollars, including salaries and expenses.

Gilmore described to me their mode of operations:

"We'd get a taxi as soon as we got into a city and tell the driver to take us to a black neighborhood. There we'd find a hotel, call Chicago so we could keep in touch, then get into the streets, talk to people on the corners, in taverns, pool halls, any likely looking hangout, ask questions about the street leaders, then go get acquainted, tell them about YOU, and find out who was interested. Sometimes we'd get leads from something like NAACP or the Urban League, or we'd hang out around the schools. We had no trouble finding the groups or gangs, then we'd move on to another city."

In the late afternoon of April 4, just a few days after the Chicago team had started its travels, an assassin shot Martin Luther King at a motel in Memphis. That evening the mobs formed in Washington, and in the week that followed, riots swept the nation. Gilmore had just arrived in Cleveland and the city was too tense even for him to work the streets. In Washington Mac and Frank called Chino, and talked with Jesse James, who had come in from San Francisco; it was all but decided to drop the four regional conferences and proceed immediately with the national conference. It now seemed too late to wait any longer. Moreover, there wasn't enough money left to pay for five conferences; in fact, it wasn't certain there was even enough left to pay for one.

At Mac's request, I had agreed only a short time before to help cut their costs by seeing if Southern Illinois University would be willing to host the regional conference for the Midwest, and the SIU administration had agreed to do so. For that, Mac estimated about thirty or forty street leaders. Now he telephoned to tell me it appeared they weren't going to have the regional conferences, and would my university be interested in hosting the national conference, to involve perhaps as many as 150 delegates? I went back to the university administration with this revised proposition, and Robert W. MacVicar, then vice-president, and Charles V. Matthews, director of SIU's Center for the Study of Crime, Delinquency, and Corrections, agreed. I relayed the decision to Mac but told him the offer was good only if the conference were held in our area, not in Puerto Rico or some other exotic place, as had been suggested by the strategists at

Milwaukee. SIU's proposed location was East St. Louis, Illinois—part of the St. Louis metropolitan area—where the university had meeting facilities. With the help of a grant from the federal Office of Juvenile Delinquency and Youth Development, SIU would pay for the delegates' lodging at an East St. Louis motel, provide meals without charge at a university cafeteria, supply local transportation, and help service the conference. YOU would use its grant funds to pay the delegates' transportation to and from East St. Louis and take care of other incidentals. Mac was appalled by the thought of how the street leaders might react to the name of our Center for the Study of Crime, Delinquency, and Corrections, which was to represent the university, and asked if I could get the name changed, at least for the conference. I told him I didn't think so, and the name stood—apparently with no adverse effects.

A few days later the YOU national committee met in San Francisco to make the final decision. Chino flew out from New York, Gilmore from Chicago, Jesse and Mac from Washington, and were joined by the western travelers. Mac was concerned about the expense involved in selecting San Francisco for the committee meeting, but that was where the street leaders wanted it, and in accordance with his customary practice he deferred to their wishes.

Nowhere near a hundred or 150 groups—the numbers mentioned in Milwaukee—had yet been visited. But the committee decided to schedule the national conference anyway, and to accept the offer from SIU. The dates: Wednesday, May 15, to Sunday, May 19, 1968. Gilmore was appointed to make advance trips to East St. Louis to work out local arrangements.

No one felt more than Mac did the pressure of time and the implications of the exploding national events that followed the assassination of Martin Luther King. Yet he was also concerned by the thought of what might happen if after holding the national conference the street leaders were to find that YOU had no promise of further funding beyond the forty-eight thousand dollars they had already obtained, which by then would be gone.

"These groups cannot be expected to become enthusiastic about moving forward on every and all fronts," he said, "then be told to put their enthusiasms on ice while the establishment in its wisdom gets ready to respond to them."

The street leaders fully agreed with this desire for money—indeed, almost violently so—and in order to be able to announce at the conference that new funding was available, Mac and Frank were searching frantically for a major grant. Their most promising source seemed to be the Office of Economic Opportunity.

Mac had hoped that the program proposal to be offered as justification for the new grant they were seeking would be a product of the youth groups themselves, growing out of the information that was to be gathered from conversations between street leaders and recorded on tape during the traveling period, then discussed and further elaborated in the conferences. But it didn't turn out that way. Realistically, the idea of systematic research using taped interviews was too much to have expected in the first place. The street leaders enjoyed tinkering with the recording machines, but putting them to use for organized research was simply out of character, and in the context of street-corner conversation, the much talked about tape recordings were largely forgotten.

As weeks passed it became increasingly evident that if a program proposal were to be developed in time to obtain a major financial commitment before the national conference, expedient steps would have to be taken. OEO was asking for a proposal, but April 15—a month prior to the conference—was the last day it could be submitted in time to get a possible commitment before the close of the government's 1968 fiscal year on June 30. Mac decided that "to keep the door open" at OEO, the proposal had to be put together at least in first draft, even though it was no longer possible to go through all the planning steps he had envisioned.

He obtained approval from YOU's national committee, and Frank Ferguson got a group of professional grantsmen to quickly write up a forty-three-page proposal. It presented today's street gangs as indigenous community organizations representing "a kind of vanguard in youth's aggrieved condemnation of adult institutions generally," and pictured YOU as having resulted from the spontaneous actions of gang leaders who were said to then be engaged in a systematic examination of youth activities across the country in preparation for a carefully planned nationwide program: to create a national inventory of youth-directed projects, provide training and technical assistance for the development of new projects, set up a system of communications among street gangs from coast to coast, and encourage the development of new gangs. It was submitted to OEO on April 15—just in time to make the deadline—and for the first year, it asked for $598,655.

This thick proposal was one of many pieces in a very large flow of duplicated material—including conference agenda—that went out from Mac's YOU Washington office during the three-month period between the Milwaukee strategy session and the East St. Louis conference. In all this material, compiled in the name of YOU, Mac continued to maintain the impression that the national organizing effort was coming entirely from the streets, and carefully relegated himself to a subordinate position. With him, this was a technique that he sincerely believed would lead to the development of a national community of youth groups which would advance the cause of democracy. But the actual effect was to take the already well-established myth that had been woven around RGS and give it a new nationwide extension.

What was actually happening was that the street leaders Mac had caused to be enlisted in the YOU promotion were being wooed, solicited, and eulogized, not only by him, but by everybody else from outside the ghetto who had become a party to the promotion—especially the government officials who were arranging Washington support—and a state of competition was being generated between Mac and the federal government for their personal loyalty. In the more innovative government offices where the personnel was young and the idea of federally supported street gangs was embraced with the greatest degree of enthusiasm, Mac was not well accepted. He was advancing revolutionary ideas, but his image was wrong. He was white and middle-aged. He used words that bore little resemblance to those of the street or of the "now generation." Some of the young government officials saw him as an invader in YOU, and plainly told the gang leaders that he had no place in any program for which they might receive federal funds. Frank attracted somewhat more favor than Mac, but he too lacked the gang-leader status that captivated the federal middle management with which they were dealing. Finally, the point was reached where the more Mac and Frank did to cause YOU to exist, the more the gang leaders expected and the more ill-mannered they became.

The strain began to show most noticeably in the relationship between Mac and Chino. As the president of RGS and YOU, and the most celebrated gang leader in the whole operation, Chino could find little time for the actual field work that was required to search out additional groups, and the bulk of the eastern territory was left virtually uncovered. This was extremely distressing to Mac, but there was not much he could do about it.

Then Chino began talking directly to OEO about the YOU budget without taking Mac into his confidence. Through the University of the Streets, RGS had its own relationships with OEO. Moreover, it carried the fabulous image which was the living symbol of YOU. By comparison, Mac seemed pretty stuffy.

The OEO romanticism toward street gangs was highly cultivated, but OEO had reservations about YOU. The YOU grant proposal had been written by professionals with no real gang-leader participation, and there was a tendency at OEO to wait and see what happened at the national organizing conference.

"YOU had a bandwagon going," I was told at OEO. "We liked the idea, but we were afraid that if we jumped in too soon with too much money we might kill it. Maybe our first grant should be kept down to something like the two hundred thousand level. Also, we were never certain to what extent YOU was the youth speaking for themselves, or Mac Lewis speaking. We wanted to be certain the youth groups were going to run it themselves."

Hearing this view expressed at OEO, Chino asserted his presidential authority, gave his authorization to cut the YOU budget to two hundred thousand dollars, and OEO called for a reexamination of the proposal.

Mac was furious.

He arranged for a special committee of three street leaders to make a "grass-roots review" of the proposal, and after meeting in Washington over a period of several days beginning on May 8, this committee refuted the president's decision and upped the original request to more than one and a quarter million dollars.

On May 13, two days before the national conference was due to open, Mac sent the amended budget to OEO with a four-page letter of transmittal which said in part:

> On April 22, 1968, Carlos Garcia, the president of the organization, made a personal visit to your office . . . [and] expressed as his personal opinion the view that the range and detail of the . . . proposal went beyond the needs and understanding of the youth organizations and that the amount in his opinion was too large. . . . Mr. Garcia had not conferred with the Board of Directors of the organization or with even a representative selection of other youth organizations presently members or expected to become members of the organization in order to ascertain their views prior to his visit.
>
> Consultation with a few of the more important of these other groups was immediately made. It disclosed the fact that Mr. Gracia's opinions were *not* shared by them in whole or in part.
>
> YOU wishes to reemphasize its hope that affirmative action will be taken on its proposal, as amended . . . and . . . *that this action may be made effective at the earliest possible moment.*

Meanwhile, in East St. Louis preparations were being made for the conference. On Tuesday, April 16, I picked up Gilmore and Mac at the St. Louis municipal airport, and drove them to East St. Louis where we met Charlie Matthews and O. W. Goldenstein, an associate of Charlie's at the Crime, Delinquency, and Corrections Center, whose work with the street gangs in East St. Louis made him especially helpful in the local arrangements. In talks with a number of East St. Louis street leaders it was quickly made clear that the local youth gangs regarded this as their city, and that without their approval no conference of out-of-town gang leaders was going to be held. Nobody ever said specifically what would be done to prevent it, but whatever action was necessary would be taken. It was just as simple as that.

Probably in the previous ten to twenty years no American city had witnessed a greater number of promising starts to deal with urban problems than East St. Louis, only to see each start turn sour. The city faced a mass of problems that kept getting worse, its ills seemed almost incurable: Soaring crime rates, a municipal government near bankruptcy, miles of deteriorated housing, a shrinking tax base, growing numbers of vacant stores, out-migration of industry, declining population, extreme racial tensions.

Only the week before there had been fresh outbreaks of vandalism and arson, the public schools were in turmoil, teachers and students were reported to be arming themselves, and on reaching the motel after driving in from the airport we were greeted by announcements of a "Black Survival Rally."

Even Gilmore and Mac expressed concern and suggested that maybe it would be necessary to switch the conference to a location in St. Louis, across the Mississippi River. However, Gilmore visited at length with the local street leaders to gain their acceptance. A common question was whether YOU would endorse violence to obtain its ends. If not, some said they weren't interested. In all the conversations I heard when this question came up, which were many, the answer was never yes, but neither was it exactly no. It was more in the form of possible alternatives Gilmore indicated might be more effective. After several days of visiting he assured me there was no problem, that not only had he obtained the backing of the local groups, he had obtained their agreement to act as local hosts, provide entertainment for the visitors, and guarantee calm in the city while the conference was in session. Considering the intensity of intergroup rivalry in East St. Louis and the fights, shootings, and related activities that were commonplace, this was no small accomplishment—if it worked.

With the help of material Mac had written for the agenda, Gilmore made out an hourly schedule of meetings and SIU had it printed. I was amazed at the contrast between the tight schedule being planned for East St. Louis, and the mode of doing business I had seen in Milwaukee.

Charlie Matthews' office made arrangements for meeting rooms, a registration and information desk, secretarial services, all the electronic gadgetry and other equipment normally used at conferences, special buses and cars, meals at the university cafeteria, and motel room reservations. Mac returned to Washington and Gilmore to Chicago, saying he would be back in time to check last-minute details.

Over the next three weeks black activists called for an investigation of the East St. Louis Police Department and the ouster of the police commissioner. Warnings of a "Black Mafia" were sounded in the press. A militant leader appearing before a cheering crowd of nearly two thousand called for black separatism, and another was quoted in the press as threatening the use of guns. Explosions were set off in two school buildings, and schools throughout the city were closed by anonymous bomb threats. Black militants brought wage complaints against the school board on behalf of a group of cafeteria workers. Several leaders who had pledged to support the YOU conference were charged with acts of criminal violence and illegal possession of weapons. Hand grenades were tossed in the streets, and several gang members were charged with attempted murder. Angry parents and teachers—both black and white—held mass meetings denouncing the militants and demanding more arrests. Merchants alleged intimidation by roving youth gangs soliciting bail money, and nearly half the city's students boycotted classes. A hundred state troopers and sheriff's deputies moved in to help city police guard the schools, the mayor issued public appeals for peace, and the governor stood by to send in the National Guard. This was East St. Louis as the day approached to begin the YOU national conference.

From the West Coast, travelers finally were sent to New Orleans, where they obtained additional travelers, who shortly before the conference made a quick search in the South. From Washington, Mac sent invitations bearing Chino's name to all groups that had been visited nationwide—a total of sixty-five—and arranged payment of their expenses, plus a daily allowance.

The invitation asked the groups to accept only on the condition that they would "participate wholeheartedly," and said in part:

> The main subject for discussion at the conference is communication between the groups in general and the usefulness of interchanges of experience. The best basis for this, at the conference or at any other time, will largely relate to the activities and projects being carried out

by your group and by the other groups. Would you, therefore, be prepared, through your representatives, to discuss and to illustrate, with pictures or other materials, your activities, projects and accomplishments to date?

Fifty groups from twenty-two cities accepted the invitation, and about 120 delegates came, most of them arriving late on Wednesday, May 15, at the St. Louis airport, where they were picked up either by members of the War Lords—the largest street gang in East St. Louis—or by Southern Illinois University staff members, and transported to the motel conference headquarters. They came from widely separated parts of the country, but geographically the representation was spotty. A six-state area in the Midwest, where most of the searching had been done, was the most heavily represented—eighteen delegates coming from East St. Louis itself—followed by an eastern contingent from Massachusetts, New York, Pennsylvania, and the District of Columbia; a western delegation drawn from San Francisco, Los Angeles, and Sacramento; and a southern contingent chiefly from New Orleans. The majority of the delegates were between eighteen and twenty-five years of age. A dozen or so were in their thirties, a few past forty. About ninety percent of them were black. Most of the others were Puerto Ricans or Mexican-Americans, and there were a few Chinese, Japanese, and American Indians. Almost all of the delegates were strangers to each other, the travelers who had done the searching being the only ones outside their own groups most of them had ever seen before. For most of them, this was the first trip away from their home city. Most of them were apprehensive. Very few had read the large flow of typewritten materials Mac had mailed out from Washington, or if they had, didn't know what it meant. Many, if not most of them, were reportedly armed for self-protection. Virtually all of them felt compelled to establish their individual status in the eyes of the others and determine for themselves whom they could trust. It had been tense on the first day of the YOU conference in New York seven months before, but here with nearly five times as many street leaders present, it soon became evident that underlying the clamor of militant and impassioned voices there was a real element of fear that could easily engulf the proceedings.

One of the older blacks, a veteran of many street battles, put it this way:

"Everybody had to prove that he was blacker than anybody else."

What could they expect to accomplish without blowing up somebody, and in the process, maybe being blown up? That was the level on which the assemblage convened. Some who were older knew well where that kind of action could get them: dead. But this was the testing most of the delegates had to experience: Who and what are you anyway? Can you do what I can do, can you be as demanding and go as far as I can?

"These younger cats aren't really grown men," one of the older leaders said to me. "Ask anybody's mother and she'll tell you. But they control the streetcorner. They make noise like men. And the thought of going halfway across the United States: Man, that's unbelievable. Why in hell would somebody pay them to do that?"

The first tangible issue on which to demonstrate their relative valor was the motel swimming pool. It didn't have any water in it, the weather was unseasonably warm, the street leaders were determined to go swimming, and according to the motel management, a city ordinance prohibited opening the pool for another two weeks. So somebody called a swimming caucus and they caucused all night, in each other's rooms, in the lobby, around the empty pool, and in the bar. The babble of voices got louder, the drinking got heavier, the commotion got wilder, and as the aggression, the threats, and the display of force mounted to a roar, other guests and motel employees became terrified.

"To swim or not to swim."

Outwardly, that was the issue, a test of strength in which the motel management—or, as it was looked upon, the establishment—became the common denominator upon which the delegates could vent their emotions. The management held out and the street leaders lost. But the collective rage expanded and after a harrowing evening, during which a shouting mob virtually took over the bar and the bartenders closed shop, the roar spread through the motel. Delegates' rooms reverberated with a revelry that sounded like insurrection, liquor bottles were emptied and fresh supplies brought in. The motel switchboard was swamped with complaints from guests who were not part of the conference—some screaming with fright—and the motel security men were helpless to keep up with the calls. Several regular customers, too petrified to go to bed, vowed never to patronize the place again.

The next morning the irate manager was confronted by a guest who detailed a story of strange individuals forcing their way into his room at 2 A.M., offering to sell him a prostitute, stealing his electric razor, a bottle of whiskey, and twenty-five dollars in cash. The guest then fled in panic to spend the balance of the night at another hotel. That was all the management needed. The conference had to get out—now. However, after listening to promises of restitution and guarantees from the conference leaders that no such night would be repeated, the management relented and said the conference could remain—on probation.

Beginning the same morning, the conference sessions evolved into a series of general assemblies alternated with meetings of regional groupings, smaller committees, and numerous informal clusters of delegates drawn together on the basis of mutual likes and newly formed friendships. In addition to SIU's East St. Louis conference facilities a few blocks from the motel, these smaller meetings went on almost everywhere: in the delegates' rooms, in the motel lobby, the bar, the dining room, and in taverns, private homes, and other gathering places around the city. Between these meetings and the inevitable partying—for which most of the delegates had voracious appetites— at least part of the conference was in motion virtually every hour of the day and night. A change of pace was provided by moving for one full day to SIU's rural campus setting at Edwardsville—about a half-hour's drive from East St. Louis—where the delegates mixed their meetings with lounging under the trees, touring the new buildings, fraternizing with coeds, eating in private dining rooms, and being guests of honor at an evening dance performance. Chartered buses transported the delegates between the motel and university meeting facilities. Cars and drivers stood on call to provide special transportation, and insofar as possible the university honored every request for extra services.

The delegates adopted a rule not to admit anyone to their meetings who was not regarded as a bona fide person of the streets, or one of their own.

"We just decided nobody from outside our type of environment had a right to be in our meetings," one of the leaders explained to me. "We made up our minds we're gonna do our thing our own goddam way, or not do it. Why should we waste our time trying to explain to outsiders what we already know? An outsider wouldn't understand anyway."

One of the few who objected to this secrecy said to me: "When it comes to strategy they want the establishment out. When it comes to getting money they want the establishment in."

In any event, the ban against outsiders was adopted and applied without exceptions, to the press, the university, the government, even to Mac and Frank, and after the opening general assembly, when a couple of outsiders did innocently wander in, guards were posted to see that the ban was enforced.

Gilmore, who had come to be looked upon as the person in charge of local arrangements, served as chairman. Chino made an opening speech. All the elaborate background materials concerning program and agenda which had been prepared in Washington, along with the printed meeting schedules, were immediately discarded, and the conference moved quickly into a wide-open, free-for-all shouting match. The central questions the delegates wanted answered were: What was this YOU thing all about, what was it trying to do, why, how, and who was trying to do it?

"Except that somebody had put out the word that a bunch of cats were getting together in East St. Louis for a YOU scene," one of the leaders explained to me, "most of the guys didn't know what was going on. This was the first time they ever heard of a national organization for guys on the street. A lot of them thought somebody was trying to decide something for them, and if that was the deal these cats wanted no part of it. They couldn't care less about any advance meeting plans. All that was irrelevant. Their attitude was, throw all that shit out the window. We don't need it. They didn't give a damn about any minutes or the fact that YOU was incorporated or who the president was. They just wanted to say what they wanted to say. And that took a lot of loud talking."

Another delegate said to me: "The arguments about YOU itself and what it should be if we decided to have it got hotter'n hell. The main thing was, let every cat have his say. But man, you had to scream your damn head off if you wanted to say it."

"There was so much confusion with everybody yelling at once," said one of the Puerto Ricans, "it was impossible even for us in there to know for sure what was going on. A lot of cats got hung up on personal stuff. They goddam near went crazy in the first meeting because three white people were in the room."

A very powerful black put it to me this way: "We just degenerated into a black-militant gathering, that's all. Hell, none of them motherfuckin' cats is any blacker than me."

Then, pulling his shirt up over his shoulders, he said: "Look at them goddam scars. Where the fuck do you think I got 'em? From a goddam gun, that's where. Man, I've been down that motherfuckin' road. I know where it's at. But now, goddamit, we got a program job we should be doin'. There ain't time for this shit. I told them mouthin' bastards to get the hell out if that's how they want it. Man, you better believe it. There's a lot of goddam stupid cats here."

One of the few delegates with college training told me in somewhat less forceful language, but with no less feeling: "They aren't interested in talking about programs. When somebody tried to say something about urban renewal he was never given a chance. If you want urban renewal, they said, burn it down. Then the establishment will rebuild it. They think all you have to do is stay militant and violent enough, and *ipso facto,* change will come. We have here what I would call two alliances: a constructive alliance and a nonconstructive alliance, and these two alliances keep clashing. I would say the constructive alliance is in the majority, but the nonconstructive alliance is a lot louder."

"Economics," said a black delegate, describing to me one of the heated exchanges. "Everybody screamed on that, screamed at the establishment. YOU can't do anything without money. But YOU ain't got any. Why? The goddam establishment has it all. YOU put in a proposal to the government before we came to East St. Louis, but that's only a hope. So the guys really breathed fire on the establishment. If the government turns us down? Goddam, the guys say, how about these big corporations that made all them millions? There's no reason we shouldn't get some of that. Our kids should have the best of whatever there is. But instead of helping us, the establishment sticks its money in its pockets, locks it up in banks, uses it for itself, and we get shit. The establishment says our kids should earn their own way. How in hell, our guys would like to know, can our poor kids do that? Our kids got nothin' to work with. Our kids are being wasted.

"The establishment blames everybody for what's wrong in the slums, everybody except itself. The establishment says to our poor black brothers there are too many Puerto Ricans, then it says to the Puerto Ricans there are too many black kids. Goddam, our people are told to fight like hell with each other for the not-enough that's left among us.

"Everybody in the family's starvin', the goddam house is fallin' down, it's so crowded we're stumblin' over each other, and the establishment says to the poor kid why don't you get an education? Hell, man, everybody's hustlin' just to stay alive. Everybody's runnin' all the credit they can get, the women are doing prostitution, everybody's sellin' dope, everybody's out stealin', everybody in the family is doing everything they can think of, and it still ain't enough. How in hell can the damn kid get an education?"

The delegate was grim. Then he started laughing.

"Man," he said to me, "you've got to laugh to be able to stand it. It would really be shit if you couldn't laugh, or keep full of booze, or dope, or somethin'. Sometimes you don't even want to wake up. If we stayed serious all the time we'd really burn down the town. Look, man, it's like one of the guys said. We can have all these dudes out runnin' around burnin' down buildings, and the establishment just sells more firehose, more burglar alarms, makes more money for rich people. Tragedy, that's what this country makes money on. So the only conclusion we could come to was that the establishment is a son-of-a-bitch."

Starting with the wild disarray of the first night, the conference moved through one ominous turn after another. In scattered groups, inside and outside the motel, delegates pooled their complaints and poured out their anger. Verbal confrontations that became almost violent were incessant. Many of the participants never got over the feeling of impending danger. Some contemplated the possibility of a shoot-out. One said he would never attend another such gathering without a bodyguard. Numerous incidents, such as an unauthorized press report, brought fresh outbursts of rage. Demands were registered for a hard line and for an organization that would be open only to blacks. At times it seemed the conference would not survive its own internal strains. At no time did it become productively engaged in program planning. Yet out of the continuum of bickering and interaction, the idea of a YOU devoted to communications, mutual assistance, and large-scale fund-raising gained acceptance, and after four tortuous days there emerged a state of conviviality that gave an outward appearance of harmony. Vice-President Humphrey telegraphed congratulations and best wishes, and representatives of the Urban Coalition, the Office of Economic Opportunity, and the Department of Health, Education, and Welfare flew out from Washington.

A twenty-one-member board of directors made up of a president and five delegates from each of the four regions—East, West, South, and North Central—was elected to manage the affairs of the organization, one delegate from each region being designated as a regional vice-president. Gilmore was elected president by acclamation.

The aura of unity crested on Saturday evening after the elections and at least for the moment a sense of national identity took hold of the majority of the delegates. Now, with officers and directors of their own choosing, YOU was theirs, and through it, they could command attention in Washington. Mac and Frank, along with SIU staff members and other outsiders who had hung around the fringes running errands and catering to the delegates' wishes, were allowed to join in the festivities of the evening, and the university vice-president was even asked to say a few words at dinner.

On Sunday the conference adjourned and most of the delegates left town. The officers and directors stayed on another day to talk over internal affairs, and to hold a Monday press conference at which they issued a public declaration calling for financial support with which to provide the nation's street gangs with "a constructive alternative to revolution."

For Mac Lewis it had been a climactic build-up that began as a dream which he initiated through the Real Great Society. With YOU now officially organized, his influence was greatly diminished; indeed, on the basis of the manner in which he was snubbed and snarled at, he appeared to be little more than a necessary evil. But this in no way diminished his continuing support. To him this meant only that the community of youth groups he had set out to develop was taking form, and that the ill treatment he was getting was a sign of progress, a further justification of his enthusiasm.

For RGS the promotion of YOU had been equally climactic, but a very different kind of experience. Having been caught up in what at first seemed like another grand adventure reminiscent of the days of Charlie Slack, RGS became the national symbol that gave the dream its public appeal. The warm glow of that symbolic position provided enough gratification to make it unnecessary to do much of the actual work that was needed after the Milwaukee strategy session, and as a consequence RGS found itself virtually unknown to the delegates at East St. Louis. After serving as the mythical founding father, its position of importance was unrecognized by YOU itself. Then came the repeated demands, so angrily voiced at the conference, for black exclusiveness—even at the expense of Puerto Ricans. These demands did not win formal conference approval, but as that racial emphasis became a dominant characteristic of the organization, there was no discernible possibility of a nonblack ever becoming its president. Over seven months of easy spending and expense-account living, spiced by high-level meetings and fun-filled nights from Washington to San Francisco—and even to San Juan—YOU became a fabulous episode in the illustrious life of RGS. But at East St. Louis a new management took over, and in a state of rejection, RGS returned to New York. Officially, it was still a member group, but suddenly it had other more pressing affairs of its own.

13

Conflict on the Home Front

During the early part of 1968, while the Real Great Society was still the glittering light in the promotion of YOU and was making the scene at gatherings across the nation, the University of the Streets, its chief claim to fame and fortune on the homefront, was struggling for existence. The East Harlem branch was rapidly extending its influence in the total RGS organization, and Bill Watman was still negotiating with OEO for a federal grant.

With the growing popularity of street gangs as vehicles for federal antipoverty funds, which had received a major boost from Vice-President Humphrey largely as a result of Chino's stellar performance at the 1968 national conference of the President's Council on Youth Opportunities, there was a solid block of interest at OEO in RGS and its grant application for the University of the Streets. But since September 1967, when it was first submitted, the application had been shifted from one OEO office to another and had become bogged down in the bureaucracy. Officials who weren't in on originating it were more concerned about other projects they could point to as theirs. Internal agency rivalries, favored treatment of projects that had specific political backing, personnel turnovers, disagreement and indecision among bureaucrats over one point or another in Bill Watman's write-up had combined to create a seemingly hopeless situation.

As a result the need for money at the University of the Streets was desperate. Salaries were cut, some eliminated. Payless pay days had become common. Staff members were quitting, and the pressures were causing serious internal dissension. Private money was coming in bits and pieces, each amount used up by the time the next amount came in, and there were always overdue bills.

This anxiety, coupled with the continuing power thrust from East Harlem, had created a situation in which people were beginning to accuse each other of being interested in the university only for the purpose of building their own influence in anticipation of the expected federal grant. Almost every day there was a new rumor, and the bad feeling caused by accusations and counteraccusations between East Harlem and the Lower East Side led to very difficult relations. The original idealism that had gone into RGS was not lost, but it was badly tarnished, and while the Lower East Side leaders continued to be away much of the time and the period of waiting for OEO dragged on, the problem of internal organization at the university went from bad to worse.

Meanwhile, in Washington Frank Ferguson reached the conclusion that the proposal for the University of the Streets had become lost in the labyrinth of government; unless it could be given a push, it would probably never come out. One day, while pondering what he might do to arrange this push, he boarded a plane for New York and got himself seated directly across the aisle from another passenger he happened to see getting on the same flight, Senator Robert F. Kennedy.

The Senator was sitting in the middle of a three-seat arrangement reading *The New York Times,* his daughter in the window seat, his briefcase and books piled in the aisle seat. Frank introduced himself and asked if he might have a word. Responding quickly to a slight affirmative nod, he moved the Senator's belongings from the vacant aisle seat, plopped down beside him, and began a glowing account of the Real Great Society and the University of the Streets. For a while the Senator kept thumbing the pages of his newspaper. Frank, one of the slowest talkers I have ever known, but determined to capture the Senator's full attention, raised his voice and stepped up his speech. Senator Kennedy put down his newspaper, listened and asked questions. Approximately forty-five minutes after takeoff they landed at LaGuardia. Frank had what he wanted, the Senator's interest, and instructions to call his top aide, Adam Walinsky, for an appointment.

Frank returned to Washington, checked to make certain the proposal was in completed form, then made the appointment and called Fred Good to join him. Fred arrived from New York with a Lower East Side street youth he had been training for public relations work, and all three of them went to the Senate Office Building to see Adam Walinsky. After about an hour of conversation Walinsky put through a telephone message to Sargent Shriver, director of OEO, that Senator Kennedy would appreciate favorable action on the proposal from the Real Great Society. Two days later, February 23, 1968, it was approved, $253,557 for the first year.

The grant, however, didn't begin until April 12, almost eight months after Bill Watman had been assured that OEO was prepared to move quickly. It was made to the Real Great Society, Inc., primarily for the work of the University of the Streets on the Lower East Side—which was viewed in Washington as a demonstration that could be repeated nationwide—but RGS/Uptown was able to get fifty thousand dollars earmarked for its use in East Harlem.

The official contract described the university as a "new model community college" to be "administered by a community organization comprised of talented neighborhood youth," and called for "a wide range of short-term courses . . . in response to the express needs of the community" to be "designed by the students themselves" with the help of staff members and other consultants. It also provided for what it called "specific courses to be offered by experienced persons"—such as those that had already been started in karate and in other fields—and for a "prep-school program" to help high school dropouts.

Thirty "work-study" positions were provided, twenty for the Lower East Side, ten for East Harlem, with a pay rate of $1.50 per hour up to twenty hours a week.

Provision was made for the development of new businesses, publication of a newsletter, the production of a documentary film, and the organization of almost any kind of neighborhood action project.

The university, said the contract, was to employ the "shadow system" and the "hunter system," adaptations of methods long used in the development of street gangs. Each leader was to have a "shadow," a youth who would follow him around and in time learn to perform the leader's job. Other youths who were to work under the supervision of "community organizers" were designated as "hunters." Their job was to search out members of the "hard-core" population and convince them to take advantage of the opportunities the project offered. These systems—because of their similarity to established street-gang practice—would, according to the contract, "set in motion the machinery" that would make it possible to "find out whether or not the members of a poverty area are able to plan for and utilize the services of the program for their own benefit."

The OEO grant should have made it possible for the University of the Streets to substantially increase its productivity and achieve on a greatly enlarged scale its potential for youth development. At least it should have taken care of the financial problems. But the RGS Lower East Side leaders were out of town, and the ruptures in the home front were getting deeper. The question was, would RGS be able to settle down to the actual work of building the project? OEO might have begun inquiries for a realistic assessment of the problems. But no one took the trouble to examine the internal divisions and power struggles then going on in New York, or to understand the how or who or what in the actual workings of the university. Instead, the bureaucrats in Washington and the salesmen from New York simply polished to a sheen the generally accepted notion that RGS was a group of "talented neighborhood youth," who, as experienced gang leaders, were peculiarly knowledgeable about working with ghetto young people, and were creating a model that could be duplicated by federally supported street gangs in urban ghettos throughout the nation. Now RGS had the kind of money it had been dreaming about, but the problems of the University of the Streets were only beginning.

The program people who had stayed with the university through all its difficulties while the famous gang leaders were on the celebrity circuit were a determined and independent lot. They were deeply committed to their work. They had done their jobs, with or without pay, and had derived considerable personal satisfaction. Collectively, they felt a strong sense of possessiveness toward the project. They were the ones who were building it. Individually, they often differed with each other, but they never tried to boss each other. Each of them regarded his portion of the venture as his, decided for himself how to run it, and did just about as he pleased.

In terms of organizational efficiency, this built-in latitude for independent action had its drawbacks, but it was the initiative and individualism of the program people which this independence allowed that had created the university in the first place. In the ten months of operation before the OEO grant was received, this loose, unstructured way of doing things had become firmly established practice.

Now with the OEO grant this accustomed pattern of operations was threatened. Legally, the University of the Streets was a creature of the Real Great Society, Inc., not an independent organization. This meant that control over the new federal funds was vested in the board of directors of the corporation, the famous gang leaders. On a strictly legal basis, everybody understood that. But inside the university it was also known that these were not the people who were actually developing the project. The program people who were developing it, though in most cases indigenous residents of the neighborhood themselves, were not directors or officers of the corporation—indeed, were not really a part of the small "in-group" of which RGS was actually comprised. They were acutely aware of the difference between what the publicity kept saying and the reality of the situation. With the exception of Fred and Bill, the program people had not been caught up in the process of myth-making, and were tired of watching the continuous outpouring of misleading publicity. These people would have welcomed a little recognition themselves.

Now, as they found themselves being subjected to the provisions of the OEO contract, their feelings of concern were substantially rein-forced. They were to be placed in formally defined "slots" in an administrative organization headed by a project director and an assistant director under the supervision of the official board of di-rectors of the corporation. The program people saw themselves being straightjacketed.

The contract provided a total of twenty-three slots—or staff posi-tions—plus the thirty work-study positions, additional funds for an accountant, and for outside consultants who could be called in at the discretion of the top administration and board of directors.

The appointment of the project director required OEO approval. Actually, the choice was in the hands of the board members, who, if they wished, were free to appoint themselves to supervisory staff positions, which they did. Thus, an interlocking membership was set up between the staff and the official body which had authority to hire and fire the staff—the corporate board of directors. In setting up to administer the grant, the East Harlem branch of RGS maneuvered itself into a strategic position of authority. With twenty percent of the grant earmarked for its autonomous use, it substantially strengthened its power base uptown. Then it got two of its members named to top administrative posts in the University of the Streets—including the position of assistant director—thus acquiring a solid measure of con-trol on the Lower East Side as well.

The matter of control became critical. The program people, eager to improve their services, were prepared to defend and maintain their position of independence. The Lower East Side wing of the inner-core group was prepared to maintain its proprietary position. The aggres-sive and more mobile East Harlem wing, having already gained a major position of control and determined to extend that control, was ready to move in.

In preparing the government contract and working it through the bureaucracy, the Lower East Side and East Harlem wings of RGS and the University of the Streets had been looked upon as a single united group. In practice, however, this complex group of people had become not one but several. About ten more people were expecting paid positions than were available, and they were jockeying to get in with the right faction. There were fierce arguments over how to distribute the money. In effect, the OEO grant became a kind of grab bag to be reached into by those who could most forcefully assert themselves. OEO provided no training, no direction, no guidance. It simply provided money, in exchange for a contract to demonstrate an innovative approach to education and community action by "talented neighborhood youth." Now, subject to the rules of government accountability, which nobody in either wing of the RGS inner-core group or at the University of the Streets quite understood, all these emotionally charged differences were lumped together and turned loose to build a model educational project for nationwide reproduction.

14

Staff Revolt

Under the OEO contract Fred Good and Bill Watman were designated as "educational specialists." Fred withdrew from all book-keeping and fiscal responsibilities, a task for which he was not temperamentally suited in the first place.

The top administrative position, that of director, was vacant. The RGS East Harlem branch put forth its candidate for the job, and he was hired. Fresh from a supervisory position in an East Harlem antipoverty agency, he came on full time at the beginning of May prepared to tighten up the university's loose organization and mold it into a structured agency operation under firm executive control.

Moving quickly to establish his authority, he put the staff on notice as to his intentions. There was to be close coordination among all units within the total program. Specific lines of communication and supervision would be clearly designated. Staff meetings with required attendance would be held on a regular weekly basis. All staff members were to submit weekly reports. Requests for funds and materials would henceforth be made in writing, accompanied by detailed justification. Regular working hours were to be strictly observed. Staff members were to leave word with the receptionist where they were going, and why, when they left the building. That was the executive mandate.

The staff response was swift and predictable. The new administration was seen as a would-be dictatorship, a vicious foreign element. Virtually no one had the slightest intention of carrying out the new directives. Staff meetings were boycotted. Required reports and memoranda were not written. Hours were disregarded. Staff members came and went as they had always done. The operation was bathed in defiance. From the Community Clubhouse in the basement through every program to the seventh floor and out into extended locations in the neighborhood, workers and students alike became distrustful of the administration. The university was split into two angry, embattled factions: the staff, supported by the neighborhood street youths who made up the student body, in one camp; the administration, supported by the RGS East Harlem branch, in the other.

The period during which this crisis was taking form—spring and early summer 1968—was an extremely critical one. The university was making its comeback from the slump that had set in the previous fall. The East Harlem wing of RGS was increasing its pressure against Fred and Bill. The leaders of the Lower East Side wing were involved in YOU and were making personal appearances in places as far away as Mexico and Puerto Rico. With their presence largely withdrawn from the scene of action, Fred, still feeling himself a part of the original group, was left as the principal spokesman for RGS on the Lower East Side.

Regardless of any official title, Fred was the leading organizer of the University of the Streets. But his leadership during this critical period greatly increased his vulnerability to the East Harlem attack. His leadership created the impression that the university was the work of the RGS gang leaders, thus adding to the myth. And it intensified an unhealthy situation with respect to his personal relationship to the Lower East Side wing of the inner core.

He had become a crutch. He had allowed the group to become dependent upon him. Had he not gone ahead as he did with the development of the project, there probably would have been no project. But the point is that, justified or not, he had gone ahead without any real involvement of the group itself. This prevented the group from seeing realistically its own limitations, or of being aware even of the existence of the problem. Fred's services were urgently needed, but the group's self-image had become so inflated it was no longer certain of that fact. From East Harlem the group heard voices that said it didn't need him. This feeling of independence, without really being independent, was cause for considerable anguish. The group was beginning to resent its closest friend.

But Fred was as captured by the myth as was the group, and by this time was in so deep that he simply continued, along with Bill, to supply the distorted material that was being printed. He and Bill were in this myth-making process together, but Fred's involvement was deeper than Bill's. Without him it is doubtful that the myth, now grown to heroic proportions, would have survived much beyond the departure of Charlie Slack.

During three years of continuous effort as both promoter and program developer, Fred had done an effective job of glorifying the RGS image. The gang leaders had come to believe the fiction he had helped create, and that fiction now had to be preserved. Ambrosia had become an addiction. The group could not afford to acknowledge that it was really the program people—nonentities in the myth—who were the actual organizers and developers of the work. In his capacity as the group's personal counselor and ally, Fred had so effectively shielded it from reality that he had not permitted even himself to accept what was actually going on.

Functionally, RGS and the University of the Streets had by this time grown into two distinct entities, and the OEO grant would have been far more effectively utilized had they been treated as such. But at this point Fred was not able to see it that way, even though other key workers in the university tried to tell him. In his mind RGS and the university were one and the same, an activity of the streets which he described as a "social phenomenon," a spiritual growth to which he had totally given himself on that night in April 1965 when he wrote and sang poetry with the Spartican Army and began dreaming about all the things they were going to do to eliminate poverty and delinquency on the Lower East Side. A thousand times he had relived the euphoria of that night, until it had become so etched in his mind that despite any disappointment he may have felt when the blunt truth forced itself upon him, his loyalty to RGS and to the spirit it symbolized to him had never ceased. He saw the University of the Streets as a tangible manifestation of that spirit.

Fred was working tirelessly to get the university more deeply rooted in the neighborhood because to him that was its basic objective. In doing this he was driven by a belief that he was revitalizing the original RGS spirit which he saw being damaged by the new circumstances then emerging. Motivated by this belief, he entered with tremendous fervor into his work with youths in the streets, such as Pee Wee and Alvin, and formed relationships with organizations outside the neighborhood, such as Kenyon & Eckhardt, as a means of enlarging the store of available resources. In these and numerous other ways he devoted all of his physical and mental energy to rebuilding from the decline of late 1967. He was greatly fortified in these efforts by the work of Owen Watson, Arnold Johnson, Leroy Bostic, and others among the program people, including many volunteers, who were also applying themselves to the rebuilding process, and by the end of April 1968, just before the new administration came in from East Harlem, Fred had the feeling that the university was moving with a greater surge than ever toward its basic goal of opening youth opportunities on the Lower East Side. At no time since he began his beautiful dream of the Real Great Society had he been more emotionally charged, more excited by the potential for development. After all they had come through, after the long struggle to stay solvent while waiting for the government grant, now the dream of that April night so long ago was coming true. Now the momentum of actual development was picking up. Now things were really beginning to happen. He was elated, and eager to push even faster.

Then, in this mood of hope and optimism, came the new university administration. Fred, along with other program leaders, saw it as an instrument of the East Harlem power thrust. They saw something terrible, a horrible intrusion from uptown that threatened the basic integrity of the experiment—its unstructured, individualized, spontaneous mode of creativity and development. The concept of allowing actions to flow out of individuals without formal administrative restraint was now being subverted by what he saw as an unwarranted move to transform the University of the Streets into just another bureaucracy.

Grimly, he vowed that the new administration had to go. Almost unanimously the rest of the workers reacted with him, and Fred emerged as the leader of a staff revolt. Thus, a seething discontent, which began the moment the new director announced his intended administrative policies, now erupted into open conflict, ideological and highly personal in tone, between two unyielding positions: one symbolized by Fred and his devotion to what he interpreted as the original spirit of RGS, which he saw being corrupted; the other symbolized by the East Harlem branch, with its ambitions for power and its determination to recast the university under its control. The director, with his support coming from East Harlem but with his operations on the Lower East Side, was caught between these two positions, and was either unable or unwilling to arbitrate the differences.

For nearly two months the tension mounted, both sides refusing to compromise. People became distracted from their work, incensed toward every move that was made by the administration or by RGS/ East Harlem. Program activities faltered. Classes shrank, many disappeared. The rebuilding process slowed, enthusiasm waned, tempers flared. As a form of administrative discipline, salary payments were withheld and staff defiance increased. In one instance a staff member seized the university checkbook and refused to return it without an agreement that the checks would be signed immediately. From continuous hostility and complaint, productive energies were dissipated and a kind of paralysis seemed to take hold of the operation. Ridden by rumor, gossip, exploding emotions, and a state of confusion that Owen Watson said made the office sound like a riot, the university sank to a new low.

"Everything we stood for was hurt," said Fred. "The real spirit of the university was going down the drain. We were losing our street kids. We were at a standstill. We weren't doing what we started out to do or what we knew how to do. The survival of the Real Great Society was at stake."

At a protest meeting early in June, staff members and street youths bluntly accused the director of attempting to wreck the university. The director countered by insisting on the need for strict administrative control, and the uptown leaders backed him.

This was just at the time that Pee Wee's court case was coming up, and Fred was working frantically to keep him out of jail. To Fred, Pee Wee's case was so central to the basic meaning of the university that any failure to support him in this hour of need was inexcusable. Scores of youths were helping Fred circulate petitions attesting to Pee Wee's rehabilitation and his value to the neighborhood. He was without doubt one of the most popular leaders in the streets, and neighborhood sentiment in his favor ran high. Fred tried to get the university director to write a letter to this effect as a part of Pee Wee's defense, but the director refused to become involved. In the eyes of the street youths, that was the height of treachery. On June 18, 1968, when Pee Wee stood trial and the effort to save him from jail was lost, Fred returned from court and confronted the director.

Almost trembling with rage, he shouted: "You fucking bastard!"

That brought the rebellion to a head.

Had there been any doubt as to the magnitude of feeling on Fred's side of the conflict, there was none now. At noon on a Saturday early in July, about fifty irate staff workers and street youths met with the director for a showdown. The leaders of the Lower East Side wing of the inner-core group were out of town.

Pee Wee's case was the top item on the agenda and in the heat of argument the director referred to him as a junkie.

The reaction was bedlam.

Finally, it was decided that a representative committee would be elected to participate in determining policy and in the hiring and firing of personnel. The East Harlem branch made one last attempt to suppress the rebellion, but by now the pressure from inside the university could no longer be resisted. The committee was elected, Fred engineered the director's separation, and the committee faded away.

With approximately a third of the one-year grant period now gone, the University of the Streets had used up a disproportionate percentage of its federal funds, and its performance under the OEO contract had to be virtually started over.

Automatically, Chino, as the RGS president, became acting director until someone else from outside could be appointed, and a relative calm settled over the staff. On the surface it now appeared that normal operations could once more be resumed. But the outward peaceful appearance was only temporary. Wounds had been opened, and although the immediate issue had been resolved, the underlying conflict was still present, indeed had been deepened and strengthened.

The program people who had won the struggle, and who were now referred to as "the staff," emerged from the revolt as a force to be reckoned with. The East Harlem portion of the inner-core group, smarting from its loss, emerged even more determined to gain control.

The Lower East Side portion of the inner core was now in a tenuous position. Symbolically, and according to the public record, it was the instrument of development for the whole operation. If the operation were to collapse, which was not a far-fetched possibility, its public image and its ability to obtain grants could be seriously damaged, maybe irreparably. To preserve its proprietary interest and its position of prestige, it now had to come forward, assert its authority, and reduce the friction that was killing the project. But the Lower East Side portion of the group was the prisoner of a myth. Its perception of the situation was extremely unclear. It was not really in charge, and now it was being pulled in opposite directions by two powerful opposing forces. Like a Greek tragedy, a drama had been started that if acted out would inevitably destroy the University of the Streets, and the Lower East Side gang leaders were not in a position to rewrite the script.

Whether the Lower East Side leaders liked it or not, the East Harlem branch now exercised heavy influence inside the Real Great Society. The Lower East Side wing held charter membership, but while it was out receiving accolades, the effective center of power within the organization had been shifted by the more sophisticated

newer membership to East Harlem, and the charter membership now
had to listen to the voices from that uptown power base. Moreover,
those voices were on a wavelength that gave them steadily increasing
appeal. They were not only from inside RGS, they were Puerto
Rican. Militant and proud, they spoke in terms of "our people," and
called for cultural unity against the outside world. They were in tune
with the times.

But on the other hand, what about the program people? Their
voices could not be ignored either. When it came to getting the work
done, they could not be just brushed aside. The Lower East Side wing
still liked to travel, but even if it could suppress that urge, was it
really possible that on its own, it could actually manage and carry out
a project of the magnitude and complexity of the University of the
Streets? And if it couldn't, then what would happen, especially now
that RGS was under government contract? This got back to the
dependency syndrome, which, as the conflicting pressures increased,
was beginning to produce sharply negative reactions.

In the struggle to throw off an authoritarian administration, Fred
had come out openly on the side of the revolt because he felt his
action was right with respect to the neighborhood itself, the primary
object of the whole project. Thus, he had taken on the role of a
crusader fighting to preserve the freedom of what he regarded as a
neighborhood effort. But he had also seen himself as the savior of
RGS, and in his determination to preserve what he interpreted to be
its basic meaning he was unconsciously fighting for his own survival.
Having made a solemn pledge to himself and to the group, having
made himself a resident of the neighborhood, having devoted more
than three years to carrying out his commitment, he had woven the
neighborhood, the University of the Streets, and the Real Great
Society into one, and made it a part of himself. That vital part of
himself he had seen in danger of destruction.

Fred's revulsion had so overwhelmed him that when the fight was
over and it became evident that even after the victory, indeed, maybe
even because of the victory, the danger was still pressing upon him,
he went into a period of depression. He took to brooding. He felt
persecuted. At times he drank too much, gave orders, screamed his

irritations, occasionally broke into tears. He became openly annoyed with the group he had all but worshiped, for not doing its share of the work. Feeling that the group had forgotten its original purpose, he began to look to other people in the neighborhood with whom to carry on the program. These were some of the negative reactions to the dependency syndrome that occurred within Fred. Some people said he was having a nervous breakdown.

For the Lower East Side wing of RGS the negative reactions were equally devastating. When Fred began openly to assert his leadership and authority instead of deferring to the gang leaders, when he assumed the role of saving RGS from its own destruction, their dependency began to sour. At that point Fred had departed from his former role as behind-the-scenes confidant, publicity agent, and program developer, and made himself the man of the hour. When he turned to the staff and to others outside RGS to uphold the ideology he had attached to RGS itself, he was unwittingly tampering with the myth he had been so instrumental in creating. He was beginning to take away some of the group's self-identity. Without either Fred or the original leaders really knowing what was happening, a long and trusted friendship began to erode, and the East Harlem branch of the RGS organization moved relentlessly to encourage that erosion.

As the breach between the staff and the RGS East Harlem wing continued to widen, it was virtually assured that the negative impulses toward Fred from the Lower East Side wing would increase, both in frequency and volume. Both sides in the conflict—the staff and the leaders in East Harlem—made claims on its allegiance and expected its support. The Lower East Side wing could try to be loyal to both sides, thus holding to the best of both worlds. But circumstances dictated that the chances of doing this were not very bright, and the two branches of the Puerto Rican inner core of which RGS was comprised drew increasingly closer together.

The hostility from East Harlem was directed at the university staff as a whole, but Fred was seen as the prime enemy and Bill was next. They were not Puerto Rican, they were not gang types, they were not even native to the ghetto, yet they exercised very great influence. They were a threat to the ambitions of the East Harlem branch. The mere fact that the Lower East Side leadership had actually accepted two such individuals as close friends, allowed them to become leaders, for a while even defended them against criticism—that was evidence enough. But the victory of the staff rebellion—that was too much.

In July 1968, Bill solved his part of the problem. He quit and joined a private Washington consulting firm doing contract work for OEO.

Said Bill: "The Real Great Society was ruined by the federal funding. The Lower East Side guys were running around the country and the East Harlem guys had their ax to grind. They wanted to control the money. Then they got on this Puerto Rican power bit. People were playing the usual poverty-program politics. Fred and I began arguing about how to interpret the contract. The tension was driving me crazy. The old spirit seemed to be killed. I started feeling we weren't a Real Great Society any more, just another government grantee, a typical antipoverty agency. So I decided that since I was one of the main instigators of the grant, if this is the kind of thing I'm to do, I might as well live in comfort and make some money in Washington as to sweat it out on the Lower East Side."

The East Harlem attack on the University of the Streets now focused on Fred.

15

The Return of Mike Good

On August 1, 1968, Mike Good, en route to a new job in Virginia, returned to New York to visit his brother Fred and look in on his old RGS friends. What he found bore little resemblance to what he remembered from his previous association, which ended in Albuquerque in May 1965

"Rumors were rampant," he said. "There was talk about putting the University of the Streets under the exclusive control of Puerto Ricans, cutting out blacks, whites, everybody else. It was an atmosphere of hate. You could feel it and hear it everywhere. Fred was so worried about what was happening to the program I decided to stick around and see if I could help get things straightened out."

Like Fred had done before, Mike canceled his plans to go on to another job and moved in with his brother in a small apartment on East Fifth Street, just a block or so from the old East Sixth Street address where he and Fred and Charlie Slack had started RGS on its rise to fame.

Mike didn't lose any time getting to work. Arriving just behind him was an examiner from a private firm under OEO contract to examine the university's financial records. Mike helped make the examination.

"He thought it would take us only a couple of days," said Mike. "But when we got into the books we discovered such a mess we worked for a week before we could put anything together that even began to make sense. It was so bad it was unbelievable. What we finally had to decide was that somebody would have to start from scratch and reconstruct a whole new set of books."

Expenditures had gone unposted, purchases were not logged, receipts were missing, and the few records that existed were largely illegible and full of errors in arithmetic. Check stubs, canceled checks, and notes scribbled on scraps of paper were scattered among file cabinets, desk drawers, and miscellaneous boxes. Payroll records were incomplete. There was not even a complete roster of payees. Time and attendance records were missing. Pay checks had been made out to cash, and it was difficult to determine how much had been paid to whom. Payroll taxes were delinquent. There was only one general account, no departmental budgets, no monthly cost projections, no financial reports. Personal loans and deposits for bail bonds were unrecorded and uncollected. Expenditures labeled "meals" had been made for beer, parties, and travel not authorized in the contract. Stacks of miscellaneous bills were overdue, including two months of telephone bills totaling more than $1,400; there were charges for long-distance calls to Puerto Rico, the Virgin Islands, and California that had no relationship to university business. When Mike went to the telephone company to clear this up, he was told that the phones would have been disconnected had it not been for the government contract. Other bills had been overpaid, in several instances more than once. Misunderstandings and disputes with a wily Lower East Side landlord had resulted in overpayments of two to three thousand dollars for rent on the building; it was impossible to establish the exact figure. Old bills incurred before the OEO contract began had been paid out of contract funds, and only after an extensive search in Washington was it possible to establish the official beginning date of the grant, April 12, 1968. At the then current rate of expenditures the federal funds would be exhausted in the following February, approximately two months before the expiration of the grant period. Nobody could be certain just when in February because at this point it was impossible to tell exactly how much money had been obligated.

Said Mike: "We estimated that it would take about two months to develop new books, bring them up to date, and figure out precisely where we stood. We could never tabulate all the past expenditures and obligations, but we thought we could come within one or two thousand dollars. I don't think there was any dishonesty, just a case of incredibly bad management and bad judgment, plus the fact that the accountant was so kind-hearted and so inexperienced in dealing with groups like RGS that he hadn't been firm enough in telling them what they could or couldn't do. He didn't insist hard enough that they keep decent records. He sort of took the attitude that it would be a good idea for them to learn by their own mistakes, thinking that he could eventually teach them where they were going wrong and then get them on the right track. But a lot of money, we'll never know how much, had been wasted."

Owen Watson described it more colorfully. "Man, them guys used a lot of bread."

The accountant was made the scapegoat, but the underlying difficulties were far deeper and more profound than sloppy accounting records, unauthorized expenditures, and inefficient business procedures.

"The basic responsibility," said Mike, "was with OEO."

Now, four months after the spending started, the arrival of the private examiner was the first move by OEO to learn what was happening to the quarter of a million dollars, and even then it didn't really find out. All it learned was that there had been financial mismanagement. It didn't learn the underlying reasons, nor did it learn to comprehend the myth. But the information it did obtain was jolting.

In Washington an OEO official said to me: "We probably should have given more consideration to the size of the grant in terms of the management capability of the group, and we should have provided training for the board members. As it is, the group may have been better off before. Maybe it was corrupted by too many federal dollars."

The examiner came up with recommendations covering twenty-four specific items he considered essential to straightening out the situation and establishing orderly business procedures. They included closing out the old bank account, in which funds from a variety of sources had been mixed together, starting a new account exclusively for the university grant, employing a new accounting firm, a new director, and a business manager.

If this caused concern at OEO, it caused shock waves at RGS. The findings of the examination with, of all people, Mike—Fred's brother —taking an active part in conducting it, were deflating enough, but the medicine prescribed as a cure was even worse. In recommending the position of business manager, the examiner suggested that if additional funds for this purpose could not be made available, the position should be established as a substitute for the assistant directorship then held by the East Harlem branch, and that Mike, because of his understanding of the situation and his interest in correcting it, was the logical person to fill the position. To correct the unbusinesslike disbursement practices, which—because of frequent delays in getting out paychecks—had become a morale problem as well as a financial one, the examiner recommended that new check-signature controls be established. This meant authorizing university staff leaders to share the responsibility of signing checks with the corporate officers of RGS.

For the position of university director, members of the staff, including Fred, wanted a black resident of the Lower East Side named Muhammad Salahuddeen whom RGS had previously rejected for that position in favor of the East Harlem appointee the staff had forced out. Widely known in the neighborhood, Muhammad had done a great deal of volunteer work for the university and thoroughly understood its problems. He had presided at many of the emotionally charged meetings that were held during the staff revolt, and in so doing had proved himself to be a skillful and fair-minded leader. But he was the choice of the program people, not of RGS. Moreover, he had the tacit approval of the examiner, who for the first time had exposed information and was making official recommendations that had the effect of deflating the myth.

Unwittingly, the examiner, with the help of a Good, had set in motion a new development that was advancing the threat to the group image and self-identity, which had become a part of the dependency syndrome. This contributed further to the growing disquiet within the Lower East Side wing of the inner core. The examiner's work also loomed as a potent new threat to the East Harlem ambitions. The impact of this double threat was substantial, for the examiner became so determined to see the situation rectified that his recommendations took on the dimensions of an official mandate. Soon it became generally assumed by the staff that Muhammad would become the new director, with Mike serving as business manager. Then, further aggravating the strain, Mike entered vigorously into the move to get these new appointments accomplished. With the characteristic candor of the streets, he told his old RGS friends that they should get Muhammad hired immediately so that the mismanagement could be corrected without further delay and the development of the university resumed. Otherwise, he argued, the whole operation was going to fall apart. And the examiner agreed. Mike's admonitions were rough. But under the circumstances they carried weight, and the inner core was steadily pushed into going along.

As the move for new management gained momentum, so did the fear of lost self-esteem that had been triggered by Fred's leadership in the staff revolt, and the determination of RGS to strike back became an obsession. Already being drawn closer together, the two wings of the group, each for its own special reasons, each being forced by the pressure of events into a defensive stance, moved with increasing speed into a position of unity against what was coming more and more to be looked upon as a common enemy—the university staff.

The negative impulses emitted from the dependency syndrome with Fred came faster. The blockage to the East Harlem power thrust grew stronger, and the backlash increased in intensity. With Fred's brother having returned to become a leading figure in an embarrassing exposure of reality, with the staff rallying around its candidate for director, Fred loomed in the imagination of the inner core as the devil himself.

The situation was complicated by the fact that all of these elements of fear and anger were interwoven into the fabric of race. In its original conception RGS was to have been open to all persons regardless of racial or national origin, and ostensibly that still held. Publicly, the rationale was: If a person was poor, lived in the ghetto, and believed in self-determination, that was all that mattered. Most of those in the inner core were not willing to say flat out that this rationale had changed. But in practice? It depended on who was asking the question and who was doing the talking. However, regardless of what might be said for public consumption, the actions of the group made it clear that its Puerto Rican make-up had become an increasingly important part of its self-image and identity. Times had changed since the beginning days of talking and dreaming at the East Sixth Street apartment. Black power had come in. But that was for blacks. Puerto Ricans had to make it on their own. They had their cultural and racial pride, and they too were demanding power. The aftermath of the Columbia youth conference in August 1967 and the rise of the East Harlem branch gave heavy emphasis to this demand. The YOU conference in East St. Louis in May 1968, which injured Puerto Rican pride, gave another push to this racial emphasis. Then while still recovering from the YOU experience, RGS in June 1968 became involved with a group of political activists in Washington who wanted to start a nationwide organization to be known as the National Training Institute (NTI).

This new organization was to create a coalition between Puerto Ricans and Mexican-Americans, and develop a network of trained organizers for community action by Spanish-speaking youths in poverty neighborhoods throughout the country, including Puerto Rico. Along with a Mexican-American action organization based in Los Angeles and a Puerto Rican action organization based in San Juan, RGS was accorded the prestigious position of acting as one of the founders of NTI, and was asked to provide NTI national headquarters and a treasurer during the period of getting started. That kind of recognition would have been rich nourishment for the group's self-image under any circumstances, but coming as it did on the heels of the affair at East St. Louis, and at the time of the conflict at the University of the Streets, this flattering influence was of special importance. A budget in excess of three hundred thousand dollars for the first fifteen months was to be raised from public and private sources, and the enterprise was given immediate status by an initial grant of eighteen thousand dollars from OEO to provide fees, traveling expenses, and other costs for planning and organization. In a number of ways the NTI idea resembled the YOU idea, except at this point in time NTI looked even better. It was intended specifically for youth of Latin-American origin, and considered in the context of events then affecting RGS, this racial emphasis made NTI a significant addition to those events.

The written proposal for NTI said in part:

> The need for programs such as NTI relates to the general problems of poverty, but more specifically to the particular problems of Spanish-speaking people in the U.S. and Puerto Rico. Spanish-speaking people have customarily been accorded a second place in American society. They have proud traditions and a common language. They are building, out of these, a determination to share a better life with other Americans. This means acquiring a degree of self-determination heretofore denied them; it means releasing the energy of their youth for creative purposes; it means getting rid of the frustration of paternalism in schools, politics, jobs, and the full range of American institutions which have always told the Mexican-American and the Puerto Rican, "You do not know what is best for you; you are not fully human." . . .
>
> Self-determination must be supported through organized efforts at community development, especially through training the younger members of the population, who have the mobility, energy and imagination to create solutions to problems of dependency. . . .
>
> Only in this direction lies the path away from passive acceptance of all the manifold oppressions which poverty and minority status force upon the Spanish-speaking population of the United States, and the colonialized poor of the commonwealth island to the south. Intercommunication between Spanish-speaking groups is behind the whole concept of NTI.

The proposal referred to RGS as a model of what could be done "to give street-gang kids an opportunity to direct their energies toward programs that build the capacity of a community to solve its problems autonomously." NTI training, said the proposal, was to be "based on the streets—the life of the streets, the resources of the streets, and the action groups that can move hard and fast on the problems of the poor." RGS was characterized in the proposal as a group that was doing just that, "right now," thus making it one of the "capital assets of NTI."

For purposes of group identity this was heady language.

As events later turned out, NTI never got beyond the initial planning and organizational stage, but during the 1968 summer crisis at the University of the Streets it was a very alive item, and had important influence on the growing emphasis on Puerto Rican identity and control. Latin people for Latin people—Puerto Rican and Mexican—became a dominant theme; Muhammad was black and the choice of the staff; the Good brothers were white; and the University of the Streets was mixed, mostly black. And so, intertwined with the syndrome of dependency, the jealousy, the personality conflicts, and the struggles for power then eating away the vital energy of this potentially important project was the fundamental issue of race.

Against this emotional background, a special meeting was convened at OEO in Washington to review the examiner's report on the university, Monday, August 19, 1968. The examiner, OEO officials, RGS gang leaders, Fred, Mike, and Muhammad—the man it was assumed would be the new director—were there. The examiner's recommendations were thoroughly aired. But when the key questions were brought up—would Muhammad, in fact, be the director and Mike the business manager—the RGS gang leaders backed away and OEO abstained. These questions, it was said, would be decided later.

Officially, the need for corrective management was now acknowledged, but action on the crucial recommendations was tabled.

"We returned to New York kind of broken-hearted," said Muhammad. "We knew what the problems were before we left home. We didn't have to go to Washington for that. We had looked forward to the trip only because we thought we would be given the authority we needed to get started solving the problems. But we weren't told yes, we weren't told no. We were just left dangling. We felt that nothing had been accomplished."

On Wednesday Fred and Mike, having heard nothing for two days, began pressing the inner-core leadership for a decision but were able to make contact only by telephone. Then, after threatening to make public the whole situation, they got a meeting in person but still failed to get a definite answer. Furious over the impasse, the leaders of the staff threatened to walk out. Fred called an OEO official in Washington but was unable to get through. The next day, still waiting to be called back, he placed a call to OEO's Congressional Relations Office and outlined the situation. Two days later the RGS gang leaders met in East Harlem and decided to appoint Muhammad director. He hired Mike.

A new bank account was opened and Muhammad got himself, Mike, and Fred authorized to sign checks in addition to the corporate officers. As business manager, Mike took over all record keeping, retained a new accounting firm, and removed all board members from the federal-grant payroll on the grounds that their university salaries were creating a conflict of interest detrimental to the project.

The staff had outmaneuvered the inner core. Operationally, the program people were now in charge. Legally, however, the RGS board of directors still held the ultimate power. It had the contract with OEO and was the officially recognized channel to Washington. In practice, the two sides had reached a stalemate. The conditions for productivity were very shaky.

16

Muhammad Salahuddeen

Muhammad Salahuddeen was not a native of the Lower East Side but he was definitely a man of the streets, with all the credentials necessary to qualify as a resident. He was born Joseph Slaughter on March 23, 1930, beside a Maryland highway; his parents were en route to Camden, New Jersey, where his father hoped to find work. Two years later his mother died of tuberculosis, leaving him to be raised by his father, then just twenty-one. His sister, the only other child, died shortly afterward. At the age of two, in the care of neighbors while his father worked at whatever odd jobs he could find in those depression years, he fell down a stairway and suffered injuries which made him a hospital charity case for seven years and left him with a noticeable limp he never outgrew.

Later, living in a northside Philadelphia slum where his father went to work in a shipyard, he made it through the fifth grade, started running the streets, learned to hustle for money, and after a good many bruises, learned to fight. There he got in with the street gangs, but because of his ability to understand and get along with people, he never found it necessary to become a gang member or to participate in their nefarious doings. Instead, he became a kind of listener to problems and was accepted as something of a counselor to whom people turned when in need of advice.

After World War II his neighborhood was flooded with narcotics and most of his friends learned to tie their arms and shoot themselves with a syringe. Racketeers, politicians, even some narcotics agents thrived on the lucrative traffic. Girls turned to prostitution to support the habit. One-family apartments became two- and three-family apartments. Usury, gambling, and robbery were flourishing businesses, and who had the best drugs and where to get them a main item of conversation. Some, trying to get off heroin, took cocaine and wound up with a cocaine habit. Others tried morphine. Muhammad himself was on, then off, then hooked again. Finally, after watching several of his friends die from drug overdose, he went to an uncle who forced him to stay in the house and quit the habit "cold turkey." For three horrible weeks he lived on sugar and water and sweated it out.

During the last two years of his teens he worked as a volunteer with a police-sponsored athletic program for neighborhood boys, developed a basement gymnasium, and organized a boxing club.

Then at age twenty he encountered a series of events that reshaped the course of his life. One day he walked through the lobby of a hotel looking for a job as a dishwasher, forgetting that Negroes were expected to enter by the rear only. He was abruptly told to get out, through the back door.

"I'll never forget that," he told me. "I was so hungry, and all the good-smelling food in that kitchen. It was something you'd have to feel to understand."

Outside in the alley an aged Negro woman, stockings half-fallen down, a ragged coat, was bending over a garbage can picking out bones.

"I felt so helpless. I stood there watching that woman, tears in my eyes. I looked up into the sky and said, God, if there is a God, what can we do?"

Later that day in a poolroom he met a black man known as Rashe

Ali who exposed him to the Muslim religion, and Joseph Slaughter became Muhammad Salahuddeen.

"From that time on," he said, "I began striving not just to live but to fulfill a life. These young men were very different. They would sit in rooms at night reading books on history and mathematics, studying Arabic, and reading the Koran. Soon I found myself studying and praying, something I had never done."

The experience was deeply satisfying, but after several weeks he was still badly in need of a job. He had fallen in love with a woman several years older than he who was carrying his child, and other than living by his wits, he had no means of support. A smart dude could always hustle it, and Muhammad knew the ropes. But he wanted to get married. He wanted to be a family man. And even though he knew that about the best he could ever hope for was an opening at the post office, he wanted a legitimate job. Late one night after weeks of being turned down, thinking of his need to get married and feeling desperate, he took three dollars, all he had, and headed for the south side of the city to put it in a card game.

Passing through a fashionable retail district on his way there, feeling sorry for himself and his bride-to-be, he happened to notice a second-floor doorway standing open at the head of a fire escape. He climbed up to look. Standing in the doorway, he decided to explore the building. At the foot of a stairway he came to a plasterboard partition and discovered a small hole. He made the hole larger and squeezed through. He was in a women's clothing store. He searched for money, but didn't find any. He began stuffing dresses into a paper bag. A policeman rattled the front door, shone his flashlight into the store, then moved on. Muhammad, breathing hard, stayed hidden behind a counter. Then the policeman came back. There was another guard. The burglar alarm began ringing.

"Somebody's in there," a man shouted.

All the lights in the store came on.

"Come out or I'll shoot."

Muhammad came out.

"You black son-of-a-bitch. What are you doing in here?"

Inwardly, Muhammad cried.

He had deserted his woman, he had deserted himself. This was the first time he had been arrested and he was scared. From jail he sent word to his father and waited to appear in court.

"I felt so sorry for my father seeing him standing there in that courtroom."

The case ahead of Muhammad's was a young man charged with auto theft, driving without a license, and hit and run. And he had a previous record for similar charges. He was white. He was released in the custody of his mother. Muhammad smiled. Maybe he had a chance.

Then the judge turned to his case. He was charged with illegal entry and given an indefinite sentence of up to twenty years. The woman he had hoped to marry lost the baby, and he never saw her again.

At the state prison in Harrisburg he played saxophone in the band, studied Arabic, Jung and Freudian psychology, and read the Koran.

"I learned so much," he said to me. "For the first time in my life I began to understand myself. I learned that whatever self-destructive steps we may take in life, we will take those same steps over and over until we begin to deal with our problems. I didn't like prison, but I began to think that maybe that judge actually did me a favor."

Muhammad became eligible for parole, but still had to meet the requirements: job, home, and sponsor. Some prisoners spent months, even years, after passing other requirements for parole waiting to get those three things. In Muhammad's case the Salvation Army arranged them. Eighteen months after being sentenced he walked through the gates with a prison suit and twenty dollars in his pocket, and returned to Philadelphia.

His job was in a small candy store his father had opened while Muhammad was in prison, 8 A.M. to midnight, seven days a week, without pay. The store couldn't afford it. After a month or so his parole officer reluctantly granted him permission to look for a paying job. He went to work as a dishwasher and rented a cheap apartment in his old neighborhood in North Philadelphia. Then two weeks later when his parole officer told the owner he was a parolee he was fired. The parole officer ordered him to find another job. After fruitless searching, broke, evicted from his apartment for being unable to pay the rent, scared of being sent back to prison, he decided to run. His father refused him the price of a bus ticket, so he hitchhiked to New York.

It was early 1952. The weather was cold. On Forty-fifth Street between Sixth and Seventh avenues he went into a place to get warm and listen to the music and there met a Muslim drummer he had known in Philadelphia. One of the brothers took him into his apartment and he went to work as an usher in a theater. That job didn't last because he was wearing brown shoes and couldn't afford to buy a pair of black shoes which the manager required.

After finishing another temporary job he got the idea of polishing cars, invested in a lard can, a can of cleaner and polish, and a package of cheesecloth and went into business for himself, soliciting customers at parking areas. Life was beginning to improve, then he started dating Yvonne.

On a rainy, miserable afternoon while at home nursing a cold and reading the Koran, Clyde, another friend of Yvonne's, came to his apartment looking for marijuana. Muhammad had long ago given up the hard stuff, but he did enjoy a little pot. Clyde had a "joint," then left. A half hour later two detectives threw open the door, forced Muhammad to lie on the floor, found the "pot," and that was his second arrest. The judge dismissed the marijuana charge, but a record search revealed his parole violation and he was returned to Harrisburg.

"No, the world wasn't cruel," he said to me. "It was just something I had to live through."

After the usual month in quarantine during which incoming prisoners are examined, recorded, immunized, and classified, he rejoined the prison band, resumed his studies of religion and psychology, and was selected by the prison psychiatrist to serve as caretaker for a gang boy who was blind. He was approved for parole after serving a year, then had to wait another year and a half for the required job, home, and sponsor.

Again, it was the Salvation Army that worked out the arrangements. Back in Philadelphia, in another slum, it was the same old routine: a job, the employer discovered his record, he lost the job. After the third time around he managed to talk his parole officer into letting him get back into the car-polishing business. In that capacity he met a wealthy white woman who took a liking to him, learned his situation, and set the process in motion that in 1955 got him released from parole. He packed everything he owned into two shopping bags and moved to New York. He was free.

"Oh, how I hated Philadelphia."

All night he walked the streets, too tired to stay up, but too happy and too broke to do anything else. It was just good to be in New York. At six o'clock in the morning he got a job, tips only, in a shoeshine parlor just off Times Square and stayed until five that afternoon, having earned ten dollars.

Afraid to spend any of his money, even for a meal, he went to Central Park to sleep. He awakened an hour later still exhausted, walked out of the park and sat down on a concrete stoop, wondering what to do next. While sitting there a man carrying a briefcase walked by, said hello, then turned and asked if Muhammad had any troubles.

"Remembering my religious teachings, 'He who has false pride cannot receive paradise,' I told him I was hungry, had no place to stay, and needed a bath."

The man took him to his home, gave him the use of the bathroom, bought him a steak, and gave him a clean shirt and five dollars.

"At first I was afraid to go with him, thinking he must be a homosexual. But he wasn't. He had a wife and two children. He was just a kind man. I have found that New York is full of people like that."

Then he said: "You know, all men are human. To know them you must know their spirit. Their color or race is not important. You have to look inside."

There was the normal struggle of life in the ghetto, but gradually Muhammad got himself together. He worked at various jobs, spent three months at a "pay college" in California where he obtained two diplomas—Doctor of Philosophy and Doctor of Naturopathy—studied at the Brooklyn Museum Art School and the National Academy of Fine Arts, became a settlement-house worker, and moved to the Lower East Side, where he supervised children's activities for a neighborhood service organization known as the Negro Action Group. Then he got involved with the University of the Streets. During the summer of 1968 he organized a neighborhood recreation program featuring daily bus trips to beaches and parks for more than one thousand children.

On a Sunday afternoon in June 1968 a dozen neighborhood leaders crowded into his tiny walk-up apartment on Avenue B just off East Sixth Street to talk about how to get more cooperation among the maze of voluntary agencies on the Lower East Side. I was there. People got into a rancorous gripe session about the government, and I was convinced the meeting wasn't accomplishing anything. For a half hour or more Muhammad remained silent while the complaints grew louder and the language increasingly obscene. Then he broke in.

"We can always escape our responsibility by talking about what the government is not doing instead of talking about what we aren't doing," he said. "Sure, we can talk about what the man is not doing. That's easy. But how about us? What are all the things we aren't doing? Look at the garbage, the trash, the stinking litter in our streets. Who put it there? Who doesn't give a good goddam? We need government help, but this is our neighborhood, not the government's neighborhood. We've got to prove to ourselves and our neighbors and our children, and to the outside world, what we can do. We've got to be a hell of a lot better example than what we're being."

In this urban jungle on Manhattan's Lower East Side there were those who viewed Muhammad as too passive, too self-introspective. In others, his infinite patience, his love of people, his desire to serve, evoked deep respect. But whatever his imperfections, it became clear to me why this man was so uniquely equipped to provide the new measure of leadership that was then needed at the University of the Streets.

"You can never appreciate a clean shirt unless you have worn a dirty one," he told me. "That's the meaning of experience. But experience is not the most important thing in life. What you learn from experience is the thing that counts."

17

Rebuilding the University

By the time the way was cleared for Muhammad to take up the precarious task of serving as the university director, August 1968 was almost over. Only eight months of the grant period remained. Muhammad knew well what he had to do: Quiet the turmoil that was sapping the project's energy, revive the efforts to rebuild, provide the staff with a sense of security, reorganize those programs that were faltering, and start whatever new programs were needed to make up for lost ground. It was a large order.

Some activities were still fairly solid. The School of Martial Arts, a leading attraction from the start, was still expanding. That fall Owen Watson built it to 147 students ranging from nine years of age to past thirty, including forty-one girls. Of those who were school age, sixty were in school with grades averaging between A and B, as Owen required. Thirty were still in a dropout status, but were doing independent study either in preparation for high school equivalency tests or for re-entry into school, also as required.

The Drama Department under Arnold Johnson had grown into a

program called the Theatre of Courage. During the summer it had used facilities at New York University in addition to the third-floor quarters at the University of the Streets. Financed by separate grants totaling fifty-seven thousand dollars, this program offered salaries of forty-five dollars a week to ghetto youths who were hired as trainees in theatrical production. This activity came about as a result of New York University's School of the Arts wanting to engage disadvantaged ghetto youths in the development of a Lower East Side cultural arts center, and the belief that the NYU people could do a better job if they worked through an experienced neighborhood organization in which there was professional artistic leadership with an understanding of ghetto life. Arnold Johnson was that leadership. Also, Mobilization for Youth, one of the largest antipoverty agencies on the Lower East Side, was interested. And so the Theatre of Courage was put together in the spring of 1968 as a cooperative venture of New York University, Mobilization for Youth, and the University of the Streets, using the Real Great Society, Inc., as the conduit for funding.

With Arnold serving as director and several professionals at New York University serving as codirectors, the Theatre of Courage was based on the assumption that violent and criminal acts of gang life are attractive to ghetto youths only when these youths have no alternative for self-expression that sufficiently interests them, and that self-development in the theatre arts can offer such an alternative. By drawing on ghetto life itself as the raw material for artistic production, it was felt that an indigenous community theatre could offer not only entertainment, but a therapeutic experience and a means of developing intelligent solutions to ghetto problems.

These assumptions closely paralleled those which Arnold had used as the basis for the drama program he had already started, but with the backing of New York University and Mobilization for Youth, he was able to make his program much more intensive. The Theatre of Courage was treated as a special school for preparing disadvantaged youths for degree-granting programs in institutions of higher learning—ultimately, for professional careers in the performing arts. Provision was made for extra studies to help those who needed to catch up, but New York University, along with several other universities, agreed to substitute student auditions for traditional entrance requirements as the basis for college admission. NYU also offered scholarships, as did several other universities.

The program offered classes in black and Puerto Rican history, acting, dance movement, and stagecraft; opportunities for the trainees to create scene improvisations through which to express their ideas; and it provided experience in play production. On the assumption that preparation for higher education and for careers in professional theatre required the most intensive individual training possible, the number of youths enrolled at the beginning of the summer season was limited to fifty-four. Later this was increased to sixty-nine. For the fall season Arnold enrolled 125 students, many of whom were continuing their work from the summer—twenty-five high school dropouts five days a week, and one hundred in-school youths for work on Saturdays. Also that fall, nine of the street youths who had completed the summer season were placed as full-time drama students in four cooperating institutions: New York University, Carnegie Institute of Technology, Columbia University, and the Institute of Film Technology at Los Angeles.

The Tompkins Square Gallery, which Leroy Bostic had started during the summer of 1967, had developed into a thriving neighborhood art center. Young people, mostly in their late teens and twenties, from rank beginners to fairly accomplished artists, came in to display and sell their works or to just browse and talk and get information and advice. Special exhibitions were staged to give recognition to art expression, budding artists experienced the satisfaction of their first sale, and efforts were made to develop leads to job opportunities or to art scholarships. The informal meetings and conversations engendered in the gallery stimulated a continuous formation of interest groups—some strictly for shop talk and mutual criticism—which got together on a more or less regular basis in private apartments and small studios around the neighborhood. A life sketch class of between ten and fifteen participants met three nights a week in a nearby loft.

Leroy had developed the Art Department almost entirely with volunteers, and had gone about as far as he could without paid help and a regular monthly budget. Also, he was short of space. Muhammad corrected the budget problem, and while steps were being taken to solve the space problem, Leroy expanded the informal classes, planned a six-day-a-week schedule, and enrolled fifty-seven students, using space wherever it could be found outside the building.

In the Music Department, Muhammad found a situation that called for complete reorganization. A group of professional musicians had developed an orchestra which had become a university showpiece, but the street youths who most needed help had dwindled to no more than a half dozen in number. Muhammad, a pretty good musician himself, was happy with the quality of the music, but the basic purpose of the University of the Streets was to provide alternatives to delinquency and deprivation. To re-establish this basic purpose, he initiated a departmental housecleaning and brought in a new music director, Kenny Dorham, a black jazz leader he knew had a way with street youths. With the help of a well-known saxophone player named Jackie McLean, Kenny assembled a fresh crew of Lower East Side musicians and began rebuilding the program to focus specifically on street youths. Instruments were provided at no cost to those who could not afford to buy their own. Each youth was allowed to come as often as he wished and progress at whatever rate his talent and capacity for work made possible. Instruction was offered during the week in simple note reading, composition, and instrumentation, and every Saturday the department sponsored a jam session. New scores were written and performed with the Theatre of Courage, and as news of what was happening got around the neighborhood, the music program began to exert a new pull. Within about two months it had between thirty and forty participants.

The "Department of Miscellaneous Studies," which in the beginning had formed most of the university program and had been overrun by hippies, and which was referred to in the OEO contract as "a wide range of short-term courses," had not served the purpose for which it was intended, and by the time Muhammad began as director was but a fraction of its former size. Because most of these informal learning groups met at scattered locations over the neighborhood, it was impossible to determine precisely how many people they still involved, and Muhammad made no effort to find out. He was not so much concerned about the number as he was about whom they involved, his prime objective being to tailor the university to the needs of the neighborhood's indigenous youth. In consultation with the other staff leaders, he therefore decided that instead of trying to rebuild the "Department of Miscellaneous Studies," a series of "short-term courses" known to be of specific interest to street youths would be developed as a part of the university's internal administrative machinery. To accomplish this and at the same time improve overall operational efficiency, several new departments were established.

The first was a Department of Business Management. Under the supervision of Mike Good, this new department worked out a monthly budget for the total project, with specific allocations for each operating unit. Systematic payroll and purchasing procedures were developed. A system of expenditure controls was put into effect, and an entirely new set of books was opened. It was never possible to untangle completely the chaos of the past, but a semblance of order was gradually achieved in the university's financial affairs. This department also provided practical training for street youths interested in accounting or business careers. Four street youths were enrolled at the start, the plan being that this enrollment would be expanded as the first students gained competence and the Business Management Department increased its ability to perform the teaching function along with its management responsibilities.

This strategy of creating "short-term courses" within the internal administrative machinery of the university was applied to every aspect of the operation.

One of the most difficult problems Muhammad had to face was the physical condition of the building. Like most buildings on the Lower East Side, it was just an old run-down structure, and from the time the university had started the previous summer, the energy of those who did the work had been so absorbed in program development and fund-raising—and in recent months, in preventing an East Harlem takeover—that only cursory attention had been given to basic physical needs.

The old wooden frames around several large glass windows in the karate room had become so weakened by rot they were dangerous.

Owen Watson and his students had repaired them as well as possible, but cracks kept opening around the edges. The wind and the rain came in, even droppings and feathers from flocks of pigeons. And there were no showers on this floor.

In the third-floor theatre, Arnold Johnson and his students had put in chairs and made an auditorium, built sets and other equipment, but there was no built-up stage, and the wiring was inadequate. With space at New York University during the summer, it had been possible to get by, but that was no longer available when NYU's fall term started. Muhammad, with the help of a group of students, came in over a period of several nights and built a stage, put up draperies, and installed new wiring and lights. But Muhammad could hardly function as the university director and keep on doing construction work.

The university had operated too long on makeshift arrangements. Most of the building wasn't even kept clean. Expecting homeless street youths to function as janitors in return for being allowed to sleep in the small penthouse on the roof hadn't been very fruitful. There had been no one to supervise them. The landlord was extremely niggardly and had done as little maintenance as possible, then only when someone—usually Fred or Owen—forced him. No one had ever made a real survey of needed repairs and alterations, and over the course of a year of steady use the building had continued to deteriorate.

Muhammad decided to change this and in so doing make another opportunity to accomplish two things at once: fix up the building, and develop a training program in construction and maintenance. Mike Good had an Irish friend named Joe Callaway who had construction skills and was willing to work part time at the university, but not without pay and there were no funds in the budget for another salary. So Muhammad took a $2,500 cut in his own salary, hired Joe, and started a Maintenance Department.

Along with cleaning the building, getting rid of the vermin, making essential repairs and renovations, and constructing needed equipment, this new department was to offer courses in carpentry, plumbing, masonry, painting, plastering, electrical work, furniture making, pest control, and general building maintenance.

As the program developed it was planned that participating street youths would be organized into four-man crews, each with a youth who had gained sufficient experience serving as crew foreman under the general supervision of the department head. Volunteer craftsmen were to be brought in to augment the training, and contracts were to be solicited from building owners, churches, and other agencies on the Lower East Side for maintenance and repair work, thus developing new job opportunities as well as additional experience. The number of crews was to be increased as rapidly as the growth of the department would permit. Eight street youths were enrolled to start with.

Lumber, paint, plaster, cement, plumbing supplies, electrical goods, pest sprays, cleaning supplies, and hand tools and power tools were accumulated. Part of this stock was purchased out of grant funds, much of it was obtained through donations arranged through labor unions and other cooperating organizations, and part of it came through agreements that were negotiated with the building owner. Mike managed to talk the landlord out of two large rooms on the fifth floor which had not previously been available, and one of them was converted into a shop for the Maintenance Department. Work benches, shelves, and storage cabinets were built.

The other newly acquired room on the fifth floor was set aside for the university's general offices. The old fourth-floor area that had been used as office quarters since the first summer of operation had become virtually unusable. There was no door to separate it from the stairway between floors, and over a period of time accumulations of furniture had been jammed in haphazardly among piles of excess printed matter and assorted junk. Streams of people wove in and out, shouting to make themselves heard. Muhammad simply moved the office to the fifth floor. Joe's Maintenance Department installed a heavy oak door to close off the new quarters from the hallway, installed lighting fixtures, fixed the plumbing in a rest-room facility, repaired the radiators, built dividers around work areas, put in shelves and bulletin boards, partitioned off an outside corner to provide a much-needed private office for the university director, and painted the whole area.

In the space left vacant on the fourth floor Muhammad established the Prep School, which had been provided in the OEO contract but until now had not been organized. Bill Lee, a Chinese-American, not quite twenty, who had served as a volunteer teacher of English and biology, was given the job of organizing this new department. Four part-time staff members, including secretarial help, were assigned to work with him, and over a period of about three months twenty-five neighborhood residents were recruited to form a pool of volunteer tutors. As soon as the new office quarters had been readied, the Maintenance Department went to work to build the Prep School facilities, including a classroom and an adjoining library and study area. The quarters were cleaned up and painted, and new lighting was installed. Chairs, tables, desks, blackboards, and audio-visual aids were brought in. Bookshelves were constructed to hold some two thousand donated books, many of which had accumulated over the course of a year but until now had been scattered in unsorted piles on the floor here and there around the building.

In keeping with the concept of self-determination, the basic principle in all programs at the university, the Prep School carefully avoided rigid schedules and other pressures inherent in the public school system from which most of its students had dropped out. Subject matter, learning pace, and time and place of instruction were adapted insofar as possible to individual student desires. Each youth was free to decide for himself how much or how little help he needed. The prime concern was to develop motivation and stay away from anything that might stifle interest. Help was offered in language, spelling, reading, history, biology, mathematics, chemistry, physics, and other subjects as requested.

Instructors were available at the Prep School each evening, and at least one of the part-time staff members was available most of each day. Also, private homes and other locations scattered through the neighborhood were used for meeting places. For example, Norman Wright, the energetic young black who made a special collection of housing materials for the university, organized a group of nine street youths who met several nights a week with a teacher at his apartment. All nine of these youths obtained high school or general equivalency diplomas and two of them entered college. Much of the Prep School instruction was in the form of individualized tutoring. Classes varied in size from one or two students to fifteen or twenty, a dozen or more groups often in session at once.

At about ten o'clock one evening that fall I dropped in at the Community Clubhouse in the basement just as a group of about twenty young men and women, most of them carrying books, were arriving for a social gathering following a series of Prep School sessions which had been going on in the building and at other places in the neighborhood. After listening until well after midnight to these young people—all of whom had previously lost interest in education—telling me about their studies and their future plans, I had to agree with them that although this permissive method of running a school created difficulties in planning, and at times caused frustrations among volunteer teachers, the school was clearly making progress.

John Arroyo, fifteen years old, one of the Prep School students, wrote this description of the Lower East Side:

> As you know it has all kinds of nationalities. Most of the people are poor and live on welfare. The houses have rats and roaches which breed sickness. . . . Sometimes when welfare money runs out people borrow food and other things from their neighbors.
>   . . . It's a bad place to bring up a child. Obviously, the education is bad, and the environment is bad too. The teenagers are influenced to take marijuana and any other drugs they can get their hands on.
>   Life on the Lower East Side is bad, but just because I tell you the bad things about it, don't think that all of it is bad. I would rather live on the Lower East Side than any other place. People are doing a lot of things to make it better. . . . The main thing I like about the Lower East Side is that you learn a lot from street life. It has taught me how important it is to keep alive.

Building this unique Prep School, focused as it was on strictly academic studies, in ways that would harmonize with the life that surrounded it, was delicate business.

A young woman who worked two nights a week as a volunteer tutor wrote in one of her reports: "For more efficiency a little more organization is needed, however, rigid organization would, I think, at this point tend to drive students away rather than attract them."

Another volunteer tutor, referring to a street youth who needed all the patience she could provide, wrote: "I work with [him] . . . on Wednesday nights on reading. He seems quite bright, but I have a suspicion that part of his interest in taking reading from me is the simple fact that I am a girl (he likes girls)."

It is difficult to make an accurate determination as to how many youths filtered in and out of this program at any given time. Some came for only a few sessions, sort of dropping in and dropping out. Some were still struggling with the drug habit. But that fall and winter the Prep School had well over sixty youths involved in its dispersed operations. Nineteen of them obtained high school or general equivalency diplomas. Ten were admitted to college.

Closely related to the Prep School was the Department of Special Programs. Headed by a Dartmouth graduate named Tom Yahn who had lived and worked for several years on the Lower East Side and had an intimate understanding of its life and problems, this department had the job of forming bridges between the University of the Streets, the courts, the police, the public schools, and numerous private agencies that tried to help with the rehabilitation of delinquents. Tom worked on getting dropouts back into school, held meetings with admission and student-aid officials in universities throughout the city, arranged scholarships, counseled youths who either wanted to prepare for college or were ready to enter, and set up cooperative arrangements with accredited institutions for special individualized study designed to help street youths get a head start for regular college courses. In cooperation with the city's Board of Education, he organized a University of the Streets teacher-training program in which a team of street youths held weekly meetings with groups of public school teachers who wanted to improve their understanding of the cultural and emotional environment of ghetto children. He organized weekend conferences between upper-middle-class youths in Connecticut and youths from the University of the Streets for intercultural human relations purposes, and worked with Fred in planning a summer camping program which would make it possible for such sessions to be held over periods of several weeks each year. He wrote proposals for university programs which needed additional funding, such as the Theatre of Courage, and helped locate job vacancies. Through these varied services, the Department of Special Programs provided an extension to the Prep School and developed important backstopping for all other programs in the university.

Another activity Muhammad established was a photography class. He knew this would have strong appeal among street youths, particularly if it could teach commercial photography and how to operate a retail business. Mindful of the high risk in starting a new business, especially a photography business, he entered into negotiations with a man named David Jackness who owned a small, successful photography shop close to the university and was anxious to retire. Muhammad's idea was that if the university could get possession of this business and retain Jackness's manager, Mark Antman, to teach the class, the risk involved in starting a new business could be substantially reduced and a great deal of time would be saved. For something between five and six thousand dollars he could go ahead. He studied the OEO contract and found an item of twenty thousand dollars with which to hire a private company to make a documentary film on the University of the Streets.

"I couldn't see the sense of spending money like that," said Muhammad. "We could get this store, give courses in commercial photography, teach kids how to run a business, eventually make new jobs, make our own film, and earn enough from the business to make the activity self-supporting. And Fred had it arranged with Kenyon & Eckhardt to get all the extra technical assistance we needed at no cost."

Muhammad took the proposition to OEO only to find that he could not use funds from the federal contract to buy a business, but that he could make the purchase if it were put down as an expenditure for materials and equipment.

So he did.

His one mistake was that he neglected to get this authorization in writing, and after having completed the purchase, OEO denied having given its approval.

But by that time the deal was made. Mark Antman stayed on to manage the shop and serve as teacher. Four street youths were enrolled to start, and the university had a Photography Department with a commercial darkroom and a real business enterprise to use as a laboratory, with Kenyon & Eckhardt making plans to help expand it into a much larger program.

In the OEO contract there was a section that referred to "community outreach," that is, reaching out into the community to find those youths who most needed help. This was, of course, implicit in all the university's activities. However, two of its programs were especially aimed at this objective: the Community Clubhouse, which Pee Wee and his followers had developed in the basement, and what the contract referred to as "community organization" and the "hunter system."

Potentially, the clubhouse was one of the most important departments in the entire project. It provided street youths with a social center they could make their own, and a recruiting arm for other university programs. Here youths could meet youths who came in with the same kinds of experiences and the same kinds of hopes and aspirations. Here, in informal conversation with friends, they could learn about the university's varied activities, talk about their personal problems and frustrations, discover which programs they might like to join, and learn how they could have a hand in shaping the university to their interests. But by the time Muhammad came in as director, the clubhouse was at a low ebb. Like everything else in the university, it was largely dependent on just the right touch by the right person. After Pee Wee was removed from the scene, that personal touch was lost. The clubhouse manager who was appointed by the previous administration did not inspire the confidence of the street youths and over a period of weeks became actively disliked by them. Already embittered because of the negative attitude of the former director toward Pee Wee, a majority of the youths had lost interest in the clubhouse, and it had deteriorated into just another hangout. Youths drifted aimlessly in and out and the ever-present problem of drugs was again on the rise.

For the other part of the community outreach function—searching

out "hard-core" members of the "target population"—the OEO contract authorized a storefront extension center and a six-member crew
headed by a full-time "community coordinator," with two full-time
"community organizers" and three part-time "hunters." This part of
the program was also in a state of deterioration. From the beginning
of the contract period in April this activity had been left to the RGS
gang leaders and had not been performed. The crew of organizers and
hunters had received no direction and had done little more than hang
out at the storefront extension center. To correct this situation,
Muhammad decided to move the crew into the main university building, where he could make sure it got training and direction, where-
upon the entire crew quit. Under the circumstances, this may have
been best, but in trying to form another crew, Muhammad chose a
coordinator no more effective than the previous one. Then, when
Muhammad moved to correct his mistake, he was pressured by RGS
into hiring a person who was equally unsuited. As a result, there was
not much he could do about this aspect of the community outreach
function except to look for other ways of getting it done.

He temporarily closed the clubhouse—ending the unwholesome
situation that had developed there—went personally into the streets
in search of ideas, and discovered an interest that up to this point had
not been tapped—football. This was reminiscent of the baseball
games Pee Wee had organized early in the spring, and out of this
discovery came the Eagles, the University of the Streets' first football
team. Fred and Muhammad went to Merle Gulick, vice-president at
Equitable Life, and he supplied enough equipment to outfit the team.

"You should have seen our boys' eyes when those football uniforms and shoes arrived," said Muhammad. "No amount of money
could have brought what that meant to them."

That fall the Eagles played seven games, lost six and won one.

"But our boys were so proud of themselves," said Muhammad.
"Hundreds of kids actually came out and rooted for the University of
the Streets."

Thirty-six young men became Eagles and twenty-six younger boys
played with the Road Runners—the university's junior team. Then
the Mayor's Urban Task Force supplied uniforms and equipment for

the first University of the Streets' basketball team. Plans were made to start boxing, swimming, and tennis matches, and with help from Owen Watson the youths formed an athletic board as a new division of the School of Martial Arts.

The sports program gave the university a new appeal and contributed substantially to reestablishing the Community Clubhouse, which Muhammad reopened under a committee of neighborhood street youths. Later that year he established a new university position—youth director—to which he appointed Alvin King, the young man who had gone to Europe on the scholarship awarded by Senator Javits, and who played end with the Eagles. Alvin had the touch, and he worked. The clubhouse began to regain its former enrollment, and again to become an important arm of the university's outreach.

Fred Good continued to serve as the principal consultant to the overall operation, filling in wherever needed, working with private companies and other organizations to generate outside backing for the project and create business and job opportunities. Like all sections of the university, Fred's unit—known as the Public Relations Department—performed a teaching as well as an administrative function. It enrolled twelve street youths in groups of four in what in essence was a laboratory course. By participating in the varied facets of Fred's activities, these students were given an opportunity to meet with public and private officials, develop projects, write papers, and learn by doing. These learnings were amplified through frequent seminars at Fred's apartment.

By integrating these "short-term courses" into the administrative operations of each university department, on-the-job training opportunities were created for the work-study positions which the OEO contract provided. Thus, in accordance with the strategy of using all university resources in ways that would produce the greatest multiplier effect, the youths holding the work-study positions were able to study in areas of their choice, and at the same time produce work that contributed to building and strengthening the university.

To obtain further penetration into the community, eight adult residents whose sons and daughters were engaged in the project were brought together to form a volunteer advisory committee, known as the community board, and steps were taken to form a coalition of organizations representing other groups in the neighborhood.

Muhammad was no high-powered executive, but his presence in the directorship made a telling impact on the university. No one better understood the neighborhood and its people, or perceived with greater clarity the conflicting forces that had caused the project to flounder during the first four months of the OEO grant. From the low point that had been reached before he came on the job, the number of participating street youths more than tripled.

Most of the staff members and volunteers, and all of the students, were Muhammad's neighbors. And they settled down and worked as neighbors. They were Puerto Ricans, Negroes, Chinese, Italians, Jews, and Anglo-Saxons. Even a few Poles and Ukrainians, people who lived as near as a block away but had never entered the building, began to show interest. Workers and students attended seminars which Muhammad held regularly to talk over problems and ideas, and although these sessions were never placid, they did produce group decisions—an achievement that had rarely happened before. For the first time in the history of the university a deliberate effort was made to achieve a measure of coordination between programs. Most of the department heads even wrote a few progress reports. There was still never a crisis-free day. No one ever hesitated to shout when he felt like shouting. The university was still a project of the streets, indeed, far more so now than ever before, and underneath the loud talk and explosive temperaments, a renewed thrust toward community service was set in motion.

Muhammad's impact was especially telling on Fred Good, and for a while painful. For more than three years Fred had entangled himself in the mythology that he helped create, upon which he had grown to be dependent, and which had distorted his ability to be honest with himself as to the significance of his role in the actual work. The myth had become so well established among those who now needed to be told why so many problems had arisen—such as the officials at OEO—that it could hardly be refuted, least of all by Fred. Any explanation he might now make could only react against him and further intensify the hostility of the inner-core group. Fred had been trapped, largely by his own doing.

Muhammad's legitimacy as a man of the streets, his quiet ability to diagnose and understand what had been going on, enabled Fred to resume his rational processes and begin to escape from his entanglement. With Muhammad's counseling he was at last able to recognize that his emotional attachment was not to a specific organization or group, but to a concept, a meaning; that this intangible was now taking concrete form in the University of the Streets, and that the university was actually the work of people who were not members of the RGS inner circle. Gradually, Fred was able to understand that while the inventions which had been used to promote the fabulous myth had been accepted outside the community, inside the community these inventions had never caught on. Finally, he was able to believe what he had known all along, that the job of making the university a truly effective enterprise on the Lower East Side required work, not fantasy, and that if this community effort were to realize its potential it would have to be just that—a community effort.

Said Muhammad: "Image making may be important for purposes of reaching resources outside the community, but when it becomes more of an ego builder than a tool of the intelligence, it not only loses its value, it becomes dangerous."

18

Vendetta

A promising fresh start was in the making but the conditions for success could hardly have been more inopportune. The conflict between those who were trying to develop the program and those to whom OEO had given the money had converted the University of the Streets into a battleground. Indeed, the schism had gone so deep that the very act of Muhammad's reorganization only added to the antagonism. There were still variations in outlook between the two wings of the inner-core group, but by this time the emotional drives that pulled them together had created a psychology that made every improvement by the staff an affront to the RGS self-image. When Muhammad spoke of the dangers of image making, he knew what he was talking about.

The East Harlem branch, more adept at in-fighting than its Lower East Side counterpart, continued to exploit the hostility which had arisen from the dependency syndrome with Fred. Over and over the rhetoric was repeated until it grew to a litany: Things weren't as they used to be. Maybe a long time ago his presence had been useful, but now that was no longer true. His job was only to help start the university, then leave. Now he was building an institution, just what the group didn't want. He was autocratic, trying to run things for his own selfish ends, didn't care about the group, belittled it, stole its reputation, injected foreign ideas into its way of doing things. The group should remember that it was Puerto Rican and that Fred had no understanding of Puerto Rican people. He was rich. He was from the middle class. He was a white colonialist. Like the Spanish conquistadores who subjugated the natives of Latin America, he wanted to dominate RGS, take over the university. He had come as a friend pretending to help, and the group had trusted him. Then, he abused that trust.

The impression thus created couldn't have been further from the truth, but as the barrage continued, both wings of RGS were so conditioned they were able to believe almost anything that gave Fred the appearance of a vicious enemy. But he was merely a target for the attack. Most of the bitterness directed toward him was applied also to his brother Mike, and to the staff as a whole.

When Fred telephoned OEO's Congressional Relations Office in late August, he conveyed to the official on the Washington end of the line the startling news that the financial affairs at the University of the Streets had been badly mismanaged, and until action was taken to open the way for Muhammad to move into the directorship, OEO faced the risk of a public scandal. This was at a time when congressional criticism of the conduct of the government's war on poverty was mounting to new heights, and in the chilling atmosphere then spreading through the bureaucracy, Fred's telephone call touched sensitive nerves. That was precisely Fred's purpose in making the call: to get action that in his mind was crucial to prevent the death of the university. But that wasn't the interpretation that circulated inside the inner core. There the response was that Fred was trying to stir up an investigation of RGS, and in the prevailing aura of distrust, this interpretation was easily accepted. Now, it seemed, he had committed the worst crime imaginable: a sneak attempt to betray his friends.

And that wasn't all.

At this same time the New York attorney-general's office was looking into charges of illegal practices concerning an arrangement between RGS and a wholesale candy distributor for house-to-house selling, and although Fred had nothing to do with that investigation, it was easy to assume that somehow he probably did.

As soon as Muhammad's administration came in and Mike was installed as business manager, the new controls on expenditures went into effect. Suddenly, it became impossible even for an officer of the corporation to just walk in and get a check without encountering questions from Mike as to whether it was proper and necessary. Mike's new payroll system requiring time slips went into effect, along with his resistance to board members drawing salaries from the OEO grant funds. The practice of handing out publicity credits to RGS for work being done by others was stopped. When reporters wanted information about a university activity, they were referred to the appropriate department head. When RGS members entered the building nobody seemed to recognize that celebrities were on the premises. Many of the street youths didn't even know who they were. As one girl put it, "They came around so seldom it got so they weren't much more than voices on the telephone." Under Muhammad's direction things really began to change, and the reaction of RGS was essentially the same as the staff reaction had been to the East Harlem administration: dictatorship—except that now it was the other way around. The injury to RGS pride was severe.

But perhaps the one most grating irritant was the formation of the neighborhood citizens' committee known as the community board. Since the earliest beginnings of the university it had been said both inside and outside the inner core that eventually the project would be spun off from RGS as an independent neighborhood activity, and in the proposal upon which the OEO contract was based, it was stated that the University of the Streets was to be "controlled by the community."

On the basis of this understanding, Fred had taken the initiative during the summer to lay the groundwork for the neighborhood citizens' board by discussing the idea with numerous local residents, including leaders of other organizations. From these discussions he identified many individuals who were enthusiastic about the idea and willing to serve. He had made no secret of these discussions, and no one, including those in the inner core, had voiced opposition.

At the August meeting with OEO in Washington, Muhammad drew special attention to the need for going ahead with the community board, and in principle everyone agreed. But in actual practice, RGS was in no hurry to go ahead. This could mean that the university, which had brought in hundreds of thousands of dollars and a heavy outpouring of publicity, might no longer be RGS property. In theory it was a good idea—some day. But Muhammad was serious about doing it now.

Therefore, shortly after he became director he and Fred asked eight parents of university youths if they would be willing to form the community board if invited, and they said they would. Muhammad presented their names to RGS and invited other suggestions. After waiting several weeks and receiving none, he decided to go ahead without further delay, and on October 19, 1968, the community board—four Puerto Ricans and four blacks, all active leaders in neighborhood affairs—held its organizational meeting with Muhammad and Fred both present, elected a chairman, and decided that the University of the Streets should become a separate corporation. Elated by this expression of interest, especially from a group of parents, Muhammad informed RGS of what had taken place, and learned that it was not at all happy. He and Fred tried to explain that a neighborhood board was basic to the whole idea of the project and would strengthen, not hurt, the university. But Muhammad soon realized that this line of reasoning was of no use. The community board represented a new threat to RGS authority. It was not RGS-appointed. It had been formed without formal RGS authorization, and the fact that Fred had been a prime mover in getting it organized seemed to confirm all the accusations leveled against him. Had starting the community board been left to RGS, it may very well have been left for tomorrow indefinitely. As it was, the community board was now a fact, but RGS saw itself being robbed.

Minutes of the RGS board of directors meeting for October 26 said it "was done behind our backs." And although that wasn't the intent, it is what happened.

On October 28, RGS informed Muhammad that it was going to fire all the leading white staff members—Fred and Mike Good, Joe Callaway, head of the Maintenance Department, and Tom Yahn, head of the Department of Special Projects—and ordered him to get them together that afternoon. Muhammad agreed to "take care of it," then through the grapevine made known what was about to happen, and the response was exactly what he knew it would be. When the RGS gang leaders arrived to deliver their ultimatum they were met, not by just those who had been marked for firing, but by virtually the entire staff and about fifty angry street youths.

It was a nasty confrontation, and had it not been for Muhammad's insistence on nonviolence, the verbal charges and countercharges might well have led to a fight. Unless the decision were reversed the staff would resign en masse and street youths would quit the university. After a lengthy session of threatening talk from both sides, the inner-core group backed down. That was the end of the meeting, and nobody was fired.

But RGS made clear its demands: The staff was eventually to become an all–Puerto Rican organization, all decisions of the community board were to be cleared with the board of directors of the corporation, and the staff was to recognize the authority of RGS—or else. Nobody knew quite what.

In response to these demands it was agreed that all staff members would train whomever RGS designated to replace them, then resign. But no candidates were ever sent for training. Joint meetings were arranged between the corporate board and the community board, but after two sessions outwardly cordial, nobody from RGS ever came back. Muhammad tried repeatedly to get the RGS leaders to participate in his staff seminars to help with program decisions, but to no avail. He couldn't even get them out to watch the Eagles play football. These rebuffs, coupled with a complete absence of any effort by RGS to help with the work, caused resentment through all levels of the university. Then the ill feeling was made even worse by a demand from the inner-core group that a course be given on the history of RGS so that all workers and students would recognize its importance. A notice was posted to find out how many people would be interested in such a course and nobody signed up. Each side traded insults with the other, and the rumor mill ground out a steady stream of inflammatory material.

After the confrontation of October 28, the feud—still fueled primarily by the East Harlem power thrust, playing on the emotions of the Lower East Side wing, picturing Fred as the archenemy— gathered momentum, and the effort to rebuild the university began to crumble.

As a result of the attempted firing of staff members and the anxiety that followed, Joe Callaway resigned as head of the Maintenance Department, and this essential part of the work became disorganized. Materials and equipment, left scattered and unattended, were lost or stolen, the physical reconditioning of the building was curtailed, and plans for classes in construction skills came to a standstill. This wasted university money and ended the development of outside work contracts. RGS took control of the income from the photographic store. That stopped Muhammad's plans for that department. Under pressure from the inner core, Muhammad was forced to hire people in key positions who not only failed to perform their jobs but disrupted university morale. Efforts were made to organize a strike for higher wages among the work-study students, which the dwindling budget could not afford. A thousand dollars in private donations for sports equipment was stolen, and an inside campaign of vilification was carried on against Muhammad himself.

Problems that would have been difficult under the best of conditions became almost insurmountable. When, early in November, a broken pane of glass had to be removed from a window in the School of Martial Arts, the whole rotten frame collapsed and all of the others had to be taken out. That closed the karate program, a mainstay from the beginning. Because of inaction by the landlord, tight conditions in the university budget, and the disarray of the Maintenance Department, there was no way of knowing when the School of Martial Arts might reopen. In his usual hustling manner, Owen Watson made makeshift arrangements with other gymnasiums, went out to raise money for repairs, and by sheer determination managed to keep the program alive, but not much more than in name only.

Against Muhammad's advice, RGS sponsored a dance one night in the Theatre of Courage, and just as he had feared, a fight broke out which caused several hundred dollars' worth of damage. It took two days for people at the university to clean out the debris and several weeks to get the theatre back into full working order.

Even the elements seemed hostile. In November, shortly after the karate room was closed, New York City was struck by a violent windstorm. The next morning when Muhammad came to work he found that the large plate-glass windows had been blown out of the first-floor display room, and there was no insurance to cover the loss. That temporarily closed the Tompkins Square Gallery and postponed the plans for an art school.

Meanwhile, the Lower East Side wing of the inner core rented a two-story warehouse on Ludlow Street eight blocks away and set itself up with separate quarters. This placed an added drain on the project's resources, and kept Muhammad running back and forth in a fruitless effort to gain the group's assistance and work out a settlement of what he described as the "cold war."

The staff began to feel that the only hope for project survival was in the community board. The university was getting no help from RGS, yet was legally tied to it. With the untenable relations that had developed and the overwhelming problems that had to be faced, the staff began to view this legal connection as an unnecessary burden. RGS had never made itself an effective instrument of communication between the university and the community, and as long as it continued to be the official contact with OEO, there seemed no prospect of the project ever becoming a viable neighborhood operation. From the beginning of the OEO grant only two members of the RGS board of directors had actually lived in the neighborhood, and only three members of the entire inner core, including both the East Harlem and Lower East Side wings—at this point about a dozen individuals in all—were residents of the neighborhood.

In the community board the staff saw the possibility of a legal body that could free the university of the major obstacles that were restricting its development. Here was a group of mature Lower East Side resident leaders who were willing to serve without pay and whose only interest in the university was to help realize its potential for neighborhood education. If the University of the Streets were incorporated and the community board were installed as its legal governing body, neighborhood youths and adults could be brought together in a joint effort to work for needed social change, and the coalition that Muhammad and Fred had already started with other local organizations—including, if possible, RGS—could be more fully developed.

The fact that the community board was formed without first having reached a clear-cut understanding with the inner-core group was referred to by Muhammad as "a very unfortunate mistake." Perhaps it was, at least from the standpoint of organizational procedure. But the conflict and the pattern of RGS behavior had been well established long before the organization of the community board. And in light of past events, it is doubtful that not forming the board would have made any practical difference. In any case, it had become clear to those who were trying to solve the problems and get on with the work that local community control had become not only desirable but a practical necessity. Muhammad encouraged Fred to push as rapidly as possible university incorporation as a separate legal entity.

The only possibility for a neutral third party to help resolve the struggle and clear the path for productive work was the federal agency that had made the quarter-million-dollar grant and which was responsible for its supervision. But that didn't happen. Instead, OEO stood on the technicality that its contract was not with the University of the Streets but with RGS, encouraged RGS in its hostility, aided and abetted its attack against the staff, and threw the official weight of the United States government into the vendetta.

This attitude on the part of OEO was made clear to me not only in New York, but at OEO's offices in Washington. Because "the gang types lost control to the staff types," OEO told me, "the University of the Streets was no longer a community organization." Muhammad and his staff, according to OEO, were trying to twist what was intended as a tool for community action into a conventional educational program. The Good brothers, said OEO, had no understanding of community development, and were using fear tactics to obtain their personal ends. Instead of transferring their expertise to the "gang types," said OEO, they wanted to dominate the group. To accomplish this, I was told, they deliberately created a dependency they figured couldn't be broken. And they did all this, said OEO, in very subversive ways: By contacting foundations and raising money they thought they could make the group indebted to them so that in the event of a rupture between them and the "gang types," they would be in a position to make the implied threat, we built you up, we can also tear you down. Fred and Mike, I was told at OEO, were just poor little rich boys with nothing better to do than spend their time patronizing the ghetto.

The line was very familiar. I had heard it over and over in New York.

Having been drugged by the romanticism that was created by the picture of urban gang leaders eliminating poverty and reforming the Lower East Side ghetto, some Washington officials had become gullible enough to believe anything that went with the fantasy-image so skillfully started by Charlie Slack. There were many once-violent gang members at the University of the Streets who were doing constructive work to help develop the project's potential for neighborhood service, and who held a very different view of the roles being performed by Fred and Mike Good, but who were not caught up in the myth, were not in contact with the federal bureaucracy, and had no influence on the attitude that governed the actions at OEO. This attitude may or may not have reflected official Washington policy, but as a practical obstruction to the effective use of federal funds in the development of the University of the Streets, it was deadly.

In the fall of 1968, OEO decided to evaluate the university. This was to be an "external evaluation" and an "internal evaluation." Whether or not this action was implemented to support the OEO position and further the attack on the university staff, it accomplished exactly that. Responsibility for the external evaluation was given to a private Washington consulting agency closely associated with OEO that had played an active role in framing the proposal used as the basis for the quarter-million-dollar grant. The agency was well aware of OEO's attitude toward the conflicting elements associated with the project. The responsibility for the internal evaluation was given to RGS and wound up in the hands of the East Harlem branch.

I asked at OEO if using one of the rival factions in a bitter local dispute might not introduce undue bias for purposes of an official government evaluation. The response was that I was asking a "loaded question."

19

Invasion

To grasp the full significance of the OEO move toward evaluation, it is important to remember that the word "staff," used to identify the program people and other workers at the University of the Streets—including those who served as volunteers—did not in actual practice mean what that word usually means. Here this word was primarily a distinction between those who were thought of as members of the inner core, the two wings of RGS, and those who weren't. In the beginning days of RGS almost everybody who took part in the gatherings at Fred's apartment thought of themselves as "members," and during the early months of the university little distinction was made between those who were in RGS and those who were not. The University of the Streets was simply thought of as a project in which various interested people were participating, all under the banner of the Real Great Society. Anybody who wanted to do something simply went ahead and did it. Everybody was staff and everybody was RGS. And from this informal cumulative effort the project evolved.

It was not until the separation into factions following the forma-

tion of RGS/East Harlem and the OEO grant that this distinction
between the small inner-core group of gang leaders and the other
people who were working at the university—including Fred—began
to have definite meaning. All of those who made up the inner core
received pay, if not from the OEO grant funds, from various other
funds, either private or public. In short, paid personnel included persons inside RGS, as well as those who were thought of as staff. The
point is that the staff was not just a group of "agency employees" in
the usual sense. It was made up chiefly of neighborhood residents
who had entered into what they had thought of as a local activity
because they had something they wanted to offer or just because they
were interested, most of them starting as volunteers.

Thus the expression "staff types" did not mean, as OEO officials
seemed to think, that the university staff was any less a local community group or any less a part of the initiating drive that had
brought the project into being than was the inner-core group. Indeed,
in most respects, just the reverse was true. On the whole, the staff was
actually more representative of the neighborhood and its indigenous
residents than was the inner core. Certainly it was far more deeply
engaged in the actual building of the project. The problem was that
OEO, in its love affair with "gang types," and its self-deception as to
what constituted the indigenous neighborhood group, interposed itself
in a local conflict. The conflict made it impossible to use the quarter
of a million dollars of federal funds in ways that would have enabled
the university to realize more fully its development potential. OEO's
taking sides was not only a disservice to the project and to the government, it was also a disservice to RGS.

It wouldn't have required any great sleuth or scientific survey to
reveal weaknesses, inadequacies, and any number of examples of
arrested development in the varied programs of the University of the
Streets. All this was self-evident. Not even Muhammad or Fred or
Mike, or any other member of the staff, would deny that. What was
needed was not an "evaluation," as that term was used in the jargon
at OEO, but an intelligent effort to end the internecine warfare,
enable the staff to feel less defensive, and help RGS settle down to
work, to apply to the project the charisma that—according to

OEO—"gang types" were supposed to have in a ghetto neighbor-hood. But OEO never supplied leadership or assistance.

As Muhammad expressed it, "OEO put on the blinders."

The fact was that in preparing for the evaluation, OEO didn't have to "put on" the blinders. It had been wearing them from the begin-ning of the project.

On November 1, 1968, four days after the abortive attempt to get rid of the Good brothers, OEO officials arrived from Washington to prepare for the "internal evaluation" of the University of the Streets. Muhammad, as project director, was allowed to sit in on the meeting. All other members of the staff were barred. OEO provided a con-sultant to prepare the evaluation design, and commissioned RGS to carry it out.

It was said that Muhammad could help select the persons who would serve on the evaluation team, but when he was told that one of the university's leading adversaries in the East Harlem wing of the inner-core group was to head it, he knew that his role in the selection was for all practical purposes a formality and that the only acceptable attitude for him was to agree. Those in charge of the evaluation then conjured up a salary cost for the team of nine thousand dollars—to be paid out of the university budget. At this, Muhammad and Mike stiffened. Mike, especially, refused to budge, labeling the request insane, and after weeks of heated negotiations the figure was cut to a sixth of the original demand. By standing firm against this attempted raid on the budget, Mike and Muhammad won the battle of dollars, but this money-saving victory only added to the conflict. The staff was well aware of the new danger to the project, and the crisis atmosphere, vastly intensified by the polarizing action of OEO, further diverted the university from its mission.

An important element in the OEO action was the evaluation de-sign, set forth in a document written by OEO's consultant. The evaluation was to provide "an honest description and analysis" of the operation, and was represented as having grown out of discussions with RGS, the university staff, and various interested "community representatives."

The evaluation was characterized as an attempt to gain "understanding of program experiences in order to sharpen the general perspective of program direction and facilitate better program planning."

The University of the Streets and RGS, according to the document, felt that

> . . . such an evaluation must be consciously undertaken by those closest to the ideals and concepts inherent in the project, in addition to using the impressions of community people capable of offering objectivity to the evaluation. . . .
>
> The general approach is marked by simplicity and honesty. . . . Every attempt will be made to maintain objectivity, specific focus and clarity. . . . Problems, issues and barriers related to program development and operations will be emphasized in order to maximize the knowledge to be gained. . . .

Then, after acknowledging that the project had encountered "complex administrative problems," the document stated, "This evaluation is designed to explore these problems, in depth, in order to gain some understanding of the degree to which administrative and other problems have hampered program development and operation."

One of the purposes cited was "to use the evaluation process as a format for training a limited number of project staff and community residents in evaluation procedures (as a built-in educational component of the University of the Streets program)."

This, said the document, was to be a means by which the "University of the Streets intends to view itself."

The evaluation design became almost eloquent. Those doing the evaluation, it said, would translate their findings

> . . . into program judgments in concert with the total evaluation team, the project director, and other staff members. . . . The project director [Muhammad] will be directly involved in all phases of the evaluation process, and findings will be reported to him on a weekly basis. Every effort has been made to assure that the entire University of the Streets staff perceive this process as an attempt to gain knowledge and direction rather than as a "Big Brother" operation.

The evaluation team, according to the document, would hold "periodic meetings" with the "total University of the Streets staff to discuss findings and translate them into policy decisions wherever possible." A report would be written jointly with the project director, and sessions would be held with the entire university staff to discuss this report and make necessary corrections before its final approval by the RGS board of directors and its submission to OEO. Thus, said the document, the final report would accurately reflect the views of the "staff and community without reservations, excuse or shame."

With these high-sounding rules written into a plan that conveyed the illusion of a serious exercise in self-analysis by all persons concerned, the plan was turned over to the East Harlem branch for execution—and the rules were suspended.

In addition to the chief evaluator, referred to as the coordinator by OEO—that is to say, the East Harlem representative who managed the evaluation and wrote the final report—the evaluation team included one of the inner-core board members, three young people at the university who were seeking personal favors from RGS, a university staff member who quit the team soon after being appointed because he said he didn't have time to work with a "stacked deck," and one of the university's street youths, who wrote a favorable report which somehow disappeared. It is not clear how in good conscience OEO could have regarded this team as representative of either the staff or the community, but except for the coordinator, the team had no real say in the evaluation anyway, and as a practical matter its composition was not really important.

Under the prevailing circumstances there was not the slightest possibility of the "internal evaluation" being used as an objective measure, or as a "built-in educational component" of the university, as was so glibly stated in the evaluation design. And given the attitude that was no secret in Washington, it would be difficult to believe that OEO was not aware of the effect of its actions.

Muhammad and his fellow workers were now firmly convinced that the only way to preserve the program was to make the university an autonomous neighborhood organization under the legal jurisdiction of the community board. This, they had learned, was going to be more difficult than they had at first thought. To use the word "university" in a corporation charter, Fred had found it necessary to obtain approval from New York state educational authorities. And he was hard at work on this problem. Mike and Muhammad were keeping a tight watch on the budget. More and more of the street youths were openly proclaiming their loyalty to the staff, and everywhere in the university there was a growing sense of urgency to be on guard. Suspected spies were running in and out of the building. Tools were constantly disappearing. The problems of physical maintenance were becoming insuperable. The maze of daily program demands seemed overwhelming. In this climate of apprehension, university workers and street youths felt increasingly their collective adversity, and as the confusion and bewilderment rose, staff resistance toward the efforts of RGS to exercise its ambitions for recognition and authority grew more and more rigid.

It was reaction and counterreaction, with OEO fanning the flames.

Unable to penetrate the staff resistance, the frustration of the inner core became maddening. Other than having gained dominance over the Lower East Side wing of the group itself, the East Harlem power thrust had failed. The move to oust the resented white leadership in the university had been stopped, and the black leadership, even the principal Puerto Rican leadership at the university, had sided with the Goods. But now OEO had supplied the inner core with a new weapon—the power to control and write an official evaluation of the project. With this potent weapon RGS could again take the offensive. Now, with the backing of the federal agency that held the power of funding, it had what it needed to humiliate and discredit the staff.

On November 11 the evaluation coordinator from East Harlem announced to the university staff that the evaluation would be completed in January 1969, and it would determine the strengths and weaknesses of the university. Based on the internal and external evaluations, OEO would make its determination as to whether the project would be funded for another year.

After nearly two months of suspicion and rumor, the OEO consultant completed the evaluation design. On December 20 at a meeting of university staff members—at which most of them were not present—the East Harlem coordinator announced that the evaluation was to begin the following Monday, two days before Christmas. Questionnaires addressed to the staff were circulated and collected. On January 10, 1969, the evaluation was finished, and the coordinator in East Harlem wrote the report, forty pages of text.

Bits and pieces of the information that had been turned in, well salted with arbitrary opinions and conclusions, were selected for inclusion. All the existing program deficiencies, plus a good many that didn't exist, were put together in a report that made the project look even more deficient than it actually was, and the staff—including Muhammad—was thoroughly discouraged. Although the report played havoc with reality, at least it was melodramatic. It was introduced by a historical account covering the period from the beginning of the university in 1967, up to the time Muhammad became director in August 1968. Based on partial truths and artfully presented interpretations, this opening had the effect of revising the project's history in a way that pictured the staff as an organization of villains led by Fred Good and Bill Watman preying on naïve Lower East Side gang leaders, with the East Harlem wing coming to the rescue, seeing through the purported exploitations by the villains, and providing the grass-roots leadership that was needed to build a successful future. With this opening, the report then trained its guns on the operation under Muhammad's direction, and after a devastating program-by-program attack, wound up by recommending that the RGS board of directors use the evaluation as the basis for redirecting the project. Then, with a final touch of grandiloquence, the East Harlem coordinator expressed thanks to the evaluation team "for helping me produce such a fine piece of work"—and, "We are proud of ourselves."

In a letter to OEO, it was stated: "The Board of Directors of the Real Great Society, Inc., has reviewed the internal evaluation done of the University of the Streets. We concur with the findings . . . the recommendations expressed reflect our own views and steps are being taken to implement them."

This statement from the board was interesting in a number of respects. The one criticism the report made of RGS—its willingness in the early days of the project to trust Fred and Bill—was credited to the Lower East Side Wing. From early 1968, when the two wings were on the verge of splitting, primarily because of this very question, to January 1969, when the report was written, the influence of the East Harlem branch had become so powerful over the Lower East Side that this kind of "self-criticism" was now acceptable.

The whole exercise made a mockery of the lofty procedures that were set forth in the evaluation design. At no time were "periodic meetings" held with either Muhammad or "the total University of the Streets staff to discuss findings and translate them into policy decisions," or to "sharpen the general perspective of program direction." No judgments were made "in concert," the project director was not "involved in all phases of the evaluation process," findings were not "reported to him on a weekly basis," indeed, not at all, and—instead of "every effort"—no effort was made to assure that the entire staff "perceive this process as an attempt to gain knowledge and direction rather than as a 'Big Brother' operation." The report was not written jointly with the project director, and the staff was not given an opportunity to discuss the final draft—or any other draft—before it was approved by RGS and submitted to Washington. But what else was there to expect? This was part of the vendetta, and making full use of the weapon it had been handed by OEO, the inner-core group chalked up a smashing victory.

The statement in the evaluation design which held that the final report would accurately reflect the views of the "staff and community without reservation, excuse or shame" was apparently just more of OEO's window dressing, for neither Muhammad nor any member of his staff got a glimpse of the report until they learned that it had already gone to OEO. At that point Muhammad contacted the OEO consultant to insist on a copy, and even then was able to get only a partial copy. Only much later after an appeal through Senator Javits was he able to see the complete report, and at no time did he get a copy of the evaluation design.

But for purposes of infuriating the staff, even the partial report was enough. Muhammad, though no less outraged than the others by what was uniformly labeled "a pack of lies," again urged restraint, and insisted that the matter could be straightened out by calm discussions with OEO. He had no conception of how wrong he was.

At OEO the report was accepted with approval. Indeed, some officials seemed downright gleeful. And not without reason. Faced by congressional criticism and the new administration of President Nixon, OEO had a report that served up the university staff as a scapegoat for another project that had gotten off the track. It exonerated OEO for its own failure in leadership, and it helped preserve its romanticism about "gang types." Then, to make the case complete, the outside evaluation was cited as confirmation of the East Harlem report. These were represented by OEO as "independent reports." However, the outside report reflected one of the most incredibly inadequate pieces of research and reporting I have ever read; it took the same line as the East Harlem report in misrepresenting the operation and the nature of the problems, and reflected the same orientation I heard at OEO before—and after—both reports were written. Muhammad, as well as the other staff members, could not recall having had any more than a few casual conversations with the two individuals who were sent to do the outside evaluation, and were not able to see the report until months later, when they appealed through Senator Javits's office for the East Harlem report.

Had the internal evaluation been conducted under the guidance of competent outside leadership as a truly objective process of self-examination and education in which all persons associated with the project could have aired their feelings and shared their thoughts and disappointments in a genuine search for understanding and insight, as OEO had pretended, it is quite possible—if not indeed probable—that a spirit of mutual accommodation and cooperation between the staff and the inner core could have evolved. Residuals of long-standing friendship and interpersonal respect reaching out from each side toward the other were still present in some degree, and even at this late date might have been reactivated.

In both the University of the Streets and the Real Great Society there was an immensely rich and potent store of imaginative ability and human energy to be put to work in the urgent tasks of youth development and democratic neighborhood service in one of the nation's most vicious social jungles. This was the grist, the priceless human resource that OEO had within its power to cultivate and turn into a united force committed to building a model of effective action in urban America. All the vital elements were there, and no combination of words could express the need of this seething ghetto on Manhattan's Lower East Side that cried out for those vital elements.

Perhaps the opportunity was best expressed by Helena King, mother of Alvin, and a devoted member of the community board:

> In this community we have so many disappointments. We see a good thing, then it is taken away. In the University of the Streets there is a future for my children, a work in which they will not be hoodlums, will grow up so they will not have to depend on welfare, not be on drugs, not run with the gangs. I see something good. It is what all of us want for our children. A chance for them to be somebody. It is the answer to our prayers.

Then this, from E. L. Timberman, president of Kenyon & Eckhardt, who had come in from outside the ghetto and seen for himself the potential that existed:

> In the University of the Streets something is happening in one of New York's most depressed areas. Hundreds of kids are being given a second chance to enter society, instead of being supported by it. The community has been given a sense of pride and the sense of a solution. The school is an enormously valuable laboratory for new concepts and techniques. Whether more comparable systems are established in other poverty areas, whether techniques are fed into the established school system, whether new ways are found to train people to get and hold jobs, the work being done has great pragmatic social value.

This was the potential for development—not to mention the investment of a quarter of a million dollars of public money—that OEO had the opportunity to salvage and bring to fruition. But instead, OEO, in its blind obsession with "gang types," decided that the university was "not relevant to ghetto problems"—as one of its Washington officials said to me—and allowed, indeed encouraged, the process of evaluation to become a one-sided accusatory investigation that served only to entrap a group of people in their own human passions.

Heavy emphasis was placed on whether the university had complied with each and every point in the project proposal, as though this were a matter of earth-shattering importance. The fact was that nobody in RGS and almost nobody in the university had anything to do with writing the project proposal, which was put together in Washington by Bill Watman, certain OEO officials themselves, and OEO's friends in the Washington consulting agency that produced the twisted outside report. During the four months before Muhammad became director the university was obviously floundering. After that it very definitely began to develop as it should have from the beginning of the OEO contract. Whether it had yet progressed far enough to be in conformance with the terms of the proposal is debatable. But OEO—either unable or unwilling to comprehend the situation— made a farce of the word "opportunity," which supposedly was its stock in trade.

As a result, the wild beasts of suspicion and fear which had threatened the project from the beginning of the federal grant were unleashed, and the antagonists became so alienated that even a semblance of peace was unattainable. To the staff, RGS had no conception of what was right. To RGS, the staff had no conception of what was right.

In a written statement intended for OEO, but which was never mailed, Fred summed up his analysis of the tragedy:

> It is my own personal belief that the leaders of the Real Great Society on the Lower East Side are not fully aware of what has happened and that their sincerity is not at all in question. By accepting direction from East Harlem, they were put in the middle of an ideological struggle which was not of their making. Old and trusted friendships were interfered with; dreams and ideals which were the result of years of being together were distorted and cast aside in favor of an obsession to develop a hierarchy which could be skillfully manipulated from East Harlem and which had no similarity to the original goals of the Real Great Society. This obsession of a few, at the expense of the individual dignity of each person committed to these goals, has been the basis of

much friction and misunderstanding, and to a degree, a reflection on the ability of our society as a whole to deal with the urban crisis. This should serve as an experience which can help us all in the future. While I believe that in the long run this friction and misunderstanding will be resolved, we cannot, and OEO cannot, ignore the importance of constant self-analysis and the promotion of an open and honest discussion of differences. Until this is done there cannot be a true reconciliation, and it is better that the University of the Streets start to function independently under a community board with the hope that our differences can be ironed out once we are no longer bound by ties which connected some of us out of need rather than out of sincere mutual respect and friendship.

Fred's devotion to his RGS friends never subsided, but there was nothing that he or anyone else engaged in the work could do now to dispel the impasse that had been solidified by OEO.

Instead of creating a mood for problem solving, the evaluation created a mood for destruction. With its inside Washington connections, RGS now had an asset that made the University of the Streets no longer important, maybe even a liability. Only a little more than two months remained in the one-year grant period, but the federal money would not last that long, and there were bills yet to be paid. The East Harlem branch had just received another fifty thousand dollars for operating expenses from the Astor Foundation. Mike, with his watchdog attitude, had become increasingly difficult to get around, and the staff was determined to make the university a neighborhood organization under the community board. RGS succumbed to its urge for revenge and reverted to the boldness of gangland. In meetings held in Washington and kept secret from the staff, the OEO backers gave their assurance that RGS could get rid of the staff, close out the university, and still be eligible for more government money. And so, with this encouragement, a plan of attack was devised and set in motion.

On the morning of January 28, 1969, Muhammad was told to come immediately to the RGS headquarters on Ludlow Street. There he was informed that as of that day the project was finished and that he and the entire staff were fired. He started back to the university to tell the others, and before he could walk the eight-block distance, a gang of about fifteen members and friends of RGS—most of whom were reported to have been armed—had arrived ahead of him with a rented truck and were moving out the furniture.

Muhammad hurried upstairs to the office. There he found staff members and street youths led by Owen Watson and a muscular young black named George Ivy, who recently had started rebuilding the Maintenance Department, getting ready to counterattack the invaders.

Insisting that there be no physical resistance, Muhammad managed to hold them back. Had he not done so there very likely would have been bloodshed.

Said Muhammad: "There I stood, George Ivy pacing up and down like a panther ready to spring, Owen swelling up like he was the whole black belt team, a couple of dozen others hardly able to restrain themselves, the women guarding the records and calling out foul names, furniture moving past me like I was in a traffic jam, the program going down the drain, and me hollering peace."

"I couldn't understand their actions," said Owen, referring to RGS. "They had done all this mouthing about help thy neighbor. I knew all along their words meant nothing. With maybe a few exceptions, they were just interested in themselves. I knew them inside out. I wanted to flatten them. And I would have, but Muhammad was so nice he kept me from doing it. One of them threatened to shoot me, so I did have the pleasure of shaking him up."

Fred and Mike were not in. They were meeting with an official at the Morgan Guaranty Trust Company of New York cultivating interest in the university, and were just getting settled into conversation when the telephone rang. It was for Fred. Karen Jordan, a vivacious Jewish brunette who had lived twelve years on the Lower East Side and served as secretary at the university, was calling to let them know that they and everybody else had been fired, and that RGS was shutting down the university. Fred told Mike and the bank official what he had just heard, then he and Mike left to grab a cab back to the university. There was the truck, and the gang hauling out furniture. By the time they could make their way inside, the building had become chaos. Muhammad called OEO in Washington, asking what could be done. Nothing, he was told. OEO said it was responsible only to RGS and if it wanted to make that decision it could do so. OEO would not discuss the matter directly with the university.

Truckload after truckload was moved to the warehouse on Ludlow Street, and by the end of the day the building was stripped—desks, chairs, tables, lamps, filing cabinets, typewriters and mimeograph machine, every stick of furniture and classroom equipment, even the rug out of Muhammad's office and a bulletin board he had screwed to the wall. The gang took tools, materials, and supplies out of the Maintenance Department, and lumber that had been purchased to replace the rotted window frames in the karate room. They threw the library books on the floor, moved out the shelves, and wrecked the Prep School classroom. They took stage lighting and equipment out of the Theatre of Courage, and moved the chairs out of the auditorium. Light fixtures were ripped out of ceilings and walls, windows were smashed, doors were torn from their hinges, locked drawers and cabinets were broken open, and papers were strewn everywhere.

But there were a few things they didn't get.

Joanne Haas, one of the most faithful workers in the project, who specialized in children's activities, and Karen Jordan and other girls gathered up the accounting books and all the file records they could carry and locked them in a large toolbox with Karen sitting on top. One of the moving gang tried to see what was in that box, but Karen wouldn't budge, and he backed off.

The plate-glass windows that had been blown out of the art gallery had been replaced only a few days before, and Leroy Bostic was just beginning to get it reorganized. The movers started taking out paintings when Leroy, a very powerful individual, came in and put an end to that. The art works in the gallery were there under contract with the artists who owned them, and Leroy was responsible for their safekeeping. Later that day RGS brought in a lawyer to make clear that the gallery was closed, that the artists' contracts were canceled, and that all paintings and other art works would have to be removed.

"We had done a lot of work to encourage these artists, now suddenly we were being told we were out of business," said Leroy.

"But the worst thing was, we were forced to break our word. It was immoral. It was illegal. The artists' contracts required a twenty-day notice for cancellation, and when RGS broke that requirement it was my word the artists thought was no good. You just don't do things like that. I wouldn't allow them to touch another painting."

In the Community Clubhouse in the basement, Alvin King, with some of his street youths, stood guard. One of the moving gang asked if Alvin thought he could beat him.

"I don't have to," said Alvin. "You just can't have any of this stuff, that's all."

And nothing was disturbed.

One of the notations in Karen Jordan's diary was this:

"Evicted! They acted like Gestapo. They removed everything they could get their hands on. Except in the clubhouse. Alvin and his crew refused to vacate. Not only that, refused to allow them to enter. Very frustrating for them to have this resistance from the kids."

But except for the clubhouse, the university was reduced to shambles.

Said Karen's diary: "The project to date has been very educational. It cost $253,000 to teach us how to be an organization."

"We have just been treated to a lesson in political science," said Fred.

"Yeah, they really pulled it off," said Owen. "They came in, struck fast, and ran." Then, shaking his head, he added, "It wasn't us, the staff, they took anything away from. It was the kids they took something away from. We shouldn't of let 'em do it, but that goddam Muhammad, well, maybe he was right. We proved we could make it work. We'll do it again."

There were at that time several hundred street youths engaged in the university's varied activities, despite the curtailment of the karate and art programs that had resulted from damage to the building a little more than two months earlier.

"I knew that legally they were the grantee, and were within their legal rights," said Muhammad. "They had done nothing for the program anyway, except put roadblocks in its way. So I said, OK, the university will be better off without them. I never dreamed they would wreck the place. But even if I had known that I would have been opposed to us using the gang tactics they used."

RGS took possession of the building and locked the doors. With no address and no income, it still didn't occur to the staff members that they were out of business. They were simply on their own, as they had long since decided they would have to be in order to get free of the conflict.

About a week later it became apparent to RGS that for its purposes the building was just a burden with a two-year lease which the staff wanted to take off its hands. Muhammad got the keys and returned to the university.

He arrived early, walked through the silence of the vacant rooms cluttered with debris, surveying the damage. He had witnessed the wild action of a few days before, but not until now did he become fully conscious of the extent of the damage.

"We had nothing but a shell," he said. "Wires dangling where there had been light fixtures, doors missing, floors littered with broken glass, and in my office—nothing, just chunks of fallen plaster. Even the elevator was out of use, jammed by a broken door."

He sat on the large toolbox where Karen had sat that day guarding the records—the one usable item that was left—wondering which way to turn. Then the others began arriving, ready to clean up, retool, and reopen the University of the Streets.

20

Aftermath

As of January 28, 1969, the day the University of the Streets was closed and the staff was fired, Mike calculated that enough money was left from the federal grant to cover two weeks' pay, handle the payroll taxes, and take care of most of the outstanding bills. In accordance with the practice which had been customary at the university of giving two weeks' notice in the event of employee separation, Mike managed—despite objections from RGS—to arrange two weeks' severance pay for the staff. With this accomplished, he relinquished his accounting records and checkbooks, and RGS took control of the university's bank account and unfinished business with respect to the OEO grant. That was the last regular staff payroll.

"What the hell," said Alvin King, shrugging his shoulders. "We'd been broke before. We figured we could get money someplace. We had too big a job to do to quit. We had the kids to think about."

On that note, Muhammad and his organization began picking up the pieces. Until the building could be put back in use, Fred's and Mike's and Muhammad's apartments served as offices. Prep School and art classes were continued in other apartments. The Theatre of Courage and the Music Department found temporary quarters in public auditoriums. The karate program—having been without its regular quarters for more than two months—continued as it had been, borrowing time in various gymnasiums. Alvin kept the clubhouse going, Leroy began reorganizing the gallery under new ownership, and George Ivy went hunting tools and materials for the Maintenance Department.

But there was now a whole new set of other problems: the lease on the building, unraveling the legal complications that were blocking incorporation, replacing the furniture and equipment, obtaining a new bank account, and—overriding everything else—finding new sources of income.

Earlier, in December, in contemplating the idea of becoming an independent organization, Muhammad and Mike had worked out an agreement with the landlord for a new three-year lease in the university's name to take effect upon the expiration of the old two-year lease which Fred had arranged back in June 1967 in the name of the Real Great Society. Under this new lease the rent was to be increased from $1,350 a month to $1,650, but they were to get the entire building—more than twice the amount of space they were then occupying.

Three days after closing the project, when it came time to pay the next month's rent, RGS agreed to cancel its lease and let Muhammad's and Mike's new three-year lease take effect. Thus, the university obtained possession of the building—exactly what it wanted—but it had not expected to be doing this on such short notice. It was still an unincorporated organization. It had no income, no money in the bank, and $1,650 for its first month's rent was now due. By subletting to other tenants who already occupied parts of the building the university had never occupied, the obligation was reduced by $843. Members of the organization combed the streets borrowing emergency funds, came up with the balance of $807, and as of February 1, the first installment on the new three-year lease in the name of the University of the Streets was paid.

But that was only a minor part of the crisis. Until the university could get a tax-exemption certificate from the Internal Revenue Service, the hope of raising enough money to keep going was little more than just that—a hope—and it was impossible even to file a request for tax exemption without being incorporated. With the help of a lawyer named Ron Moss, Fred had gotten the incorporation papers drawn up and filed, with the members of the community board as directors. But despite what seemed like endless correspondence, telephone calls, and personal contacts, he still had not been able to satisfy the requirements of the State Education Department, which under New York law had to approve the use of the word "university" in a corporate title, and everybody in the organization was determined to stay with that name.

Then a grant of one thousand dollars came through—a real windfall. But the check was made out to RGS. Mike tried several times to get it endorsed over to the university, and each time was turned down. He then went to the foundation that had issued the check, and with its help eventually got the endorsement. Then he ran into another obstacle. Because the university was not incorporated, he could not find a bank that would allow it to open an account. To resolve this problem, he went to their old friend Merle Gulick at Equitable Life, explained the situation, and on the strength of a call from him was finally able to establish a bank account at Chase Manhattan.

The legal and fund-raising problems were further complicated because of problems with the mail. It wasn't being delivered. On the day of the invasion RGS put in a notice at the post office to have all mail for the university sent to the address on Ludlow Street, and in spite of repeated attempts, Mike had not been able to convince the postal authorities that the university was a new organization at the old address, and as such was entitled to receive its mail. After a week or more, the post office, not knowing whom to believe, ceased delivering university mail even to the Ludlow Street address, held everything, and gave Mike five days to produce evidence that his organization was qualified to receive mail addressed to the University of the Streets. He took in as exhibit A their new Chase Manhattan bank book. But the post office officials were not convinced. Eventually, with the help of an attorney, he obtained a written agreement as to how the mail should be distributed, took that to the post office, and after three weeks of haggling got this problem solved.

Meanwhile, other members of the university organization were out hustling furniture and re-establishing the office on the fifth floor. Hand tools and lumber were being gathered, and reconstruction was beginning to get under way. Then a fire broke out on the third floor. Tables and chairs collected for classes were destroyed, and the walls of a large room that was being worked on were charred and blackened. The furnace broke down, necessary parts couldn't be found, furnace smoke forced a two-week closing of the clubhouse, and for more than six weeks the building was without heat. By early March the university, with its new bank account but still not incorporated, was back in the streets borrowing money. The rent was overdue.

Karen Jordan wrote in her diary:

From the outside, the University of the Streets may seem like an exciting and romantic involvement, when in fact it's hard, frustrating work in a cold, dirty office. Every day is aggravating and hard on your head. Postage meter stolen, walk to the post office. No heat. Water leaking down the wall. Hassles. People interfering, bumming money and cigarettes. Phone ringing with important and unimportant calls. Poor pay—most of the time no pay. Why are these people here? What do they get out of it? None are professional social workers or do-gooders. Every day some of them swear they'll quit and don't. But there is always a vibration in the air. A pregnancy. A report card from school. A new apartment for someone. A job for another. The unity is spectacular. The staff is tight and straight with each other. There are waves of rifts here and there, but like a marriage. Always with the knowledge that nobody stays mad very long, that it will be dealt with and worked out on the basis of what seems most expedient. If morale stays like it is the project, when it reopens, will be fantastic.

Back in the fall of 1968, about three months before the invasion, Fred had become acquainted with several leading members of a New York management firm that worked with governmental and private organizations in the general field of public affairs. These people expressed interest in obtaining suggestions and advice concerning the experiences of the University of the Streets for possible application to other public-service programs in New York and elsewhere, and indicated a willingness to assist Fred with his fund-raising efforts. Fred devoted a tremendous amount of time familiarizing these people with the project, and through them met a number of wealthy socialites who also expressed interest. One of them paid the cost of sending one of the university's street youths to a private college, where he made an excellent academic showing and successfully completed his personal struggle against the heroin habit. In December 1968 Fred was led to believe that as a result of the interest these people had shown, the university might receive a Christmas gift of sixty thousand dollars. As it turned out no such gift materialized, but Fred was encouraged enough to believe that his association with this management firm would eventually lead to the support the project so desperately needed. As a result of this contact, various prominent individuals, even European royalty, visited the university and afterward wrote glowing letters of praise alluding to possible offers of financial assistance. One of these visitors, Senator Javits, toured the project just four days before the invasion, asked questions about its financial needs, volunteered paint for a major job the Maintenance Department was planning, and invited Fred and Muhammad to visit his Washington office to discuss possible further government funding.

When, after the invasion, the university was without even a typewriter with which to prepare written proposals for funding, Fred spent the better part of two weeks at the management firm's office using its equipment to get out mimeographed descriptions of the university program which the firm offered to circulate for promotional purposes. Conversations with this firm and with Senator Javits's office went on over a period of months, always with the hopeful indication that material assistance was just around the corner, but like many hopeful corners, this corner was never turned.

This was typical of numerous apparently promising possibilities that were pursued day after day, gradually became more and more elusive, then evaporated.

"We had promises from everybody," said Owen Watson. "But they weren't for real. Crap, that's all, just crap. Still, Fred had to follow 'em down, because we couldn't always know who was for real and who wasn't. We started workin' for nothin' and we ended up workin' for nothin'. We figured if we stuck together we'd make it. We had to, for the kids. We kept telling ourselves this was something people could put their money in and do some good."

Most of the promises did seem pretty hollow, but this kind of testing had certain values. As Karen Jordan put it: "We had twenty-four staff workers, all poor and getting poorer by the minute. But the financial crisis was the healthiest thing that could have happened, because this weeded out the trouble-makers who had been shoved off on us just to get paid and act important. Only the dedicated ones stayed."

Near the end of March, when it seemed they were about to lose the building for nonpayment of rent, another windfall came in.

On the twenty-sixth Mike and Karen had a meeting with Bruce Gelb, president of Clairol, Inc., with whom Fred had talked previously, and informed him of their circumstances.

"We just told him we were at our wits' end," said Karen, "that all we had were promises, promises, no action."

Gelb made them a gift of $1,650 for a month's rent. And that wasn't the last time he came to the rescue. On another occasion when things were looking pretty dismal he came in with a check for the rent, saying he had had a dream that night telling him they needed the money. In addition, he supplied some much-needed furniture, and made arrangements for personnel and materials for two ten-session courses for forty girls in feminine grooming and personal development.

CIT Financial Corporation came through with ten sets of steel bookshelves, two large work tables, twenty stools, a lectern, three desks, three file cabinets, and ten swivel chairs.

Then, with work almost complete on getting new window frames in the karate quarters, notice was received that because they had used wood in the construction, they were in violation of city building codes. All the work would have to be torn out and redone in steel. Estimated cost: two thousand dollars, and the landlord wouldn't pay it.

For every problem that was solved it seemed that a dozen more arose to take its place. The process of planning became more and more a day-to-day affair, and Muhammad began holding staff meetings early each morning at which workers could report to each other what happened yesterday and map strategy for the rest of the day. I attended several of these meetings, and never ceased to marvel at the talent: playwrights, musicians, artists, mechanics, teachers, karate experts, street youths—young men and women—and the staff girls, like Karen and Joanne, all of them almost always broke, but without the slightest doubt about the future of the university.

One of these meetings, which was fairly typical, was early in April.

Muhammad announced that because they had spent the last of their money putting lights in the Prep School, this was another week they wouldn't be able to make a payroll. Getting the building reopened for programs, he explained, seemed more important than a payroll. There were about fifteen minutes of grumbling while Muhammad remained silent waiting for it to subside.

"If anybody needs money," he said, "you can get out in the streets and hustle a few dollars. Too many of our kids have a habit to support. If we don't get them, the habit will."

That seemed to settle the argument.

There was discussion about building a kindergarten and day-care center on the fourth floor. George Ivy said he would start looking for materials.

A plan was suggested for getting buses from the city to take youngsters on outings to Central Park, and someone said he would take care of that.

"How's the clubhouse doing?" Muhammad asked.

"It's doin' OK," said one of the street youths. "The cats are workin' and so are the chicks."

They decided to raise money by holding a raffle, a dance for "cats" and "chicks," and a concert by the Music Department for older folks.

"We've got to raise five thousand dollars in the next two weeks," said Mike, then went over the bills.

All agreed to do their part, and the meeting adjourned.

Fred kept hoping that next week they would get their incorporation papers approved so they could get the tax-exemption certificate, thinking that would ease the difficulty of fund-raising, but the approval didn't come, and each week it seemed more complicated.

Finally, it was decided that to obtain clearance from the state Education Department they would change the name in the corporation papers, but stay as closely as possible to the University of the Streets. So Fred took the initials and tried that—U.O.T.S. The lawyer telephoned Albany and was told that probably it would work.

On April 15 the state Board of Public Welfare gave its approval, as required under New York law for charitable organizations, on the twenty-fourth approval came from the state Commissioner of Education, and on May 7, 1969, the corporation was formally established as a nonprofit membership organization, authorized by the state of New York to "combat social and economic poverty" . . . study the causes of poverty and delinquency . . . provide educational alternatives for high school dropouts . . . teach building maintenance, photography, art, music, drama, advertising, business management, and other subjects related to the needs of the community . . . develop athletic programs to create a more friendly and cooperative attitude among young members of the community, provide classes for older members of the community, provide exhibition space for art works, film showings, poetry readings, dance programs, and music concerts . . . award scholarships . . . foster closer relationships with state, city, and other local community organizations . . . and to acquire property and collect and dispense funds. On May 27 the Internal Revenue Service issued the federal tax-exemption certificate, and the University of the Streets—U.O.T.S., Inc.—four months after being pronounced dead, was legally qualified to do business.

A few days later they were served notice to vacate the building. The rent was said to be two months in arrears. But this time they had a defense. According to their lease, the other tenants who were subletting space in the building were to have paid their rent to the university, though by informal, verbal agreement these payments had been made directly to the owner. When the arithmetic and misunderstandings were all worked out, they were able to show that instead of owing the landlord, it was the other way around. They had accumulated a credit of $272, which—with the $843 then due from the other tenants for the current month's rent—meant that not only was the university not in arrears, it owed only $535 for the current month. With the help of more free legal services, while frantically stalling off the eviction over the better part of a week, that problem was resolved.

Then in early June a grant of $7,500 was received from the Rockefeller Brothers Fund. Between program demands, the need for at least a few short payrolls, and all the borrowing that had been done, this wouldn't go far, but once more the project was safe at least temporarily. During the summer and fall the university managed to bring in enough in small amounts—from foundations, business firms, politicians, and private individuals—to keep going, though not enough to get out of debt, and its credit was always overreached. Then Mike and Karen got married. To cut costs, Fred moved into a room at the university. Everybody in the organization was cutting corners. All of them were borrowing money and whenever possible eating with friends.

Fred, Muhammad, and Tom Yahn made two trips to Washington knocking on doors at the government. They got nowhere at OEO. They tried several other agencies, with no luck. At Health, Education, and Welfare, and at the White House, they found what seemed like real enthusiasm for possible future support, but that would take time.

By the end of October, after repeated near misses with bankruptcy but with a gradually increasing number of friends, the University of the Streets had raised approximately twenty-five thousand dollars— an average of about $2,800 a month since the day it was wrecked by RGS and abandoned by OEO. The School of Martial Arts was back in the building. Most of its programs were still holding on and new ventures were being planned. The potential for development was still very much alive.

But after that fatal event in the last days of January, nine months before, known at the university as "the invasion," there was one capital trademark Muhammad and his organization no longer had— the myth that was started by Charlie Slack, which in certain circles of romantic thought made the difference between whether to fund or not to fund. The image of self-directed gang fighters in the vanguard of the war on poverty had been so thoroughly embraced at OEO that the actual developers of the university simply could not be accepted. To have done so would have spoiled the illusion. And so having endorsed the project's destruction, OEO rejected those who threatened the image and aligned itself with the destroyers. With the university grant thus out of the way—the mishandling of which had become a possible source of embarrassment that some quarters in the agency were just as happy to be done with—those quarters that were imbued with the myth were now free to generate another grant for RGS, and were not about to listen to an organization known as "the staff," which had been pictured as the enemy.

As to whether OEO would have refunded the university had there not been a break between the staff and the inner-core group, I can only guess. Undoubtedly the bureaucrats who were involved would now say no. However, three months before the break I was told at OEO that although there were officials in the agency who were less than enthusiastic about how well the project was going, "It will be difficult not to refund because of its public relations image." In any event, with the termination of the "staff types," an immediate move was put in motion in OEO to arrange further funding for RGS, the results of the "inside" and "outside" evaluations being used as justification.

While the new grant proposal was being put on paper and the way was being cleared for maneuvering it through the internal OEO machinery, RGS—by now quite adept at getting around in Washington—made arrangements for other federal money that could be tapped more quickly at the Department of Labor's Coalition for Youth Action, an office that was less encumbered by federal red tape than most other government offices, and which had made street-gang grants something of a specialty. There, as of March 24, 1969, RGS was given $30,296. According to a six-page supporting proposal, this grant was for a "self-directed, nonprofit youth group" that depended on "the strong leadership of a few individuals" who recognized the need to train new potential street leaders so that its work could develop "in any direction." Exactly what this training would be, and for exactly what work, the proposal didn't make clear. But that didn't seem to be particularly important.

When I asked the official who had handled this grant at the Coalition for Youth Action what the proposal meant, I was told: "The Real Great Society is very flexible and free-wheeling and is difficult to link with a definite membership."

Freely admitting that the proposal didn't say much, the official explained, "It's vague because we were not able to get them to be more specific about just what they had in mind. But we decided that this group is probably one that works best with flexibility."

I was then shown a collection of glowing RGS publicity accounts—with which I was already intimately familiar—and was told that the new grant was considered a good investment because RGS had proved its capability for community action with a "fabulous project" on Manhattan's Lower East Side called the University of the Streets. This federal grant-making officer was not only unaware of the actual history of the university, but also did not know what RGS had done to the project just a little more than two months before the grant was made.

"Some day," said the young official, "I would like to get up there and visit that project."

"You should do that," I replied.

By July, 1969, OEO had completed its new paper work, and gave RGS another $125,000. The purpose: To do planning on the Lower East Side for economic development. By the time I began cutting off my research four months later, this project had yet to get off the ground. In December I was told at OEO that it was still in the "gearing-up stage." In the meantime the factions within RGS itself were again splitting apart, and there was no evidence to indicate that this split would not continue. What may happen in the future I do not know. But on the basis of past performance, there seems little likelihood that RGS will become a major force for constructive social change on the Lower East Side; at least not through the simple expedient of another grant.

The University of the Streets had learned another lesson. Linked to the famous image that pictured it as a project initiated and operated by gang leaders, it had been a popular item in various quarters at OEO, but once it became disconnected from that image and the magic days were gone, the sober truth had to be faced: At least in these grant-making circles of the war on poverty, it had been much easier to elicit money on the basis of myth than on the basis of reality.

Said Fred: "The only thing at the university that counts now is what we produce. Now everybody is at work. What we are doing now is exciting because it's constructive, but it is not romantic. There are no more games and there is no romance in building something real."

As this is written it has been a year since anyone could look forward with certainty to pay day. But the university is still there. Funds are still dribbling in, and in the minds of the workers themselves there is not the slightest doubt that the project will survive. They sound and act like very stout people, and they just could be right. Since its earliest beginnings this has been a project that has thrived in adversity. Obviously, it would be unrealistic to suppose that as time goes on there will not be changes in the make-up of the working crew, as there have been in the past, or that new elements of internal stress will not arise. Against the background of the Lower East Side it is difficult to imagine any project in this area that would not alternate between peaks and valleys, and there could well be slippages in this one. But as we Americans continue our search for solutions to our urban crisis, it seems to me that this much is clear: Whatever the future of the University of the Streets may be, the history of this ghetto enterprise has already provided important clues to some of the essential differences between actions and arrangements that are likely to work and those that probably won't.*

* In September 1970, the Department of Health, Education, and Welfare approved grant funds totaling approximately $250,000 for vocational training at the University of the Streets.

21

Summation

An elaborate game of myth-making between the gang and the establishment, played with large shots of illusionary publicity and heavy doses of mismanaged money, choked the early potential of the Real Great Society. The gang leaders wanted recognition and independence with no strings attached. What they got was a passkey to never-never land. After being sufficiently romanticized, fawned upon, and showered with gifts, RGS was rendered incapable of dealing effectively even with itself. Living from one grand splash to the next, never quite going to work, never actually performing the development in the streets for which it was being credited, it deteriorated to a kind of glorified payroll operation. Most of its benefactors, particularly those in Washington who threw open the doors to the federal treasury, lost whatever ability they might have had to assess realistically what was happening, and thus denied themselves a factual basis from which to devise the practical guidance and training that was needed to capitalize on the very real opportunities that existed. Gradually, from continuous feeding, the cancerous growth of fantasy and distortion became uncontrollable, and RGS became hopelessly addicted to the artificial stimulant of make-believe.

Money was squandered, but the greater tragedy was the squandering of important human resources—the frittering away of creative energies in protracted in-fighting, the dissolution of cooperative relationships between individuals whose diversity of talent was needed in the work, and the loss to thousands of Lower East Side street youths that resulted from the waste and destruction. By substituting myth for reality, effective organization and management became impossible, and the University of the Streets—the core of the opportunity for neighborhood development and education—was rendered impotent during much of its period of operation, then placed in a position of near-total eclipse. That was the ultimate contribution of the Washington bureaucrats who first accepted, then compounded the myth.

Then the myth was projected into the nationwide promotion for which RGS became the symbolic entrepreneur—Youth Organizations United. Exactly what was accomplished by this national extension of the myth-making game that would justify the cost, excitement, and expectations of the affair at East St. Louis is an exceedingly painful and difficult question. By the time that affair was over, the price tag just for getting YOU organized, including fees and traveling expenses, had climbed to more than eighty thousand dollars. A substantial part of this total was paid out of accounts at Southern Illinois University, another substantial part was paid by Mac Lewis out of his personal funds, and much of it was being carried in the form of unpaid bills. The two grants that had been obtained for organizational purposes— $33,525 from the government and fifteen thousand dollars from a private foundation—had been spent, and the promotion had run up a debt of more than fifteen thousand dollars.

But at no time was this insolvency interpreted as a signal for caution or as a reflection of the extravagance that had caused it. The one common belief to emerge from the heat of the East St. Louis conference was that YOU and its member groups had a special claim on the public treasury, and the overspent budget was seen merely as evidence that this special claim had not been paid. Whatever the street leaders wanted, they had a right to expect. That was the overriding mood. And in the euphoria of East St. Louis, buttressed by the solicitation from backers on the sidelines—including the Vice-President of the United States—there was no reason to feel any other mood. YOU had begun to look like a paying proposition. Money had been made to seem like a simple commodity the establishment would supply. All the street leaders had to do was collect it. With this guiding spirit, a committee of six was appointed to move into Washington and stay there until the negotiations started at OEO were completed. To supply fees and maintenance payments for this stay in Washington, the Coalition for Youth Action at the Department of Labor, which had provided the previous government money, came up with another ten thousand dollars—designated as a planning grant. The Department of Health, Education, and Welfare supplied invitational travel expenses, and Frank Ferguson took up the task of raising private funds to pay off the bills that had piled up at East St. Louis.

During the summer of 1968 Frank's efforts at private fund-raising, coupled with those of other interested outsiders, brought in almost thirty-six thousand dollars. But that was regarded as chicken feed. The main target was the federal government. To bring this target within range, a group of federal employees, with Frank actively assisting, worked out an agency consortium: the Office of Economic Opportunity, the Department of Health, Education, and Welfare, and the Department of Labor. In the wary circles of Washington a major grant to a national association of street gangs carried a very real possibility of political repercussions in Congress, and even the most ardent bureaucrat recognized that as exceedingly high-risk business. However, under the consortium arrangement, no one agency would have to carry the risk alone. Then through a series of further maneuvers assisted by the Office of the Vice-President, the YOU proposal was lifted to a point in the bureaucracy just under cabinet level, where it could gain the benefit of additional executive muscle but without arousing too much attention at the top until all necessary details were in order.

With this strategy in motion, the YOU committee of six arrived in Washington and was enthusiastically received. Here was the opportunity, it was said, to bridge the gap between the establishment and the streets. Using as the basic design the proposal that had been submitted to OEO just before East St. Louis, various alterations were made in the grant application and an informal agreement was worked out for the first-year budget: seven hundred thousand dollars—OEO to come in with two hundred thousand, HEW with two hundred thousand, and Labor with three hundred thousand, the total grant to be channeled through Labor, which was less vulnerable politically than OEO.

Through all of June and into the first days of July the members of the YOU committee lived in a downtown Washington hotel and now and then flew home and back. From the standpoint of negotiations or actual work, there was little for them to do. In essence, the decision to make the grant had already been reached. Beyond that it was primarily a matter of internal agency business—managing the paper work and getting the application formally approved before the midnight close of the government's fiscal year on June 30. Everything was moving along, the red tape was being unraveled, the YOU committee members were having a pleasant stay in Washington, influential friends were at work on their behalf, and the actual issuing of the grant seemed all but certain.

Then the glow was suddenly shattered and doubts formed over the whole enterprise. On June 20, 1968, a subcommittee of the United States Senate chaired by Senator John L. McClellan of Arkansas opened public hearings concerning an OEO grant of $927,341 that had been made about a year earlier for a training and employment program with two Chicago street gangs—the Blackstone Rangers, which YOU had attempted to get as one of its sponsoring groups, and the East Side Disciples. OEO was accused of supporting street-gang activities alleged to include intimidation, fraud, and other criminal behavior. The hearings became extremely controversial, with a flood of allegations being made and denied, but the end result was a clamor of indignation from OEO's opponents in Congress. OEO's next-year budget was then under consideration, confirmation of its then acting director—Bertrand Harding—was pending in the Senate, and the 1968 presidential election was not far off. Suddenly, the high risk that attended the funneling of federal money into street gangs took a sharp turn upward.

At that point the YOU proposal was being readied for formal signing, and even after the news broke from the McClellan hearings, Labor and HEW still indicated every intention of going ahead. But OEO backed down and the other agencies followed suit. Whether the decision for this last-minute withdrawal was made by Joseph Califano, then a White House assistant, or by President Johnson himself is a moot question. But the YOU proposal was vetoed by the White House and the finished contract then about to be signed became a worthless piece of paper. Early in July, in a meeting with representatives of the three agencies in the consortium, YOU was advised to lay low until after the heat from the McClellan Committee had blown over, and in a month or so negotiations could be rescheduled. But months passed and the rescheduling never came. The bureaucracy was running scared.

YOU felt cheated—after what had happened, understandably so. Shortly before the Johnson administration left office, YOU mailed to the White House what had come to be looked upon as its uncollected claim. Entitled "Commitment of the United States Government to YOU—For Performance Prior to Jan. 20, 1969," this, in part, is what the notice said:

> YOU has an unwritten, but top-level, explicit "I.O.U." for $700,000 from this Administration. It is uncollected. It was given on July 2, 1968, by Mr. Bertrand Harding, Acting Director of OEO, in a meeting of the representatives of the different Departments of this Government that had been engaged in negotiations with YOU. It was given incident to the decision made by the Government, in the last three days of June, not to fund YOU at that time. A comparable promise was given personally, on behalf of HEW, by Secretary Cohen. . . . The IOU, or obligation, was given following a full month of formal negotiations. A Labor Department Planning Grant had paid for the presence at that negotiation of YOU's six officers. . . . The IOU, or obligation has, affirmatively, been repeatedly recognized by the Government. Both Mr. Harding and Secretary Cohen, in statements to YOU, and to outsiders, have affirmed the nature of this obligation. The staffs of OEO and of

the Departments have constantly and consistently acted in recognition
of the existence of the obligation both in their occasional dealings with
YOU and, far more frequently and explicitly, in their dealings with
outsiders. A written request for the fulfillment of this obligation was
sent by YOU to Mr. Harding under date of October 17, 1968. This
date was two months after the earliest due date of the IOU as
expressed in July. Nearly three months have since passed. . . .

YOU kept waiting. January 20 came and went and no reply or
check ever came in response to the IOU. Months later, with President
Nixon in the White House, the drive for federal funds was still going
on, and Labor's Coalition for Youth Action contributed another forty
thousand dollars, which helped keep YOU alive.

As time dragged on, this claim became the central preoccupation
of the new national organization, and nothing much was done to go
ahead with the proposed national program upon which the claim was
based. Perhaps this inaction may be attributed to the lack of response
from the government, a matter which resulted in considerable anger
and disillusion. However, the basic purpose of YOU was to supply
leadership, motivation, and a means of communication; and from a
strictly fund-raising point of view, it had fared better than was
generally acknowledged. Over a period of approximately two years
beginning with the initial grants in 1968, cash contributions from all
sources—private and public—are estimated to have totaled at least
three hundred thousand dollars, in addition to which there were a
number of noncash contributions, such as room and board at East St.
Louis and rent-free office quarters, printing services, and many hours
of professional assistance in Washington. Also, through its Washington contacts, YOU was instrumental in arranging other direct grants
to various local groups.

YOU is a unique social invention. Effectively cultivated, it could
supply constructive national leadership for a vast body of young
Americans whose deprivation has given them cause for rage and
frustration, and who have lost their way. If this new national organization can avoid becoming a haven for brooding, resentment, and self-
righteousness, or a protective screen for destructive behavior, it is

possible that this leadership role could yet be performed. There is also the possibility that YOU may lose its way too, betray this leadership role, squander its talents and resources, and result only in more desperation, more waste, and more violence. What direction the organization may yet take in response to this challenge will depend not so much upon the size of its treasury, but upon what is done to it by its own internal forces, and what is done to it by forces outside itself—primarily by its friends and supporters in the establishment. Thus far the indications of that direction are mixed.

A few weeks before the affair at East St. Louis, when YOU was looking for member groups, a black street youth said this:

> First, I would like to talk about my fellows. Well, we have about four in for burglary, a couple for molesting, a couple for robbery, you know, a little bit of everything. But what we're trying to do is get settled out. We're trying to get these slums fixed. As it is, these clubs are fighting against each other, which is not right. They pop in, and what I mean by pop in, they're shooting guys down for nothing. They go and burglarize in different neighborhoods. And it's not right. What they should do is unite. Then we might get somewhere, like fix the playgrounds, you know, build something instead of tearing everything down. We got maybe 150 members in my neighborhood that are wild and free. They're tired of being in the streets and getting shot at and knocked up. Being frank, this stuff is going from worse to worser. I guess if we just stop and think, it ain't helping us none. A lot of the fellows would like to get back in school, you know, get their education. Maybe YOU could help us.

I have talked at length and in depth with numerous gang youths in various cities who have described to me in vivid detail their delinquent patterns of living, then asserted in apparent complete sincerity their determination to reverse direction. Repeatedly, I have accepted this stated determination and have been convinced that the gang was in fact becoming a constructive neighborhood force, only to learn a short time later that the very youths in whom I had placed confidence were committing further crime, or not holding up their end of the work in projects for which they had been given grant funds. I have conducted hundreds of these interviews and have been "conned" more times than I like to think about. I suppose this only confirms what many practitioners whose daily work is concerned with helping street gangs move toward constructive ends have told me. Yet in spite of these repeated disappointments, despite having discovered over and over again that programs which appeared to be making progress were in fact not at all what they had been said to be, or after promising starts had relaxed and gone backward, I am still convinced from my own field observations that many of these gang youths had every intention to move in alternative directions, and probably would have if effective guidance from both peers and outsiders had been available. If YOU can make itself a source of that kind of support, as say, Alcoholics Anonymous has been to its members, and worry less about collecting claims from the government, it is possible that YOU could become a new and major part of the nation's effort to reclaim its lost ghetto youth.

One of the YOU travelers in attempting to explain to a street leader the idea behind the organization said this: "Now the whole purpose of this thing is once these clubs and these gangs and whatnot get YOU organized, we can find out some of the things they would like to do, like educationwise, culturewise, scientificwise, things along this line or that line for their particular benefits. It's going to be directed right at youth for youth. Eventually, we plan on having a national credit union to help guys put together their ideas, like open a market or something. They would be able to borrow the money and put their thing into effect and run it themselves. Understand? Maybe they'd be concerned with photography, or arts and crafts, or anything they might want. This is what we want to do, help these kids do something they can benefit from."

Some months after East St. Louis, one of the leaders said to me: "Our groups are hung up with their daily life in the raw. But they're there. They are the ones all the books, TV, the newspapers, keep talking about. We don't have to go through something else, like Urban League, or CORE, or NAACP, to get to them. We are them. We can go into any ghetto in the United States, talk, identify with the people, live in their houses, eat their food, really get with them. We know their problems because their problems are our problems. Our guys aren't specialists in anything, we don't have twenty degrees like all these people that keep studying the American Negro, but we know the ghetto. We don't think we have all the answers, but we are the guys this whole damn thing is all about. Unless YOU can do its thing there's going to be a hell of a lot more things like the Black Panthers. We know how to deliver what our guys need."

Another YOU leader put it this way: "The most important thing is to create sound communications. The question is not race, but getting independent from the establishment, yet being able to work in it. That we can do. Not having that is why there are burnings, shootings, killings, all that. No one organization can do this job, only if a lot of organizations work together as human beings can the changes get made this confused country has to have. YOU can be the link that until now has been missing."

One of the common failures among promoters and grant-makers in attempting to help today's street youths deal with ghetto problems is to accept literally any positive statement they make and accord it a greater measure of validity than careful assessment would warrant. However, assuming a sufficient discounting of the rhetoric, I believe that in this national organization there is capacity for productive action—if that capacity is properly nourished and cultivated.

This capacity is an important positive.

If adequate attention were given to its own inner resources, YOU could make a significant contribution to essential environmental change and constructive youth development, for in this association there is a combination of positive attributes that probably does not exist in any other national organization in the same particular mix or in the same particular degree. Certainly, whatever may be said about the depredation of today's street gangs and ganglike groups on ghetto youth—which is considerable—this much can be said about YOU: If this organization either cannot or does not effectively marshal its inner resources for constructive national leadership, and if appropriate ways cannot be found to reinforce those resources, America will have lost a real opportunity. This does not mean that the "white power structure" should suddenly rush in with a free flow of grant funds and unrestrained promotion. It is precisely this kind of ill-considered intervention that has already jeopardized the opportunity. But as the YOU leader said, these groups are there. They exist. The question is not, should they be supported in their efforts to improve their life conditions, but how and under what circumstances? Potentially, YOU is an instrument through which urgent deliveries could be made—if these questions, how and under what circumstances, are dealt with on the basis of realism, not romanticism.

During the summer of 1968, after it became evident that major federal funding had been indefinitely postponed, a group of YOU leaders, with the help of professional advice, formed a commercial operation to function separately from YOU itself, known as the General Metropolitan Communications Corporation—or Gen Metro. Nonvoting stock was sold to outsiders, and voting stock was sold to anyone in YOU who wanted to buy it. With twenty thousand dollars in capital assets—mostly from the outsiders—this new company began offering its services to private or public organizations wanting to disseminate information or conduct consumer or other surveys in inner-city areas. Washington was designated as the company's national headquarters, but through YOU there was a potential supply of personnel with which to staff offices in other cities as the business allowed. This venture into business, with competent assistance, is showing signs of success. It is a small start, but it is not dependent on a grant, and it is a project in which self-sufficiency and independence, at least on a limited scale, could become realities.

This independence has been another positive.

It is to be hoped that these positives will become strong enough to offset the negatives, for the negatives have been formidable. In the typical RGS pattern, an outpouring of publicity—vocal and written—was applied to the promotion of a YOU image that to a very large extent was pure fiction. The fact is that YOU did not originate from the spontaneous action of gang leaders; indeed, at many points along the way it came very close to not happening at all simply because in the period that led up to East St. Louis there was so little spontaneity.

The effort to start the organization in the first place came not from the streets, but from the establishment. Then, even after this initial thrust, it is doubtful that there would have been enough effort from the streets to actually go ahead had it not been for continuous prodding and the payment of fees. After East St. Louis the street leaders became even more assertive than before in their talk of independence, but even then much of the actual work was still done by outsiders.

The organization was said to be made up of street youths who had turned away from crime and committed themselves to community service. There were such leaders as this, including some very remarkable individuals. But in the months following East St. Louis many of the leading participants either dropped out of community service or became outright obstructions to such activity. Others reverted to their delinquent past—or simply continued it. At least two were convicted of murder. The promoters simply chalked such activity up to circumstances and ignored it, even though it involved not merely teenage boys fighting in the streets, but adult men with criminal records. For youths, and adults as well, who live in a daily environment of crime, destruction, and prejudice—especially those who have spent substantial portions of their lives in prison—the route to constructive alternatives is not easy to follow, and rehabilitation requires infinite patience and understanding. Moreover, it would be unrealistic to expect no delinquent or criminal acts from at least some of the members of groups such as those that make up YOU. Dealing with groups such as this is, after all, the fundamental business of YOU. But to pretend that a level of achievement has been reached whether it actually has or not, and to allow fiction to become a substitute for fact, is inimical to building an effective national youth organization dedicated to reform, and can only make honest problem-solving hopeless and impossible.

Advertising had it that by the fall of 1968 the number of YOU member groups had increased to more than 325 local organizations representing more than four hundred thousand ghetto youths. Actually, it is doubtful that many of these groups knew that, or were even aware of their own existence.

These and other fictions grew into major negatives. Much of this kind of promotion was done by YOU's friends in the establishment, some by YOU itself. But however the responsibility may be divided, the fiction of numbers, of spontaneity, of volunteerism and reform weakened the organization internally and diverted it from its mission. With the passage of time the relationship between the Washington office and its nationwide constituency became pretty thin, the spirit of unity that had surfaced in the closing hours at East St. Louis cooled, and, as in many organizations, the national headquarters tended to become a function of a small, controlling clique. Under the influence of Washington's public relations and promotional circuits, this small group was led to see itself as a commanding national spokesman for hundreds of thousands of ghetto youths, and steadily, irresistibly was drawn into the luxury of fantasyland. This had the effect of strengthening the grant-dependent mentality, and YOU became more and more another captive of Washington politics, waiting upon the benevolence of the establishment—the very mode of living it so vehemently denounced. With the impressive outward appearance of a nationwide community of street gangs in the vanguard of social and political reform, the organization gained a substantial following of "establishment-type" supporters, and its principal architects were unceremoniously dropped by the wayside, just as the Goods were dropped by RGS. Frank Ferguson, knowing he was no longer wanted, quit during the summer of 1968. Mac Lewis became even more unwelcome. The YOU leadership became irritated by his constant presence, felt pressured by his advice, at times misinterpreted his motives. He never stopped dreaming of a nationwide partnership between the gang and the establishment, but by August 1969 the strained relations had become so intense that he too was out.

However, YOU's supporters, from ever-ascending levels of influence in the establishment, continued to grow in numbers and added increasing weight to the efforts in fund-rasing. Finally, the Nixon Administration was persuaded to take the risk. In June 1970, the Department of Health, Education, and Welfare authorized a first-year grant of $393,414 for a proposed program similar to that which had been turned down by OEO. On paper it sounds promising. I deeply hope it will be equally so in practice. For if with this new financial hold on life, YOU can now resolve its internal problems, cut through the fiction, and supply the constructive leadership that most of the nation's street gangs do not have inside themselves, it may yet perform one of the most urgently needed services in America today.

22

The Dangerous Future

The historic advance of democracy in America has been diluted and held back by prejudices and practices that have deeply hurt the nation's racial minorities, and the nation itself. The slum, now referred to as the ghetto, that massive blot on the urban landscape, is but a physical manifestation of this hurt. A more vicious manifestation has been the steady eating away of human dignity; millions of citizens, largely because of race, have been unable to realize the hope that America is capable of offering, and live as social rejects in their own country.

Our racial minorities have not been alone in this state of deprivation, but they are the ones who have suffered most from sheer prejudice, and in the case of Negroes, from the aftermath of an institution that shackled their forebears. America has managed to tolerate this deadly social disease, though not without the agony of a Civil War and the corrosive hatreds that have come as a part of today's wave of reform, which threatens to become equally devastating. These explosive upheavals, producing positive and negative results, are but a part of the price the nation has had to pay for the gap between its commitment to democracy and its attempt to live up to that commitment. Today many have lost faith in the possibility of closing that gap by anything short of bringing down the establishment. Extremists on both left and right are stockpiling weapons, and violence has become routine. Never in history has a nation so loudly and persistently proclaimed to itself, and to the rest of the world, its own racial injustices and its determination to correct them. Not in a hundred years has America been as torn internally by racial tension and the danger of armed revolt.

This national unrest is casting heavy shadows over the ghettos which supply the great majority of our minority children and young adults with their daily experiences. For most of these young Americans life in the streets begins early and often continues through the twenties and beyond. Many of them are uncounted in the census, unregistered in the schools, unlisted on most public rolls—except perhaps those of the police or public welfare. Collectively, they are a volatile and rapidly expanding new population whose comings and goings are largely unknown even to their own parents. Cut off from the paths of growth, education, and employment regarded by other Americans as normal, and with no identity except that which their inner slum world provides, these roving millions of youths are conditioned by circumstances to adapt to the raw environment in which they exist. Many of them cannot read or write, yet despite that added handicap, a surging and confusing awareness is getting through to them that in this highly developed nation there is much to be had that somehow has eluded them. And growing numbers of them, by one means or another, legal or illegal, intend to get it.

The overriding attitude of these street youths is embittered and harsh. They are not willing to abide by the traditional acceptance that has characterized their elders. Many of them are no longer restrained by the law and are entirely capable of producing a level of crime in the streets even more horrifying than that which already exists. It is within this frustrated youth population that the modern street gang evolves and takes form—a process of socialization which endows its members with personal status and group identification, a vastly enlarged potential for acting out the vengeance of the day, and enough power to mount a reign of terror that could precipitate a national emergency. One can only speculate on the human and physical wreckage of which today's ghetto youths operating as street gangs are capable. Add to this capacity for destruction the equally vast constructive energy of which such groups are also capable, and the dimensions of one of America's most critical national problems become discernible.

The problem cannot be overstated. But solutions to the problem will not be achieved by assertions of righteous indignation and a retreat from reality. And the opportunities that exist will not be cultivated by distributing federal and private grant funds on the basis of exaggerated or distorted claims, or by playing the currently popular game of myth-making enhancing the grandiloquent image of gang leaders and misleading well-meaning members of the establishment. This myth-making game played between the gang and the establishment is not only wasting human and financial resources, but of far more importance than that, is intensifying the dangers to the future of the American city.

No one knows precisely how many street gangs or ganglike groups are now operating in the nation's cities, or how many ghetto young people they include. But the presence of such groups—uncounted thousands of them, by whatever name they may be called—has become a significant part of today's urban scene, and the practice of making them beneficiaries of millions of dollars of uncontrolled federal and private grant funds has become nationwide.

Street gangs have appeared in America since early in the nineteenth century, usually beginning as normal play groups, or as informal streetcorner clubs arising spontaneously out of friendships and mutual interests among small bands of youngsters who obtained thrill and satisfaction from being together. Sports were among the favorite activities, and in the course of competition, fighting became a common part of the pattern. Then petty crime, boasting and acting tough, demonstrations of physical power, imagined feats of bravery, willingness to take increasingly higher risks, to commit more daring acts of crime, were added to the pattern. Gradually, as the group came into conflict with forces outside itself, as it encountered increasing opposition from other similar groups, from parents, from other neighborhood adults, and finally from the police, it began to feel that it was surrounded by enemies. Its members drew closer to each other for protection, it developed internal codes of loyalty and secrecy, and it became a gang. Some of these earlier gangs were less violent than others, but violence and crime were common elements.

In a classic seven-year study published in 1927, entitled *The Gang,* the late social scientist Frederic M. Thrasher reported the existence of 1,313 identifiable street gangs in Chicago alone. Emerging primarily in immigrant neighborhoods—Irish, Italian, German, Jewish, and others—these old-time gangs laid claim to what they regarded as their respective territories, or "turfs," and these territorial claims led to frequent outbreaks of physical combat. Most of these gangs consisted of only a dozen or so members each, and most of them remained intact over relatively short periods of time, changing or fading away as members fell out with each other, outgrew their teens, were arrested, got married, went to work, or—in the course of upward social mobility—their families left the neighborhood. Gang life did in many instances become a prelude to adult crime, but in most cases it was limited to the years between childhood and adulthood, and eventually there came a period of legitimation when the gang began to disappear and its members moved into accepted pursuits of society.

During World War II street-gang activity sharply diminished. It came back strongly after the war, then began tapering off again during the late fifties and early sixties. But this was only a period of adjustment between eras. As the nation was swept increasingly into the current urban transition, larger and larger numbers of families that had made up the source of supply for gang membership joined the exodus from the inner city. The old composition of gangland was going out, but a new one was coming in. Vast areas were being left to steadily increasing decay, and to a different population—one that had virtually no way out, blacks, Puerto Ricans, Mexican-Americans.

The age-old conditions of poverty, deprivation, and crowded living that had helped drive slum-trapped youths into street gangs in the earlier years were expanded to an infinitely larger scale. These conditions were coupled with the normal processes of street association and peer-group identity, and a new wave of gang formation began, the majority of the youths now being supplied by the families of the racial minorities that were occupying in increasingly larger numbers the vacated residential areas. Basically, this new wave of street-gang formation was simply a resumption of the old gang phenomenon, but as the sixties progressed other motivations more compelling than those of the past came into play. As the bitterness inherited from years of racial discrimination combined with today's assertions of racial pride, militance, and revolt, an environment more conducive to street gangs than anything the slum had offered before came into being, and more and more the new gangs took on these modern attributes.

As in the past, today's street gangs are found in a variety of forms, some posing much greater danger to the community and its youth than others. Most of them, like their earlier counterparts, are no larger than the number of youths who can know each other well, and because personal alliances are continuously changing, the gangs themselves are in a constant state of flux. Many of them break up and regroup almost from week to week, depending on the success or failure of their exploits of the moment, or upon the pressure of the police and other outside forces—including rival gangs. Many are no more than loosely formed bands of youth plying the streets making noise about self-protection, preying on innocent victims, breaking into buildings, fighting among themselves, committing random acts of vandalism, looking for excitement and easy money. Despite claims to the contrary, most of these gangs are not viewed with substantial favor or support in their own neighborhoods. Frequently, their supposed strength is little more than a figment of their imagination, or a creation of inflated press reports. Many of them are merely clusters of militant youths or young adults who congregate around various neighborhood hangouts—including federally supported youth centers —where aggressive conversation often serves as an added encouragement for delinquency.

In the country as a whole, this assorted maze of ever-shifting youth gangs and ganglike groups probably accounts for the bulk of today's street-gang activity, and except for the upsurge of emphasis on race and the special problems of racial minorities, is not much different in principle than it was in the past. But the indiscriminate supply of grant money has added a new dimension to the gang phenomenon, and has produced at least two entirely new gang varieties.

One of these new varieties, the small, closely knit group consisting of only a handful of members which operates as a state-chartered, nonprofit corporation, is given an identity far out of proportion to reality, then kept alive by the grant funds. Gangs such as this may or may not be engaged in violent or criminal activity, although the potential for such activity is never far beneath the surface, but because of the fantastic illusion that is built up around them and the enormous waste of valuable resources this illusion makes possible, these gangs often become a serious obstacle to effective neighborhood action and youth development—the exact opposite of what the grant-makers have intended.

The other new gang variety that has been heavily cultivated by grants and inflated image-building is the older and much larger street organization that may have as many as several hundred, or in some cases even several thousand members. Through mergers of smaller gangs, through a process of absorption in which weaker groups are simply taken over, and through relentless campaigns of recruitment in which youths are often forced into membership, these conglomerates of the streets—sometimes called "gang nations"—are highly structured organizations. They are ruled over by firmly entrenched hierarchies of extremely bold and aggressive individuals who usually have substantial criminal records and range in age from the early twenties to past forty. Like their counterparts in the smaller grant-supported groups, these individuals are in effect professional gang leaders—not uncommonly a lucrative occupation.

As in the case of the smaller groups, many of these large organizations have been chartered by the state as nonprofit corporations and enjoy the benefit of a vigorously promoted story to the effect that at some point a few years back the leaders grew tired of violence and crime and decided to turn their efforts toward constructive activities that would enable the neighborhood's youth to avoid the painful consequences of poverty and delinquency. Typically, this story pictures the gang leaders as people whose experiences in gangland have given them special insight into ghetto problems, then describes the gang itself as an indigenous community organization which is said to have become a healthy political force directed toward needed social change.

This story is elaborated with incidents of riot prevention and other positive actions—such as the opening of new businesses—and given wide circulation in newspapers and magazines. Usually it is aired on radio and television, sometimes on a national-network show, and by means of this publicity the gang acquires a glamorous reputation. Increasing numbers of allies from the establishment flock to its support, the gang opens an office and recreation center—perhaps several of them—and its leaders collect generous salaries and expense accounts and travel around the country. This pattern of development has been worked so smoothly and so often it has become standard. Built up from certain bits of truth, the story which is used to make this pattern of development possible is remarkable not only for the way it distorts the examples cited as evidence of positive action, but for its effectiveness in screening or dismissing as excusable or irrelevant the wasteful, destructive, and in many instances, outright criminal activities of the gang. But the story almost always works. And the grant money almost always keeps coming in.

The fact is that many of these large street gangs wield raw power over wide areas of the city and engage in strong-arm tactics that make them objects of fear to anyone who dares disagree with them. They have even been known to appear at funerals of youths they have killed to threaten the families of their victims. Often paramilitary in character, many of these gangs are heavily armed with an array of weapons virtually unknown to the violent street gangs of the past. The rumbles that were common in former years no longer occur to any great extent, but acts of terror, repression, guerrilla warfare, and other forms of violence far more deadly than the old-time rumbles are common occurrences, and often involve the gangs' most prestigious leaders as well as its rank-and-file younger members. However, premeditated murder—which appears frequently on criminal dockets related to street-gang activities—is usually carried out by the younger members who, if convicted, are likely to receive lighter sentences than the older members, who would be treated as adults.

Among these modern gangs brutal physical assault is a commonly accepted means of expanding the number of dues-paying members and of enforcing loyalty to the organization. Bribery, taking the law into the gang's own hands, rigid codes of secrecy—often concerning even the actions of rival gangs—blackmail, and intimidation of witnesses scheduled to supply evidence in court are regarded as normal. This is not to say that all of today's street gangs are equally violent or criminal in character, or that no positive action toward constructive change can be attributed to any of them. However, these are some of the commonplace items that are usually ignored or blurred over in the classic stories of reform that have been used to activate the current flow of grant funds.

The large gang organization poses a much greater threat as a neighborhood bully than does the smaller gang-type group. But when it comes to soliciting grant funds, the two varieties have much in common. Both of them know how to hustle. "Hustling": a pattern of getting money that street youths learn in the ordinary course of growing up. It may consist of buying and selling "hot" merchandise, peddling numbers for gambling racketeers, pushing dope, operating dice games, procuring prostitutes or homosexuals, using the right words to talk a few dollars—or even a quarter—out of anybody who might succumb, or outright stealing. These and similar skills that fall under the heading of hustling are an ingrained part of street life. Street youths even try it on each other, often even on their best friends.

Today's gang leaders have become expert at taking the practical art of hustling, expanding its scale, and using it on government agencies, foundations, and business firms to promote the grants so important to their continued operations and power. No modern, professional grantsman is their superior; the gang leaders obtain professional grantsmen to write their proposals, then add their own special touch to the hustle. Sweet talk, patriotic talk, inspirational talk, insulting talk, abrasive talk, blustering talk, demanding talk, intimidating talk, misleading talk—whatever kind of talk it takes, depending on the listener and the situation—the gang leaders know all the words and how to use them. When to keep the peace, when to make a show of strength, when to be threatening—whatever seems to work best at any given moment is brought into play. Alliances useful for the moment are made with politicians, artists, writers, clergymen, academicians, businessmen, foundation executives, government officials, even revolutionaries, and each alliance is worked for all it is worth. From their numerous allies, and from their own experience, the gang leaders have learned what makes the establishment listen, and have become practiced in the art of supplying it.

In some ways these modern street gangs may resemble almost any effective sales organization or legitimate political group; in other ways they may resemble the Mafia. To accept them at face value, as twentieth-century Robin Hoods, or as indigenous community organizations whose prime interest is constructive works, and to ignore the full range of their maneuvers and activities is to move so far out of touch with reality that intelligent grant-making becomes impossible. I do not wish to imply that under no circumstances should grant funds—including federal grant funds—be made available for projects that involve street gangs or gang-type groups. But in the current game of myth-making, it is often difficult to determine which is the greater problem: the gangs themselves, or the agents of philanthropy whose favors and concessions are now having the effect of rewarding and supporting even the most bizarre gangland behavior.

What is needed is a long, hard look at what works and what doesn't work, and a careful examination, case by case, of specifically which gang or which group is most likely to serve the legitimate interests of each given area. Anything short of this is certain to deny valuable financial resources to nongang groups that would make better use of them for the development of ghetto street youths. By pretending that a gang is responsible for constructive developments it has not actually achieved, the gang is given a reputation it has not earned and thus feels no need to earn. By ignoring or explaining away destructive acts, or simply attributing them to unfortunate circumstances and looking the other way, the gang's allies and benefactors ensure the continuation of such acts. By pretending that a gang is responsible for work that is actually done by outsiders is to deny the essential role of the outsiders, blind the gang members to their own inadequacies, and indulge in a charade that impairs honest learning and development. Those who make themselves parties to these varied forms of deception—no matter how noble their intentions—are simply reinforcing the gang's worst side and stimulating its predatory aggression. Unwittingly, in some instances not so unwittingly, this kind of help is further complicating the problems of ghetto youth, erecting needless barriers to solutions, and strengthening the dependency of the gang on tactics of manipulation or force.

The environmental conditions in which America's ghetto young people find themselves need desperately to be changed. But that change is not likely to be achieved by pretending that a street gang is something it is not, then believing whatever the gang says, and submitting blindly to the hustle. Soft-headedness in the name of ghetto problem-solving, or in the name of delinquency prevention, can only add to the misery of the ghetto, and further extend the corrupting influence of the society at large. Indiscriminate support of today's street gangs—financial or otherwise—is no help to the ghetto, and no help to the ghetto youths who belong to the gang. By falling into this modern-day gang trap, a grant-maker makes himself a setup for the hustle—in the eyes of the gang, a stupid, perhaps even loathsome creature.

But the hustle continues, and the grant-makers who are allowing themselves to be victimized—both in government and out of government—seem to have no clue to what is happening. New jealousies, hostilities, and power struggles are stirred among rival gangs—often among leaders in the same gang—because some are getting more recognition and financing than others. The capacity for havoc is being increased, the phony image is being enlarged and perpetuated, honesty and reality are becoming more and more difficult to detect, and streams of well-intended money continue to flow into dead ends.

The first requirement for the productive use of grant funds is mutual trust between the grantor and grantee. Each must have respect for the other, a quality that can exist only if it is truly warranted, not merely contrived or assumed. Each must be completely honest with the other, genuinely committed to the good works for which the funds are intended, and willing to carry out to the best of his ability his end of the bargain. Ulterior motives and hidden desires must be revealed and fully confronted. Each of the parties must have a clearcut understanding of the ultimate goal, and be able to comprehend without undue speculation what by-products or special purposes the other hopes to accomplish in the course of attempting to reach that goal. A relationship such as this cannot be achieved under a cloud of deceit, false advertising, and pretense.

Nor can it be achieved by merely writing a list of project activities, job descriptions, and budget specifications, as is done in formal grant contracts with the federal government—no matter how detailed. These government documents may be necessary for the purpose of complying with federal laws and regulations, but any notion that such documents necessarily ensure real understanding is wishful thinking. Frequently the grantee, especially if it is a gang, is not even very much involved in preparing the proposal and is no more than vaguely aware of what it says. Usually the proposal is written by the gang's outside friends—either paid or volunteer, often by the government's own employees. In many instances the grant is approved largely because of influence or pressure brought to bear by an important political figure who may have no real knowledge of the situation, but who also has fallen for the hustle. The verbiage contained in these government grant documents is usually more a matter of pleasing the bureaucrats than a meeting of minds, and often falls far short of describing the reality of the operations. However, these documents are a central part of what is called "negotiating"—meaning, in many cases, a series of meetings in which the giver and the receiver attempt to manipulate, or "con," each other—a procedure free of trust and understanding between human beings, but ideal for the hustle.

In the case of the gang and the government, this procedure may result in a relationship in which the government becomes a paternalistic master and the gang a cynical and belligerent servant. The gang says it wants nothing to do with charity or handouts, but this is just another part of the myth. Actually, it will take all the charity it can hustle, and the federal góvernment has become a likely target. The gang, cast in the role of servant and making full use of its wiles, waits expectantly for money, then feels abused if it doesn't get it, or—if it does—resents the feeling that it is being secretly watched by the all-powerful master. This relationship reinforces the basic suspicion the gang already feels toward society, encourages the gang to outsmart its federal master, and results in more chaos than any government granting agency can manage, regardless of auditing procedures and the technical language in the official contract.

The only relationship between grantor and grantee that will work in the streets is that which is based on complete understanding, absolute honesty, and a sense of full partnership on both sides, all of which goes back to the matter of trust and respect, or as they say in the streets, "knowing where it's at."

If the gang leaders lie about their intentions or behavior, the grant-maker is obliged to be aware of that fact and candidly tell them they are lying. Any attempt at deception or exaggeration must be labeled, and firmly rejected. But this calls for a relationship that can exist only in real life between real people, not one that is a product of pretense, or that is merely written out on paper and "negotiated." The gang leaders must be able to discover from the outset that any letdown in actual work on their part without legitimate reason will not be tolerated, and that they cannot violate the spirit or intent of the grant and continue to be eligible for funds. They must know that the grantor is not a setup for a hustle, and that they cannot depend on him to shield them from illegal or criminal acts, regardless of how angry or alienated they may feel toward the establishment—including the police. The grantor will lose the day if he tries to moralize, but he will also lose the day if he fails to make it clear that understanding is a two-way street, that in addition to his earning their respect, they must earn his respect, that just as he will make no promises he does not intend to keep, he expects the same treatment from them.

Unless these conditions are accepted by both grantor and grantee there is no legitimate basis for the grant. Street youths have no use for either an individual or an institution they can play for a sucker, or for the do-gooder who thinks he can buy them with favors. Their demands will only increase until, if they can get away with it, they will pump him dry, or perhaps with his help they are able to hustle other sources that are just as lucrative. In the old Moroccan city of Tangier the street hustlers have a name for the tourist who succumbs to their solicitations: donkey, a person the hustler can lead around. The grantor who allows himself to become a donkey for a street gang will not win the gang's respect and after being sufficiently used is likely to be discarded. This is at least one situation in life in which sheer kindness and good will in the absence of equal measures of realism, toughness, and firmness are likely to produce contempt—a condition in which the effective use of grant funds cannot be achieved.

In addition to being obstinate and willing to go only so far in playing games, the grantor who works with a gang must be scrupulously fair, open-minded, willing to listen, and able to acknowledge that he too can be wrong. As a good partner he must be willing to allow the gang the degree of freedom for action and decision-making appropriate within the framework of any honest partnership. He must be willing to be patient and to make allowances for honest mistakes. He must comprehend the character of life in the streets and be prepared to make judgments in that context. He cannot expect perfection and must be willing to accept something less than ideal standards of financial accountability. But if he bends so far that he has no values of his own to offer, and does not insist on fiscal responsibility and reasonable evidence of growth in effort and capability in that direction, he will cause more harm than good.

This means that in dealing with street gangs the grant-maker has a responsibility which he dare not neglect: to see to it that adequate provision is made for effective guidance, counseling, and training by a person who is competent both in terms of personal acceptance and knowledge to perform this role. In the context of today's street gangs, leaders do arise from time to time who are interested in moving toward constructive development. However, these leaders need reinforcement for their best intentions, and the counselor who is made available by the grant-maker must be able to supply that reinforcement. The current notion that a gang, because of its experiences in the streets and the indigenous nature of its organization, is uniquely qualified as a sponsor of ghetto youth projects is full of practical limitations. The counselor must know how to work with these limitations and how to stretch individual and group capabilities for constructive action. He must be able to judge when and what additional outside skills would be useful, and must be able to move speedily and effectively in supplying them. The counselor's role must be a respected friend and helper, not a crutch. Yet he must also exercise an element of control that will extend far beyond the puny effects of any contract specifications or auditing procedures. To do this, he must be a free agent, not beholden to the gang, and he must carry enough authority to be decisive.

Authority: that does not mean in this case authoritarian. It does mean the power to veto proposed expenditures and to cut off funds, and this power must be thoroughly understood by all parties to the agreement. Hopefully, the counselor will have no cause to exercise that power, but if the concept of trust and habits of responsibility are to be fully developed, the possession of this power is essential. The job of the counselor will obviously be extremely delicate and exceedingly difficult, perhaps even hazardous, and in the case of black youths who make up the majority of today's street gangs, very few whites will be suitable candidates. The suspicion of the day is simply too deep. But not just any black will be suited either. The person who performs this counseling task must be able to develop a close working relationship with both grantor and grantee, perceive their respective aspirations, and not aid or abet any action that would violate the essential purpose of the grant, or have the effect of condoning irresponsible work habits, delinquency, or crime. He must be flexible and democratic, and committed to the resolution of social problems. He must be understanding of personal needs, and have the ability to give and take. But he must also be firm, and make clear where he stands. The supply of workers who meet these qualifications is not large. However, they do exist, and many others are capable of being trained.

These requirements for the effective use of grant funds to help young Americans rise out of the deprivation and delinquency of the ghetto and put to work their inner talents for constructive personal and civic development may seem unduly stringent. They are not. They are merely the practical minimum.

The magnitude of the problem confronting millions of today's ghetto youth is not a racial problem, or a ghetto problem, or a youth problem. It is a national problem. It concerns all Americans of whatever race, or age, or status. It concerns the ultimate survival of everything in this country that is right and humane. It is a problem that people and government must resolve, and soon, if we expect to realize our fundamental purpose as a free, democratic nation.

The so-called establishment has got to give—money, and recognition that the young men and women who live in ghettos comprise a vast reservoir of human energy, creativity, and productive ability for an effective attack on the problems they and the nation face. These young men and women must find ways to make their capacities flourish, and the nation must find ways to support and encourage them in that effort. This responsibility, which staggers the imagination, must be shared by many institutions—including those engaged in grant-making, public and private. It is a responsibility that will call for countless, inevitable risks. But the stakes are high and the risks are worth taking—provided stakes and risks are real, not myth; and provided further, doers and helpers are partners willing to earn each other's trust and respect, not noble givers and dependent receivers brought together by hustling. A gang may or may not be the appropriate route to a ghetto's street youths, but whether it is the appropriate route, or an alternative agent—as for example, the University of the Streets—is the appropriate route, is a determination that can only be made by thorough and objective local inquiry, not by listening with romantic attention to the enticing sounds of the hustle.

None of these requirements for effective assistance to ghetto youth are likely to be fulfilled as long as the incredible fantasy woven around today's street gangs continues to enjoy widespread acceptance in public and private grant-making circles. Unfortunately, myths once established die hard. The wild promotional flings that have made today's exaggerated gang image possible have been going on since the mid-1960s. Much of the distorted publicity has been put out by some of the establishment's most respected, high-level organizations, widely known for their dedication to the needs of urban America. Leading newspapers, magazines, the electronic media, celebrities in the entertainment world, have helped spread the fantasy. Stories have been told, embellished, and retold about once-violent gangs turning away from violence, doing good in the ghetto, guiding younger boys and girls away from crime, struggling against repression, asking only to be given a leg up in their new self-inspired role. It is a beautiful and heroic picture. Its appeal is magic. But until the bubbles quit fizzing and the promoters and grant-makers get sober, there is little reason to hope that the picture will become real.

Index

About the Author

RICHARD W. POSTON, research professor at Southern Illinois University, has pioneered in the field of community development for more than twenty years in the United States, Latin America, Asia, and Europe. Founder and former director of the community development services at the University of Washington and at Southern Illinois University, Mr. Poston was one of the principal organizers and early chairmen of the Division of Community Development of the National University Extension Association. As a consultant to the Peace Corps and a director of training programs he has trained more than two thousand volunteers for overseas service.